SELF·MADE
AMERICANS

SELF·MADE AMERICANS

Personal Interviews
~ *with* ~
Dreamers,
Visionaries
& Entrepreneurs

MARGERY MANDELL

Gift to the Future2000, Inc. *Publishers*
Rhinebeck, New York

Gift to the Future2000 books may be purchased for educational, business, or sales promotional use. For information please call or write: *Gift to the Future2000, Inc.*, P.O. Box 625, Rhinebeck, NY 12572. Tel: 914-876-6365 Fax: 914-876-7927

Interior design & production services:
Dunn+Associates Design, Hayward, WI
Sara Patton Book Production Services, Maui, HI

ISBN 0-9634249-9-8
Gift to the Future2000, Inc. Rhinebeck, New York
Manufactured in the U.S.A.

CONTENTS

ACKNOWLEDGMENTS

This book wouldn't have been possible without the efforts of a lot of people. Many thanks to all the publicists and assistants who did their best to create time in my subjects' busy schedules for me to do my interviews. They are, indeed, the power behind the throne. I'd also like to thank Jim Brown for his vision and his support throughout this project and to Alexia Dorszynski for her graceful editing and meticulous attention to detail. Most of all, thanks to my children, Jacob, Alix and K.T., for exhibiting a rare degree of patience and to my husband Mark for his appreciation for the well-chosen word and for always being there to pick me up at the airport.

INTRODUCTION

eddy Roosevelt called them "rugged individualists"; Ralph
Waldo Emerson celebrated them as "self-reliant"; Henry
David Thoreau described them as "marching to the beat
of a different drummer." They are part of America's cultural heritage — the men and women who have inspired the
widely held perception, both here and abroad, of an American
as someone unafraid to pursue individual goals, regardless of
the obstacles created by class or culture, educational background or financial means. Some, alluding to the 19th century
American Unitarian clergyman who wrote popular novels
about poor boys who make good, think of them simply as
"Horatio Algers." Others think of them as representatives of
"the log cabin myth" — individuals made larger than life by
our common need to believe that achieving the "American
dream" of fame and fortune is only legitimatized by a struggle
upwards from the depths of rural poverty. As the end of the
20th century approaches, however, the only log cabins left are
of the pre-fabricated variety and the skills that led to the
celebration of America's pioneers as cultural icons are arguably
obsolete. The physical strength to survive the raw elements
and the courage to settle down and build a life in a vast and
unknown territory are hardly considered essential tools on the
information superhighway.

But when I set out to write this book I believed — and still
do — that the pioneering spirit still exists in this country and
that there are many people whose accomplishments illustrate
and celebrate that spirit. I prefer to think of them as "self-made

Americans" — those who have brought a dream to life, realized a goal, or built an empire of sorts through their own ingenuity, originality, fearlessness, and even stubborn stick-to-it-iveness. Identifying these attributes was not difficult; determining the source of their strength proved to be considerably more elusive.

Self-Made Americans: Interviews with Dreamers, Visionaries and Entrepreneurs is a collection of profiles of 25 men and women who think of themselves as being in at least *one*, and sometimes *all*, of the above categories. When I originally approached my subjects on the topic, their reactions varied. Some said, "Look, I'm no visionary. I'm just an entrepreneur who saw a good business opportunity." Others told me, "I don't really think of myself as an entrepreneur. I believed in an idea — I had a vision — and I wanted to make it happen. Financial success naturally followed." One man, whom I ultimately did not include in the book, announced with great candor: "When I made $5 million, the media called me an entrepreneur. When my income grew to $20 million, they called me a visionary. If you ask me, I'm still the same fool I always was." I quoted him often as I conducted my interviews. Many of my subjects laughed, recognizing at least a glimmer of truth in the notion that, more often than not, public figures are not born but media-made. Artist R.C. Gorman spoke for them when he told me, "I am rather ordinary; it's other people who created me as a legend."

Ultimately, I had to decide which of these men and women to include in the book. *Forbes* magazine's 400 richest people in America, *Fortune* magazine's 500 largest companies in America, *Black Enterprise* magazine's 100 largest black businesses, and other heavily publicized lists offered ample possibilities. And in fact, I did turn to all of these magazines for some ideas. But I was looking for more than the measure of my subjects' net worth. In many cases, success can be easily measured by fame or fortune. Sometimes, however, success is far less tangible and may mean attaining the intellectual or emotional satisfaction that derives from "making a dream come true" or turning a theoretical concept into a physical reality.

Several subjects, like Jaron Lanier and Jhoon Rhee, have been included not because they are rich beyond measure but rather because they have crossed new frontiers, pursuing goals not readily accepted or understood by society and bringing into existence systems or programs whose success may not easily be gauged by measuring financial gain. However, all those included can certainly be described as innovative. My subjects had to be people who recognized a way of doing something within their field that had never been done before. Robert Mondavi, for instance, was one of the first wine-makers to bring an understanding and appreciation of fine wine to the American palate. Jan Davidson was one of the first teachers to lobby for the myriad benefits of bringing computer technology into the American classroom. Emilio Estefan brought Latin music into the American pop music mainstream, and R.C. Gorman was one of the first Native Americans to express the Navajo experience through a popular and accessible art form.

In part, I was looking for men and women, like Robert Johnson, Scott McNealy, Bettye Martin Musham, and Josie Natori, who started with the seed of an idea and then nurtured it — with creativity, careful strategy, and devotion against sometimes daunting odds — until it was, if not a mighty oak, at least a good-sized tree. Others, like Chase Hibbard or Joel Glickman, inherited some sort of basic business or the capital for a business, and then, using the same kind of ingenuity and stick-to-it-iveness, revamped that business into something bigger and uniquely their own. A third set were individuals we generally think of as artists rather than entrepreneurs — people like R.C. Gorman, Emilio Estefan, Senator Ben Nighthorse Campbell, and architect Jack Travis — who have managed to combine their artistic talents with a good business sense and used their vision to build a successful enterprise. In Senator Campbell's case, he not only developed a successful jewelry business but went on to seek a broader sense of purpose in the political arena.

All of these individuals shared the ability to conceive a vision of their own future that sometimes departed quite radically from what their backgrounds might have determined for them. Neither a lack of formal education nor the provincialism born of poverty nor the restrictions imposed by well-meaning but myopic parents stopped them from pursuing what most of them called "instinct." Some admitted that childhood poverty helped to motivate their drive for success, but none felt that it helped to give specific shape to their vision. Some thanked a formal education for teaching them basic organizational skills, but few felt it gave them the essential tools to operate their businesses effectively. Many saw their mothers or fathers as role models for developing a strong work ethic, but none felt they inherited specific goals from their parents. My subjects were Harvard Business School graduates and eighth-grade drop-outs; they were richly supported by their parents and forced to work in the fields before they turned ten; they spent their childhoods squeezed into boxcars and playing in the backyards of sprawling suburban homes. All of these factors most certainly played a part in each of my subjects' unique stories, but it was their "instinct," their drive to continue, that unified them as a group.

I wanted to create a list of profiles that reflected both genders as well as a diversity of professions, cultural backgrounds, and geographical origins. As a result, I found many of my subjects through newspaper and magazine articles, through organizations such as the U.S. Pan-Asian American Chamber of Commerce, the Indian Pueblo Cultural Center, the Hispanic Business Association, through local Chambers of Commerce, or simply through word of mouth. The geographical breadth proved fairly easy to capture; every state in the Union has its success stories. As for the professions, I chose high-profile positions that represented some common fantasies for success. How often have I flipped on my computer, helped my child play with a trendy new toy, or popped a tablespoon of Ben & Jerry's Rainforest Crunch ice cream into my mouth and thought, "Gee, why didn't I invent that?" In short, I sought the most successful people I could find in the professions about which I was the most curious.

Finding sufficient multi-cultural diversity was not as easy as I had hoped — or, in fact, expected it to be. I called many tribal councils and Native American associations in order to locate American Indian entrepreneurs. Most of my contacts came up with few suggestions. I was fortunate to obtain the cooperation of R.C. Gorman and Senator Ben Nighthorse Campbell, both of whom were very generous with their time. The names of Asian-Americans and Latinos were also difficult to come by. I felt Josie Natori was an ideal example of a self-made American who still retained a strong sense of her cultural heritage. Jhoon Rhee, on the other hand, paid homage to his Korean roots through his teaching of Tae Kwon Do but was in some ways *more* American than any native-born American I know. It isn't every day that you meet an Asian-American whose role model is George Washington and who has choreographed a flag-waving martial arts ballet to the American national anthem. For Patrice Tanaka, on the other hand, identification with her cultural background took a back seat to identification with gender and profession. "I think of myself as a woman first and then as a woman business owner," she told me. "After that comes being a New Yorker, then being Hawaiian and, finally, being an Asian-American woman . . . The longer I'm around, the more sensitized I have become to being a woman. I believe women have to reach out and help other women if we are ever to attain the kind of power that men have."

Some of the biggest Latino names, like Wayne Huizinga of Blockbuster Entertainment or Roberto Goizueta of Coca-Cola, were very difficult to reach. Their public relations people politely insisted that their clients had already donated their names to the growing list of "Great Hispanic-Americans"-type books that are profilerating in the current climate of political correctness. The challenge made discovering Phil Roman's Mexican heritage and hearing the story of Emilio Estefan's journey from Cuba and subsequent rise to superstar status in the United States doubly interesting for me. Emilio Estefan's story also brought home quite clearly the ways in which the immigrant experience can play its part in the successful pursuit of a dream. The opportunity to start from scratch, to leave one's roots behind and have what Estefan called "nothing left to lose," was quite clearly a liberating creative force for Estefan — as well as for Jhoon Rhee, Josie Natori, and even, one generation removed, Robert Mondavi and Phil Roman.

The names of successful African-Americans were much easier to come by, but the people often proved inaccessible. I contacted many of America's wealthiest African-Americans — including Oprah Winfrey and Chicago media magnate John Johnson — but they were unwilling to spare the time to talk with me. Fortunately, Manny Jackson, Sylvia Woods, Jack Travis, and Edward Gardner offered me as much time as I needed to get my story. On the other hand, Robert Johnson, the CEO of Black Entertainment Television, was willing to grant me an interview but ultimately offered me very little of his time. I decided to include him anyway because I felt that he has had a significant impact on our popular culture.

In contrast to others I interviewed, all of my African-American subjects stressed racial issues in our discussions. Just about all of them were involved in community projects to help other African-Americans get ahead and were anxious to project the image of successful black entrepreneurs in America, something most of them felt was still sorely lacking in the media.

Overall, it was easier than I expected to assemble a list of exciting subjects. Approximately forty percent of the people I contacted agreed to be included in the book. Many, especially those less touted by the media, told me they were flattered to be asked and gave me as much time as I needed to obtain a thorough interview. Lots of the more familiar names — people like Ted Turner and Dolly Parton — or trendy cultural icons who had already been the recipients of heavy media coverage, like Seattle's Starbucks coffee king Howard Shultz, Microsoft's Bill Gates, or Nike CEO Philip Knight, simply refused on the grounds that they couldn't find time in their busy schedules. Perhaps they felt they didn't need any additional publicity, or maybe they were simply talked out.

Nevertheless, I was surprised at how many very successful people were more than happy to participate in the project. Communications magnate Michael Bloomberg, whose empire was recently estimated at over a half a billion dollars, answered his own telephone and scheduled an appointment with me without asking for a formal proposal in writing. He generously spent the better part of his workday with me. So did J.R. Simplot, whose Northwest agribusiness is one of the largest in the country. J.R. graciously drove me all through Idaho, proudly touring his holdings and sharing engaging stories of his rise to fortune. Similarly, Robert Mondavi met with me at his vineyards and gave me as much time as I required. His son Tim, who is a partner in the family wine business, took several of us out for a delightful lunch, during which he regaled us with hilarious tales of pretentious people in the wine business.

Once they agreed to the project, many executives were surprisingly willing to stretch their tight corporate schedules and allow lengthy conversations. Sometimes, the interviews ran longer than originally scheduled. Few, however, would make the time to meet with me, in person, more than once. As a result, these profiles are designed to capture the essence of my first impressions, the brief period of intimacy my subjects shared with me — and, I hope, to offer some considered explanations of dreams conceived, obstacles confronted and overcome, and ambitions realized.

I allowed each of my subjects to define the content of their individual profiles. In some cases, like Joel Glickman's and Edward Gardner's, the story focuses on the specific strategic ways in which they built their companies. In others, such as Chase Hibbard's, Rod Friedman's, and Sylvia Woods's, there is greater emphasis on emotional issues such as drive, inspiration, and motivation. In still others, like Jaron Lanier's and Stanley Selengut's, the story is more about the pursuit of a vision and the ways to make a dream come true. In short order, I came to sense what a particular subject felt was most important. Consequently, it seemed only right to let my subjects inspire others by focusing on the feelings and principles about which they felt the most passion and had the most clarity.

By the time I had completed my fourth interview, I began to see common threads in the personalities of my subjects.

For one thing, all of them made a similar first impression. They all had a degree of energy that was palpable when I walked into their offices and introduced myself. I'm not talking about literal physical energy, although most of them had that, too. J.R. Simplot literally bounded up the stairs two at a time; Manny Jackson and Phil Roman both looked astoundingly young and fit for men well over fifty years old; Josie Natorie could pass for a woman in her twenties or thirties; and at 82, Robert Mondavi seemed as trim and spry as he must have been in his soccer-playing days at Stanford. But they all shared an internal energy as well. These people literally vibrate. They fill a room with the focus of their vision, the energy of their ideas, and the need to make things happen. There's no question that it was downright exciting to be in their presence.

All of them, I would have to say, had enormous egos, and, for an interviewer, that was a mixed blessing. These self-made men and women consistently attributed the successful realization of their ambitions to an unfailing belief that what they were doing was "right" — either socially responsible, morally uplifting, financially rewarding, or all three. That's not to say that many of my subjects were not racked by insecurity and an irrepressible need to prove themselves over and over again. But it seems that the combination of self-righteousness and self-doubt created a kind of combustible force that produced the energy, dedication, and creativity necessary to pursue their visions for as many as fifteen and twenty hours a day, seven days a week, for many years at a stretch. In fact, *all* of my subjects confessed that their businesses occupied their minds anywhere from seventy-five to one hundred percent of the time. This probably accounts for the high divorce rate among them as well. Of the twenty-five people profiled, about half had been divorced at least once and many of them two or three times. Several never married or didn't wed until well after turning forty. Gloria and Emilio Estefan, married for 15 years, were an inspiring exception.

Few subjects admitted to having had a mentor. Although everybody paid homage to the quasi-Buddhist concept that we are all teachers and all students — typical was Scott McNealy's comment that "I learn from everyone. I learn what to do and what not to do" — it seemed to me that most of my subjects simply thought they were smarter than anyone else and uniquely visionary as well. People who march to the beat of a different drummer have a hard time thinking of themselves as following in anyone else's footsteps.

They also shared a common attitude towards money. Although everyone conceded that money is the current on which their ideas run, not a single subject said that he did what he did for the money. It seems that money, *per se,* loses its inherent charm fairly quickly. "Once you have enough to buy whatever you want," explained Robert Johnson, "money alone doesn't hold much power to motivate." Again, the responses provided variations on a theme. Many said they simply had a good idea and were driven to do it as well as they possibly could. They also shared an abiding belief that they could "make an impact," that is, create a business that could cure social evils or, at the very least, improve our lives so that more time would be available to devote to social and political causes.

A few had reached the point — mostly as a result of age — of conceding that few single individuals can really make a difference in the world at large and felt that making the lives of members of their own family better was good enough for them. Still others, like Michael Bloomberg, were less lofty in their perspective. Bloomberg described success as an "aphrodisiac." It makes sense that for anyone who harbors feelings of insecurity — and certainly some of my subjects did — and attains a modicum of success, the feeling of potency born of that success inspires an effort to create more success and so on up the list of the *Fortune* 500.

Many friends and colleagues have asked me, "What were these people really like? Did you like them — as people?" The answer is, yes, I liked them. I liked them all for giving me their time and their thoughts and their support so that I could write this book. In fact, many of them conducted our conversations the way they manage their businesses. Some subjects arrived late and raced through our conversation with a tense eye on the clock; others offered me lunch and as much time as I needed to get the profile right.

As for their being *nice* people . . . Well, I didn't really think that was a relevant issue for this volume. I'm certain that many of my subjects held political beliefs quite different from my own. I'm also certain that running a successful business calls for tactics that probably wouldn't make anyone a candidate for sainthood. However, these were individuals who latched onto a dream and pursued it as far as it would go. I think many of them are as successful as they are because they trust so deeply in the inherent rightness of what they are doing and the way they have gone about doing it.

There's no question that there's something exciting, inspirational, and fascinating about that kind of dedication. We could all use a dose of that in our respective walks of life.

"I hear America singing," Walt Whitman wrote. "Each singing what belongs to him or her and to none else." *Self-Made Americans* records those songs so that all of us may learn from them.

– MARGERY MANDELL
Spring, 1995

SELF·MADE
AMERICANS

"To win, you have to be able to make decisions rapidly — something that doesn't have to do with IQ but with judgment and balance and the ability to visualize the future."

HERBERT KELLEHER

Founder and Chairman of Southwest Airlines Inc.

⌒

The elegant, soaring lobby of Southwest Airlines headquarters, just outside Love Field in Dallas, Texas, is nothing less than a secular cathedral. Spokes of sunshine fan through the impossibly high glass and steel-beamed ceiling onto deep teal blue leather couches, huge, potted ficus trees, and an assortment of large, sparkling amethyst geodes that look more like natural outcroppings than corporate sculpture installed to accentuate the teal and purple carpeting.

In the center of the room, lit like a religious artifact, is a glass box displaying a crystal airplane. It is the Department of Transportation Service's Triple Crown Award, handed to Southwest Airlines for the past two years for most on-time flights, best baggage handling, and highest rate of customer satisfaction.

An inscription, painted in six-inch white letters on a glass wall enclosing the elevator bank reads:

> *The people of Southwest Airlines are the creators of what we have become — and of what we will be.*
>
> *Our people transformed an idea into a legend. That legend will continue to grow only so long as it is nourished — by our own people's good will and burning desire to excel.*
>
> *Our thanks and our love to the people of Southwest Airlines for creating a marvelous family and a wonderful airline.*

Herbert Kelleher, the chairman, president, and CEO of Southwest Airlines and the man who presides over this architectural testament to man's ability to rise to such heights of impassioned dedication and excellence, is neither a god nor a high priest nor a cult figure — although he is often portrayed as one in the popular media. He is, however, an original, whose unique management style and innovative sales and marketing strategies have nurtured the growth of Southwestern Airlines from a three-plane company offering flights to three Texas cities to the nation's seventh-largest domestic carrier, worth close to $5 billion. With the recent acquisition of Morris Air, Southwest now flies over 178 Boeing 737s to 52 airports in 51 cities across America. While the major American airlines have lost billions over the past five years, Kelleher's company has consistently turned a profit, and, at the same time, won numerous awards and accolades for meeting the highest levels of customer satisfaction.

"If you're customer-driven internally, then that reflects externally," offers Kelleher as a simple explanation for his success. "If you proceed from the thesis that the essence of any business is its people, then I don't think you need any management training. The intangibles are much more important than the tangibles. The spirit, the desire, the humor, the ability to subjugate your own ego for the collective success of the company and for the enjoyment of the people, is what makes us work . . .

"My experience has been that, by and large, if you extend trust and responsibility to people, then they respond very well. To the extent that you don't do that, you need a bigger bureaucracy and hierarchy to police them. Bureaucracy is expensive and retards flexibility and speed. I analogize it to a crusade. The Southwest Airline people are crusaders. They are totally involved in what they are doing, and, in the process, are uplifted to a spiritual perspective."

"Crusader" is perhaps the best word for "Herb," as even the lowliest employee and the least intimate of visiting writers is encouraged to call him. As he sinks back into one of several teal leather armchairs in his office, there is almost nothing corporate about his appearance. Dressed in chinos and a striped shirt with sleeves rolled to the elbows, he is at once the father figure, the guidance counselor, the coach, and the college student in the dorm lounge, engaged in a late-night ideological discussion with friends.

The body posture is a careless sprawl; the intense blue eyes are completely caught up in the spirit of the moment. The Merit Ultra Lights get lit, one after another, evidence of a five-pack-a-day habit that belies his otherwise completely centered demeanor. Contrary to his popular media image as the zany entrepreneur, Kelleher is a man who clearly enjoys thinking about motivation and inspiration, strategy and efficiency.

"People ask me all the time to define my management style," he says. "I doubt that Jackie Kennedy would have called what she had 'style.' How I run this company is not style, it is a process of relating to people. There's nothing stylish about it.

"All of our management training is in *leadership*, not in management. One time, I was lecturing at Yale's Graduate School of Business, and one of the students said to me: 'You're not talking about a company, you're talking about a religion.' Well, people perceive you however they do. I don't want to be perceived. I want to *be*. And what I want to be is considerate, kind, empathic, loving, concerned, and forward-thinking.

"What that graduate student called a 'religion' begins in the hiring process. We're looking for people to serve and who enjoy serving. We look at the people who work for us as 'customers.' Our thesis is that if the employees are not just treated in a way that is fair but in a way that honors their individuality, then that will be translated into a public-service attitude. You don't do it for business reasons. You do it because you want to treat the people right, and, coincidentally, that turns out to be good business."

Indeed, for the past few years, the press has had a field day touting Southwest's employees for going out of their way to amuse, surprise, entertain, and serve their passengers. Flight attendants have been known to rap sing the flight safety precautions, perform stand-up comedy routines in-flight, dress like Santa's elves during Christmas flights, and even hide in the overhead luggage bins so that they could pop out to surprise boarding passengers. (This last prank was recently abandoned after a passenger reportedly clutched his heart in shock and pleaded for oxygen.) Team spirit is strong. If things are slow at the airport, Southwest's pilots man the boarding gate; ticket agents also haul luggage, and, on a few occasions, have even accompanied aging passengers all the way to their destination cities to ensure their safe arrival.

A born prankster, Herb is frequently part of the act. He has been seen dressed up as a leprechaun so that he could pass out peanuts and Irish coffee aboard a Southwest flight on St. Patrick's Day, and ever since the time he dressed as the King for a personnel recruiting ad, he has enjoyed impersonating Elvis Presley. ("If he's dressed as Ethel Merman, ignore him — we're trying to break him of that," the ad's copy read.) The same spirit infuses his employee relations. Every February 14, for example, he sends each of his 13,000-plus employees a Valentine's Day card. He is known for being able to put the right names to most of those 13,000 faces and even get the grandchildrens' names right too, if pressed.

In-house festivities like Casual Month, during which employees come to work dressed any way they like, are estab-lished spontaneously. Company parties, like the annual Hallo-ween party for which employees transform their building into Freddie Kruger's Texas vacation home, are an institution. Herb is a chain-smoking, Wild Turkey-imbibing presence at these and at just about every birthday and retirement party that is celebrated. To prove it, along every hallway in South-west's three-story headquarters hang Polaroid collages of Herb and his employees clowning around at one company gathering or another.

"I feel that you have to be with your employees through all of their difficulties, that you have to be interested in them personally," Herb once told *Fortune* magazine, which ran a cover story suggesting that he just might be "America's Best CEO." "They may be disappointed in their country. Even their family life might not be working out the way they wish it would. But I want them to know that Southwest will always be there for them."

Born and raised near Camden, New Jersey, Herb cites his mother as the first source of inspiration in a philosophy he describes as "helping people to coalesce in pursuit of a common goal that serves a higher good."

"I had a sister and two brothers, all of whom were much older than me," he recalls. "I was third-generation Irish. My mother was a housewife, very ethical and moral. She was interested in business and politics and people, and she had a tremendous sense of humor. When I was young, my mother and I used to stay up until two in the morning, talking about ideas and ethical issues. Looking back, I've just never had inner needs that took precedence over outside wants. I just always wanted to make other people feel happy and secure."

Herb's father, a general manager for Campbell's Soup, died when Herb was just a teenager, but this didn't stop the young Kelleher from spending most of his high school and college summers working in the Campbell's plant, holding positions that ranged from production analyst to time-and-motion studies man.

"I had the opportunity to learn about industrial processes which were entirely outside my ken," he recalls. "And I got to work with a broad cross-section of people in a very hyper environment. I would watch the way the people worked, and I could see that the ones who were particularly successful were the people who treated their workers like individuals."

A star athlete who excelled in football, basketball, and track, he graduated Haddon Heights High School and attended Wesleyan University in Connecticut, where he studied English literature. Although the results of a college aptitude test suggested a career in journalism, he went instead to New York University Law School, on the encouragement of Arthur T. Vanderbilt, a distinguished legal scholar and Wesleyan trustee who took a liking to him. Kelleher did exceptionally well at New York University, making law review and earning the prestigious Root-Tilden scholarship. "I wasn't sure what I wanted to do. I was feeling my way, and a law school education seemed like a practical choice," he said. "I'm never bored, no matter what I'm doing, so it was no surprise when it turned out that I loved the law."

After a stint clerking for New Jersey Supreme Court justice William Wachenfeld, he took a job with Lun, Biunno and Tompkins, a Newark, New Jersey, firm. "Wachenfeld was a great inspiration to me," Kelleher recalls. "He was tough but gentle and had a great sense of humor. He was zesty and full of life and regaled me with wonderful tales. Some of what I am today came from watching people like William Wachenfeld and seeing what works to help further the cause, whatever it may be."

In the early 1960s, Herb moved to San Antonio, Texas, his wife's hometown. "We were spending a lot of time in Texas because my wife's family was there," recalls Herb. "Texas was a young state, and I visualized a lot of entrepreneurial opportunities there. It doesn't matter what the business is. I just like to start things. It's the sacrifice and the creativity of building something from nothing that excites me."

After working for a local San Antonio firm, Herb and several colleagues started the law firm of Oppenheimer, Rosenberg and Kelleher. In 1967, he had a meeting with client Rollin King, an entrepreneur and pilot in the process of dismantling his own small commuter airline service. That meeting would ultimately change the face of the airline industry.

According to the oft-told tale, King had tried to build an airline by concentrating on small towns, but there wasn't enough demand. He asked Herb to meet with him one afternoon to discuss the possibilities of starting a conveniently scheduled, low-fare, "no frills" airline, something like Pacific Southwest Airlines in California, to serve Dallas, Houston, and San Antonio.

"He drew a triangle with the three cities on a napkin," recalls Kelleher, "and asked me to do the fund-raising. At first I thought he was crazy, but after I reviewed the history of PSA, a company that was jetting people up and down the California coast at bargain fares, I said, 'Let's do it!'"

In November, 1967, with $500,000 bankrolling them, Kelleher filed an application with the Texas Aeronautics Commission (TAC) asking approval for a new airline to serve Dallas, Houston, and San Antonio. Starting a new airline or adding routes to an existing one was no mean feat in the highly regulated aviation industry in those days. TAC's unanimous approval came in early 1968 and was immediately followed by a continued challenge from Braniff, Trans Texas, and Continental Airlines, who called for a restraining order to prohibit the delivery of Southwest's certificate from the Commission. The restraining order was the first action in a three-and-a-half year legal battle to gain airport access.

"It was a bitter, prolonged litigation that took us all over the United States," Herb laments. "We knew very little about the airline industry, but that really worked in our favor. We weren't constrained by tradition. Venturesome instincts and a legal background can be a very potent combination."

Kelleher ultimately won a series of decisions that would allow Southwest to begin service with a "fleet" of three planes. On June 18, 1971 Southwest Airlines' first flight took off for Houston from Love Field, the smaller, more centrally located Dallas airport, which offered more local, domestic service than the sprawling Dallas/Ft. Worth International. That same year, King and Kelleher, who had no intention of leaving his law practice at the time, hired Lamar Muse, who had been president of several other airlines, to run the company.

Muse recruited a team of veterans from Braniff, American Airlines, and Trans Texas that became known as the "Over the Hill Gang." Muse also raised $1.25 million to buy airplanes and purchased four 737-200s from Boeing. He then went to the financial markets with a successful $6.5 million stock offering for Southwest Airlines.

After a shaky start, the airline broke into the black within two years and has remained profitable every year since. In the early days, the company adopted a clever marketing strategy based on its location, billing itself as "The Love Airline" and providing stewardesses clad in a sexy assortment of fishnet pantyhose, hot pants, and miniskirts. As times changed, the cabin attendants outfits remained casual, if more politically correct, and the marketing strategy switched to include humorous ads featuring Herb in various zany situations, a two-tier fare system that offered lower-than-usual rates during off-peak hours, and sales campaigns that offered the consumer everything from fare slashes to a free bottle of premium liquor to fly to Southwest over its competitors.

Southwest's common stock was first listed on the American Stock Exchange in October of 1975 and assigned the ticker symbol "LUV." In 1977, "LUV" moved to the New York Stock Exchange. A year later, Muse resigned after a dispute with the board of directors, and Kelleher became chairman of the board. A short while later, the board named Howard D. Putnam president and CEO of Southwest, a tenure that lasted until 1981, when Herb assumed those titles, too. It was then that the company began looking to the future.

In the mid-eighties the company saw more growth. Profits soared to $50 million by 1984, allowing the company to purchase Muse Air, a competitor that had been founded in Dallas by Lamar Muse, the former Southwest CEO, and his son, Michael. Destination cities now included Nashville, Birmingham, Detroit, Indianapolis, Oakland, Burbank, Reno, and Sacramento. In 1990, the company moved into its 245,000-square foot "cathedral" near Love Field.

Southwest's long sought-after acquisition of twenty gates at the ultramodern Terminal Four in Phoenix in 1990 was another turning point. Phoenix proved to be the key to the airline's rapid expansion in the Southwest. Hundreds of Southwest pilots and flight attendants are now based there, along with a reservations center, a marketing office, a personnel office, and various ground operations.

"I always thought of myself as a risk-taker," says Kelleher about his leap into a business about which he knew nothing. "The airline business, in particular, is capital intensive, fuel intensive, and people intensive. If your principal capital asset travels at 545 mph, then you better be able to move quickly and compete quickly. Everybody's wares are displayed equally in this business. Passengers can walk into any airport and more or less pick whatever carrier they choose. To win, you have to be able to make decisions rapidly — something that doesn't have to do with IQ but with judgment and balance and the ability to visualize the future."

But, adds Herb, what keeps him going are certain personality traits that have been his for as far back as he can remember. "I've always liked to do things for other people," he says. "My primary objective is to keep my people happy and secure, and this struck me as a business in which that would be possible.

"Also, I love excellence. It doesn't matter what kind of job it is, I like to do things competitively and well. I don't mean to compete in a way that puts other people down. I compete with myself to do the best possible job. All my life I have set contests for myself. Even little ones. If I went to the bathroom, I would simultaneously start peeing and flush the toilet to see if I could combine both actions so that they would finish at the same time. If I'm pulling out of my garage in the morning, I push the button on the automatic garage door opener at the same time as I begin backing out to see if I can make it out before the garage door closes on my car. It's part of what makes life fun. I'm absolutely never bored.

"But having said all that, what drives me is the will to go to war if I'm attacked. People often think there's an unusual dichotomy between my sentimentality toward my family — that is, the people of Southwest Airlines — and my willingness to fight. I'm not sentimental about people who attack Southwest. The way I see it is, 'You choose the weapon; you select the place; you provoke a fight with me; and in the place of your choosing, with the weapon of your choosing, I will kill you.'"

What drives Herb is precisely what has made Southwest the maverick airline that it is.

The man who loves to set "little contests" for himself created a commercial airline with the fastest turnaround time in aviation history. By eliminating seat assignments, offering no in-flight meal service other than peanuts or crackers, and requiring that baggage be rechecked for all connecting flights, Southwest can usually turn around an aircraft at the gate in fifteen to twenty minutes, about a third of the time it takes most other carriers. The company also frequents the less congested secondary airports such as Chicago's Midway, Dallas' Love Field, and Detroit's City Airport. This not only helps to reduce turnaround time, but the midtown locations of most of these smaller airports offers a distinct advantage to today's demanding business travelers whose tight schedules and budgets dictate that they avoid airport traffic and expensive cab rides.

In addition, the company avoids the traditional hub-and-spoke system used by most big airlines, instead flying frequent round-trips between pairs of cities that are geographically close. Southwest planes make about ten flights a day, more than twice the industry average. The company also uses only one type of aircraft — the Boeing 737 — which simplifies flight-crew training and plane maintenance and reduces the need for a large inventory of spare parts. Maintenance is further minimized by keeping the average age of the fleet to a mere 7.3 years. This efficient use of the company's major capital asset saves millions of dollars.

Furthermore, the average Southwest flight is about 375 miles at an average fare of $60, far lower than any other airline. As a result, increasing numbers of people who once drove to business meetings several hours away have discovered that it is faster, more efficient, and sometimes even cheaper to fly Southwest.

Another key innovation is Southwest's distribution system. Most airlines rely on independent travel agents to write up their tickets. Southwest by contrast, has no linkups with the computer reservation systems used by travel agents. Agents who are asked to book a Southwest flight have to book by telephone, and many try to pick another carrier or tell customers to call themselves. As a result, nearly half of all Southwest tickets are sold directly to passengers, which saves the company close to $30 million in travel agent fees.

Finally, Southwest's success is not just the result of innovative cost control measures and clever marketing, but of its corporate culture. Over 80 percent of the employees are unionized, and the average worker's salary is only a few dollars less than would be the case at the larger airlines. To maximize service, flight attendants and pilots are paid by the trip, rather than the hour. But the company offers a generous profit sharing plan that allows for about fifteen percent of net profits to be returned to workers. Then, of course, there's the opportunity to work for the airline that still thinks of itself as "The Love Airline." There has never been a lay-off in Southwest's history, and only a single strike (by the machinists) in the last decade. Job satisfaction is so high among workers, admits Herb, that many think of it almost as a religion.

The "love" extends beyond Southwest's immediate family, too. Since 1980, Southwest has sponsored "Home for the Holidays," a program that has enabled thousands of senior citizens to visit friends and relatives during the Christmas season — for free. They have also adopted the Ronald McDonald Houses, a network of facilities across the country that provide lodging and services to the families of seriously ill children, as their corporate charity. Southwest employees volunteer for such services as cooking meals for guests, hosting the annual fund-raising LUV Classic golf tournament in Dallas, and escorting children from the Los Angeles Ronald McDonald Camp for Good Times on white-water rafting trips.

Despite its astronomical growth over the past few years, Southwest shows no signs of slowing down. Although the Wright Amendment — legislation created by former U.S. Representative James Wright when Southwest first tried to fly outside of Texas in the mid-1970s — prohibits any carrier in

Love Field from flying routes out of Dallas to destinations beyond the four states contiguous to Texas, it doesn't stop the company from flying direct to such popular destinations as New Orleans, Albuquerque, and Little Rock. Other cities are accessed through connecting flights.

And the number of Southwest's destinations is still growing. In 1993, Southwest acquired Morris Air, a small airline company based in Salt Lake City and providing "no frills," low-fare service to the Northwest and Upper Plains region of the U.S. Through 1995, the $129-million acquisition will add flights from Salt Lake City to Boise, Seattle, Denver, Phoenix, and other cities.

For now, Herb seems to be enjoying every bit of his success. When he's not attending corporate bashes, cheerleading his Southwest "family," or advising the Clinton administration on the future of the aviation industry, he reads voraciously, visits his family's home in San Antonio, and spends time with his wife of 40 years in their Dallas townhouse. Any given day may find him accepting yet another award for his innovative contributions to the airline industry.

His children are all grown, and, so far, none of them show any signs of joining Dad's business. As far as Herb is concerned, that's just fine. Youngest son David, who took three years off to be a bartender, is now a student at the University of Texas in San Antonio; daughter Julie works with birds at Sea World in San Antonio; son Michael runs a successful software business in San Antonio; and daughter Ruth, whose son John Herbert is the apple of Herb's eye, is a lawyer with Oppenheimer, Rosenberg and Kelleher.

"I grew up in an era when there were an amplitude of heroes around," reflects Herb, glancing at the photographs of Harry Truman, Winston Churchill, and FDR that hang, like devotional icons, from his office walls. "The country was unified in an effort to do what they called 'saving Western civilization.' I think this feeling is missing today. This is more of an anti-hero age. We focus now on idiosyncrasies rather than on leadership."

Does Herb Kelleher think he's a hero for our times? "I don't believe in being messianic," he says earnestly. "I don't want to advise people; I want to inspire people. I believe in leadership by example. I don't want to preach, I want to be a model that other people want to emulate." Others are already trying. Numerous small upstart airlines have tried to copy Southwest's low-fare, short-haul approach, and many of the major airline carriers are working to compete with Southwest's operations. The difficulty may lie only in finding others with the intelligence, the vision, the dedication, and, perhaps, the love to get it right.

"I've always felt that you have to love what you do and go for it. The only limitations are the ones you place on yourself. If you get rejections, there's no reason to quit because if it is something you really want, it will happen."

PHIL ROMAN

Founder and CEO of Film Roman Inc., animators for
The Simpsons, Garfield and Friends, **and** *Bobby's World*

A sk Phil Roman the secret to success in life, and he's likely
to say, "Be dumb." At least that's what the disarmingly
candid and hopelessly modest president and CEO of
Film Roman, Inc. says about what motivated him to
create one of the most original and financially successful independent film animation studios in the United States today.
Over the past 35 years, Roman has assiduously pursued a career
in animation that led him eleven years ago to the founding
of the company that produces the animation for such contemporary icons of pop culture as *Garfield, The Simpsons,* and
Bobby's World, a show he created with comedian Howie
Mandel. And his success on network prime time and Saturday
morning television is only part of the story. Film Roman has
recently been appointed the official animation company for
the 1996 Olympics in Atlanta.

"When you're a kid and you decide that you want to be a
fireman or a policeman, you don't think about whether you'll
make enough money to support a family. You think about
having fun every day by doing something you enjoy," Roman
insists. "And that's what drove me . . . Doing what I enjoyed."

Roman makes it all sound so simple. Despite the plush
surroundings of his mahogany-paneled office on one of three
sprawling floors of a large brick building on Chandler Boule-
vard in North Hollywood, he is relaxed, accessible, and nothing

like the stereotypic executive in the television industry. There are no disingenuous kisses on both cheeks, no rapid-fire negotiations with someone named "Baby" on a cellular phone, no Rolex watches or Gucci loafers.

Perched on his desk and scattered around the office are plush toy versions of the characters he has either admired or actually animated over the years. Bart Simpson smiles incorrigibly from between two piles of paper; Felix the Cat coolly supervises the coffee table; the Pink Panther peers surreptitiously from behind the telephone. Casually dressed in chinos and a cream-colored cotton shirt, Roman seems far younger than his 64 years. The years bespoken by his steel-colored hair are all but canceled out by a bright smile, black shoe-button eyes, and cheeks that seem to blush perpetually. Just beneath the surface gleams the face of the ten-year-old Mexican-American boy whose mother took him and his two younger brothers to see the movie *Bambi* at the local movie theater in his native Fresno, California.

"We didn't have much money while I was growing up," he recalls. "My mother and father came from Mexico, met in Fresno, and got married. They didn't have much education, so they became field laborers. Fresno was at the hub of the San Joachin Valley, an agriculture-based community of Italians, Armenians, Okies, and Hispanics [who] came north from Mexico in search of work. During the summer we would all go out and pick grapes for two or three cents per tray. That's how I earned enough money to buy school clothes and books. In fact, when I first started school I didn't even speak English. Then my mother insisted that I attend Catholic school because she believed I would get a better education.

"We had no telephone and no electricity. For entertainment, we would 'watch radio.' Then one day my mother took us to see *Bambi*, and I was completely mesmerized by the movie. After I saw it, I would draw Bambi on everything — scraps of paper, my notebooks, the school blackboard."

From that time on, Roman was determined to become an animator.

"There were no art schools in Fresno, so I took correspondence courses in drawing," he continues. "Once I graduated high school in 1948, I spent a year working as an usher at the local Warner Brothers' [movie] theater. I would sit and watch all of the cartoons and learn the names of all the famous cartoonists like Chuck Jones and Fritz Freleng." Eventually he would have the chance to work with all of them.

Throughout that year, Roman continued to draw, penning cartoons of the people who worked in the theater and of the ever-changing array of patrons who passed through its doors. Intent on pursuing his career, one day he simply decided to hop a Greyhound bus for Los Angeles to find an art school that would train him. He arrived in the City of Angels with no friends, no place to live, and only $60 in his pocket. It never occurred to him to fear failure. His enthusiasm and single-minded purpose — what he now calls "being dumb" — carried him.

Thanks to a recommendation from his old boss, he found a night job at another Warner's Theater almost immediately. "Then I opened up the Yellow Pages, found 'Hollywood Art Center,' and gave them a call," he adds. "One of their teachers was Ted Donnicksen, an ex-Disney animator, so I thought it would be a good school for me." Roman convinced the school to take a small down payment while he worked his way through the rest of the tuition. "Maybe they responded to my enthusiasm," he says when pressed to explain the school's willingness to advance tuition to a complete stranger with a very small portfolio. "I know that's what I look for now when I hire kids. I want to see that they are really interested.

"I've always felt that you have to love what you do and go for it. The only limitations are the ones you place on yourself. If you get rejections, [that's] no reason to quit, because if it is something you really want, it will happen."

In 1951, a year after he started school, Roman left to join the Air Force. "To show you just how stupid I was, I volunteered to go to the Far East," he says, alluding to the Korean War. In fact, he was stationed in France for a time and was then transferred to Illinois, where he trained in radio technology.

He returned to Los Angeles in 1955 and attended the Art Center School, which offered one of the top animation programs in the country, on the G.I. Bill. Although he had planned to stay on and obtain a degree, within a year he applied for and landed a position as an assistant animator at Walt Disney Productions.

"I learned a lot during my time there," he reflects. "I worked on projects like the film *Sleeping Beauty,* and I worked with very good people. Art school taught me to use my head and my imagination and develop my creative skills, while Disney taught me how to make my work look consistent, how to adapt to different styles and develop my technical skills."

After a couple of years, however, the magic of Disney began to wear off. "I had wanted to work at Disney all my life," Roman reflects, "but after a couple of years it became tiresome to work with so many people above me. The organization was huge, and I didn't have a lot of opportunity to grow. Everyone told me I would be crazy to quit, but I didn't care."

Once again citing "dumbness" as the reason, Roman quit Disney in search of work that would be more creative and allow him to develop as an animator. He took a job with a small animation company in San Francisco that gave him experience in doing background, lay out, and sound recording as well as more commercial work. "I learned the guts of the business," he says, "until I was laid off a couple of years later."

As Film Roman's public relations department now explains it, the "guts" of the business involves a host of skills and the people to implement them.

Producing a cartoon is a long, complex process. It can take as long as six months to make one episode of *The Simpsons* and several years to produce a feature-length cartoon. What's more, it takes a minimum of 12,000 drawings, penned and painted by more than 200 animators, layout artists, and background painters, to create a 22-minute television cartoon.

A cartoon is made up of many individual drawings, or frames. Each frame shows the characters in a slightly different position than they were in the frame before. When all the frames are shown very quickly, one after another, the characters look like they are moving.

Each episode starts with a "show bible". A team of writers and artists work from an idea developed by the team, producer, or network, detailing the story, characters, situations, and settings that will remain integral to the show for as long as it is broadcast. For each episode, a script with the show's dialogue, screen directions, and sound effects cues is written. At the same time, artists' drawings or models of the characters are created to illustrate how the characters will look from many angles in many poses.

Next, a visual script, or storyboard, is sketched. The storyboard is a plan or blueprint for the entire production. Then the voices of the characters are prerecorded and the director then tells the animators what to draw in each individual frame to determine the overall tempo of the cartoon. Using the storyboards, layout artists design production-size backgrounds, props, and costumes for each scene. They also map out or stage each scene, noting position and action poses for each character. Animators then make key drawings of the character in action, and assistant animators complete the in-between drawings that smooth out the characters' movements from one point to another.

The animators' drawings are carefully photocopied, color-coded, and painted on clear acetate sheets, or cels, that represent each frame. Background painters complete the color detail for every landscape or interior setting. Each drawing is shot on film; then they are edited together, dubbed with the soundtrack voices, music, and effects, and transferred to videotape.

The early 1960s were the toughest time in Roman's career. Massive lay-offs at Disney left the market glutted with talented animators — at a time when there were not enough other jobs to employ them. Animated films were slowly being replaced by animated television series, but the new marketplace had not yet developed. The animation industry was in turmoil.

"I enrolled in night school to become a stock broker," Roman says, "but I never gave up looking for animation work. I would do anything, because I knew it would all be useful, but mostly, because I liked it all. TV work taught me how to budget my time, while commercials and film work gave me more experience in full animation." He succeeded in landing a number of free-lance jobs that provided the experience and the connections that would ultimately make his career.

First he worked as an animator on *The Incredible Mr. Limpet*, a Warner Brothers' live action/animation feature starring Don Knotts. This led to a job working as an assistant for animator Chuck Jones, who was then at MGM. "This was another example of my being dumb," Roman says with a laugh. "It was a step down for me to work as an assistant after being an animator on a feature film, but I [had] always wanted to work with Chuck Jones. Sure enough, it proved to be a great experience. Little by little, Chuck gave me more and more responsibility."

Roman spent seven years working at MGM, contributing to such animation classics as *The Phantom Tollbooth* and *The Grinch Who Stole Christmas*, as well as the classic cartoon television series *Tom and Jerry*.

"Every place that I worked," says Roman, "I had a filing system in my brain. I told myself which things I would do and which things I wouldn't do if I ever had my own studio . . . I learned a lot from Chuck. He [had] a very creative mind, and he made classy, funny, entertaining cartoons. I learned a lot about humor and timing. I also learned a lot about management. Chuck was an artist, and he respected the artists who worked for him. He gave them a lot of room to do their best work. Many studios treat their artists like machines. Chuck cared more about quality. He treated people like people and that really stayed with me."

When MGM closed its animation studio in 1969, Roman found himself without work again. Undaunted, he continued to seek out free-lance work and worked as an animator for a number of Dr. Seuss specials for the DePatie-Freleng animation company, for ABC and, finally, for Bill Melendez Productions. Under Melendez, he worked as an animator and then directed several Emmy award-winning *Garfield* specials, as well as numerous Emmy award-winning specials starring the Peanuts' character Charlie Brown.

"Bill was another great influence for me," recalls Roman. "Much like Chuck, he was an animator himself and had a lot of respect for the artists in his studio. Best of all, he gave me a chance to direct, which was something I had never done before. I learned how to set up scenes, plan the various poses and attitudes of my characters, and create storyboards. Being a director requires being a storyteller. You have to pace your story and make your characters interesting. You have to work with everyone — the ink and paint people, the musicians, the animators. That to me was the ultimate. I welcomed the opportunity to learn something new about what I enjoy doing, and directing was new."

By 1983, Roman was ready to start his own company. "I was 52 years old," he explains, leaning forward, elbows on knees, for emphasis. "I had always wanted to open my own studio. I finally felt if I didn't do it [then], I'd never do it. I had to get it out of my system, so I gave my notice to Bill. I knew it was a risk, but, as usual, I didn't do any studies or hire any consultants. I just decided to do it."

He and his wife Anita, whom he had married in 1970, took a vacation to Europe and when they got back, Film Roman, Inc. was born.

"We started with a small office not far from here in Toluca Lake," recalls Roman. Since the Romans have no children, Anita had the time to help her husband get organized in the beginning. "We were very small at first — just three employees: a production manager, a secretary, and a lay-out person. I did almost everything myself — payroll, pre- and post-production, and direction. We subcontracted animators, musicians, camera services, ink and paint people, and editors. Our first job was a

Garfield special. It won an Emmy award, and after that Film Roman got the license to do all the animation for *Garfield*."

By 1987, the Film Roman staff had grown to twelve, and the company geared up to do a year's worth of *Garfield* shows for a half-hour Saturday morning series. Their efforts were so successful that they earned a contract for a one-hour *Garfield* series for the following year. Roman purchased 8,500 square feet of a larger building in Toluca Lake, and, by 1990, Film Roman had taken over the entire building.

"We decided to start branching out to create properties we would own ourselves," Roman continues. "We began with *Bobby's World* and an educational show called *Zazou You*. Though teachers loved *Zazou*, we found that it was very difficult to make educational programming for children. Kids turn to television for entertainment, and if the balance between education and entertainment isn't just right, kids will get turned off. On the other hand, if they like something, they'll watch it over and over again. I realized that our strength is in doing things that entertain, so that's where we put our emphasis."

As each year passed, almost all of the old shows were renewed and new projects were taken on. The highest profile project has been *The Simpsons*, which Film Roman took on after three seasons. The show's enormous popularity virtually catapulted the company into the spotlight. Since 1991, the company has produced countless commercials and television specials, the animated feature film *Tom and Jerry — The Movie*, and several series besides *The Simpsons*, including *Mother Goose* and *Grimm*. Another show, *Cro*, is a co-production with the Children's Television Workshop. It features an Hispanic female scientist, a clever woolly mammoth, and a Cro-Magnon boy and is intended to explain basic scientific concepts to children. After a successful run on public television, *Cro* has now been renewed by ABC. Other programming includes *Mighty Max*, which is based on a British toy and features a kid with a baseball hat that gives him the ability to travel through time, and *The Critic*, written by the same writers that brought us *The Simpsons*. The firm's commercial clients include

Pizza Hut, Kentucky Fried Chicken, Toyota, Butterfingers, and Japan Airlines. Meanwhile, the company is still producing the Saturday morning *Garfield* series, which has long been the company's bread and butter.

Between 1987 and 1993, the Film Roman staff literally doubled each year. Today Film Roman employs 250 people, produces $35 million in sales, and occupies close to 40,000 square feet in a new office building in North Hollywood. Scripts, storyboards, direction, lay out, background, editing, and the posing of scenes are all done in-house. The labor-intensive animation — i.e., ink and paint — are done in animation houses in Taiwan and Korea. Film Roman also goes to outside companies for computer animation and the kind of high-tech specialty work needed for commercials.

One of the more interesting projects he has begun in recent years is *Film Roman Presents . . . Animated Classic Showcase*, which is based on the library of Soyuzmult Film, the largest animation studio in Moscow. Roman purchased the collection in partnership with Joan Boorstein and her husband, the Soviet actor Oleg Vidov. The library contains 1,300 titles, many of them award-winning films. "I was impressed by the quality of these films, which were patterned after the old Disney cartoons of the thirties and forties," Roman explains. "We restored them and added English dialogue and new music and sound effects and sold them as a series of twelve one-hour specials for first-run syndication.

"I try to make the environment here a place where I would enjoy working," says Roman of his management style. "Like my friends Chuck Jones and Bill Melendez, I try to give our animators as much room as possible to do the best work that they can. I enjoy helping kids and do my best to give opportunities to Hispanic interns. I walk the halls a lot and say hello to everyone." In fact, company policy allows for a rotating exhibit of employees' art work on the walls of Film Roman's hallways. There's an "opening party" on the first of every month, when the exhibit changes to allow new employees to display their work.

Roman has tried to avoid the traditional studio structure. Instead, his firm uses more of what Roman calls a "unit" system, in which artists are assigned to a particular project rather than to a department. Although Film Roman does have an ink and paint department, a background department, a Xerox department and the like, each artist still tends to work within the particular show to which he or she has been assigned.

"It's important for me to teach my animators how to budget their time well," says Roman. "You can't baby a thing to death, because you have budgets and deadlines to meet, especially for television. You have to know what you want ahead of time and plan for it. That's one of the best ways to weed out the talent in a company. If they can give you what you want, when you want it, then you know you've got someone good."

In the near future, Roman hopes to take his company public. "We've reached a point in the business where we're competing with the big studios. Guys like Warner Brothers and Disney have deep pockets. My pockets have holes in them. Thus far, we've been able to compete — not because we throw a lot money at our projects, but because we're creative. But we have to plan on purchasing the rights to our products for international distribution and for merchandising, and that takes a lot of cash.

"The good news *and* the bad news is — we're successful," laments Roman, only half-joking. "The thing that got me into this business — drawing and animating — is what I can't do anymore. By now, I'm wise enough to know that the only way to stay even is to plan ahead. I spend most of my time finding new product, going overseas to find co-producers, and running the business. Fortunately, we have an excellent management staff who won't let me use my 'dumb' policy anymore. They help me in areas where I'm the weakest, and together we decide what's best for the company."

But there are rewards. "I wake up in the morning and come into the office, and I still get delighted to see what we've accomplished," Roman adds with characteristic humility. "The networks know who we are. Children's Television Workshop chooses us for programming. Even the Olympics Committee respects our work. We've become a force to be reckoned with in the business . . . Whatever I did, I did because it was something I wanted to do. If you do something the best that you can do, then there's no reason why you shouldn't succeed. My portfolio is what's on the screen every day. There are no lies up there. And that's pretty rewarding."

Dumb? As a member of Roman's prime-time audience might say, *NOT*.

"Life is too short, and I want to spend my time around people who are fun to be around. I look for people who will add to the party, people who can create good energy in our workplace community."

PATRICE TANAKA

CEO and Creative Director of
PT&Co., a public relations firm

T he clutter in Patrice Tanaka's office is downright architectural. Books, videotapes, and pillars of manila folders
and spiral-bound files form a crenelated castle on the
eight-foot expanse of her glass desktop and spread over
two neighboring file cabinets and the moat of gray-carpeted
floor space between them. A neon-yellow plastic iguana coils
in mock-menace on the computer keyboard, and Thomas
Moore's *Care of the Soul*, Mark Pendergrast's *For God, Country
and Coca Cola: The Unauthorized History of the Great American
Soft Drink and the Company that Makes It*, a cookbook of
macrobiotic recipes, and a videotape entitled *Harley-Davidson
— The American Motorcycle* are scattered amidst the cream-
colored stacks of papers like icons of the eclectic interests of
the castle's queen.

Tanaka emerges from behind the desk, her five-foot frame
barely as tall as the mountains of files around her. "I've carved
a little patch of work space for myself back here," she says,
pointing to a square foot of bare glass, "and — believe it or
not — when I can't find something on the computer, I know
just where to find it in these piles."

In spite of the cool minimalist black pantsuit and stylish
contemporary jewelry, Tanaka comes across as warm and
accessible. When she talks about Patrice Tanaka & Company,
Inc., the public relations agency she founded in 1990, she is

just as likely to be serious and articulate about her goals and ambitions as she is apt to crinkle her Hawaiian features into a big grin and let out a truly infectious giggle, the warm, spirited laugh of a woman who is comfortable with herself and her goals.

And Tanaka has reason to be self-confident. In the last four years, the 42-year-old Honolulu-born public relations specialist has built an award-winning firm with offices in Dallas, Los Angeles, and New York and corporate clients that include Avon Products, Coors Brewing Company, Godiva Chocolatier, Lipton, and Liz Claiborne. Last year, PT&Co. was named one of the twelve "hot creative shops" by *Inside PR*, the industry's leading trade publication, and in 1994, the firm was number four on the magazine's newly created "[Top] Ten Innovators" list. In a short time, the company has not only built annual billings of nearly $3 million but has consistently been recognized for its innovative public relations programs, its commitment to client service, and its unique management style.

Tanaka attributes much of her success to what she calls "breakthrough public relations."

"The job of a public relations firm is to work with clients and help them communicate to their target audiences through the media," she explains. "Since there are literally thousands of public relations firms vying for the attention of the media, our job is to *break through* the clutter of all the other voices trying to get their attention by presenting something that they've never heard before . . . Our goal is to create the kind of campaigns that are so unique and so innovative that we create grief for all the other public relations firms. When our campaigns are really good, we can raise the bar one notch higher by creating effective public relations campaigns that have never been done before."

As an example, Tanaka cites an immensely successful public relations program for Korbel champagne that involved placing a classified ad in the *Wall Street Journal* stating that Korbel was seeking a director for their newly formed Department of

Romance, Weddings & Entertaining to serve corporate America. The unique ad earned Korbel countless feature stories on television and radio and in national newspapers and magazines and generated a string of romance-related initiatives that garnered media attention for Korbel well beyond the traditional New Year season — no small feat in a media environment that has grown increasingly unsympathetic to alcoholic beverage products in recent years.

But good business is only a small part of what inspires PT&Co.'s public relations work. "To develop a public relations campaign requires flexibility and creativity," Tanaka adds with characteristic thoughtfulness. "To be able to create something that didn't even exist the day before is very exciting work. [But] big ideas are not necessarily tied to big bucks. The trick is to spend $100,000 in order to generate $1 million worth of publicity . . . Of course we want to represent big name clients and create ground-breaking campaigns in order to be respected and admired within the industry, but we [also] want to use our public relations skills as communications practitioners to be a catalyst for transforming society. I don't mean to sound overinflated about our goals, but I've always been intrigued by the idea that if used properly, the media could have a powerful positive impact on society. Some of the campaigns that we find most satisfying to create are cause-related marketing programs."

Indeed, in the past few years, PT&Co. has had great success with a media campaign against domestic violence sponsored by the fashion company Liz Claiborne. The program included powerful ads created by conceptual artists such as Barbara Kruger and Carrie Mae Weames, as well as the establishment of domestic abuse hotlines and fundraising efforts to support women's shelters across the country. Similarly, PT&Co. created a campaign for the Coors Brewing Company to raise money for women's literacy programs nation-wide. Both campaigns performed the dual function of attracting "breakthrough" media attention while working to increase awareness of important social issues among consumers.

"Anybody who creates something from scratch would like that thing to be the most or best possible," says Tanaka, who believes that the notion of making business a catalyst for social good applies not only to a company's ultimate product but also to the way that company is operated. "I never started PT&Co. just to be a business. In fact, I was never motivated by money. I was motivated more by the desire to keep together a group of people whom I enjoyed working with and to maintain a harmonious community among men and women I had hand-selected for their humor, intelligence, resourcefulness, creativity, and generosity of spirit. I honestly believe that the nurturing of greater spirituality can take place in the workplace."

PT&Co. is wholly owned by its employees, including CEO and creative director Tanaka, president Ellen LaNicca, and six vice-presidents, in addition to two employees in Dallas and one in Los Angeles. All corporate decisions are based on the input of the company's eleven shareholders and on the feedback from specific committees designed to deal with every aspect of running the company, from employee benefits policies to office equipment to commissions policies.

"I have worked hard to create a workplace where I would want to work if I were an employee," adds Tanaka, "one that is comfortable, challenging, and dynamic, one where high standards prevail and where people are encouraged and expected to do great work. I have tried to strike the right balance between making the agency's shareholder group feel that as owners they have some 'special' status without making non-shareholders feel like second-class citizens. I think every person we hire — whether a shareholder or non-shareholder, whether an executive or a non-executive — makes a significant contribution to the agency.

"There are a lot of public relations firms in New York. [With only 25 employees], we are a relatively small firm and can't afford to pay the kind of salaries that some of the big firms can. What we can offer, however, is a great environment with good employee benefits, high job satisfaction, and a nurturing and comfortable environment. I try very hard not to dictate any one right way to do things and to give employees enough feedback so that they may 'own' their responsibilities. I don't view employees as disposable commodities. If a person doesn't work out in a particular job, I try to re-design their role at the agency to maximize the employee's strengths and minimize their less-than-strong suits so that they can succeed and make a valuable contribution.

"What I always look for when I am hiring people is a certain spark, something that says this person is passionate about their feelings and has the self-confidence to express them. I look for people with an obsessive drive to do the best they can possibly do . . . People who are creative and resourceful and independent are, by very definition, difficult to manage since they don't respond well to standardization. Each of them has to be accommodated and to be motivated in individual ways. But the effort to accommodate them is worth it to me. I made a decision a long time ago that I don't want to stay up every night worrying about my clients. I want to share that responsibility with everyone in the firm. If we each worry a little, then I only have to worry 1/25th of the total amount of worrying. The only way to share that burden is to hire people who own their responsibility, and the only way to get that is to give them what they need individually."

"What they need individually" can mean anything from allowing an employee to stay home one day a week to care for her new baby to creatively extending the company's already generous three-month paid maternity leave to allowing another employee to relocate to and work from Puerto Rico so that she could be close to her dying mother. Tanaka considers *Working Mother* magazine's 1994 award to her company as one of the country's fifteen best family-friendly work places to be one of the highlights of her career.

One of the biggest mistakes managers make, contends Tanaka, is "not remembering back to when they themselves may have been unhappy working for a difficult boss and vowing at that time to 'do things differently when I'm a manager.'" It was, in fact, just such an experience that helped Tanaka to establish her own management policies.

After graduating with a journalism major from the University of Honolulu in 1974, Tanaka worked for a local newspaper before taking a job in the public relations department of the Intercontinental Maui Hotel. "I grew up in Hawaii, but I never really felt a true connection with the place," she recalls. "I was raised on movies that were filmed in New York in the forties and fifties, movies like *How to Marry a Millionaire.* Although my grandparents were Japanese and I was made to go to Japanese school when I was small, I always knew I wanted to come to New York and live an exciting life like Lauren Bacall and all the other American 'dames' I'd seen in the movies.

"My mother was a great role model for me. She is very outgoing, warm, and sociable, and she worked for many years in direct sales, selling everything from brassieres to food supplements to household products. She exposed my brother and sister and me to as much mainland culture as she could. We would go to the ballet when Rudolf Nureyev came to Honolulu or to afternoon tea at one of the island's fancy hotels."

When Tanaka took the job at the Intercontinental Maui, she told herself she would work there for two years and then move on. "I believe we work on things consciously and unconsciously," she reflects with a hearty laugh. "I actually worked at the Intercontinental for two years to the day and then decided to simply bite the bullet and move to New York."

Tanaka moved to New York in 1979, and, with the help of some travel writers she had met while doing public relations for the hotel, landed a free-lance job with Jessica Dee Communications, a small Manhattan-based public relations firm. Tanaka quickly rose to be second-in-command under Dee, whose tough, uncompromising management style created an extremely stressful work environment that led to heavy employee turnover. Tanaka is clearly ambivalent about what turned into ten years under Dee's tutelage. "We were a very good team," says Tanaka. "We played good cop/bad cop. Jessica was a terrific businesswomen and did the selling while

I serviced all the clients . . . But I don't think she was a team player. She never worried about her employees' needs, financial or otherwise. I would watch her and think, 'If we can be this successful with all of her flaws, imagine what might be possible without that kind of narcissism.' I vowed that if I ever ran a company, I would give everyone a piece of the business. Like Jessica, I too am a flawed human being. I can be short-tempered and moody, impatient and inflexible. But I understood that if I ran a company I wouldn't want the success of my company to be limited by my own personal limitations. I would give everyone a say."

Tanaka's opportunity came in 1990, three years after Dee had sold her public relations firm to Chiat/Day, Inc. the highly successful advertising company. "Traditionally, the relationship between public relations and advertising is antagonistic, and Jessica lacked the personal skills to help build a better relationship with the parent company," she opines. "She left within a year or two of the takeover, and, as next in line, I took charge of the Jessica Dee subsidiary.

"Those of us who remained continued to feel the frustration of working under the ad agency," she continues. "What's more, the recession was just kicking in and I suspected that any day, Chiat/Day would begin making cutbacks that started with lay-offs in the public relations subsidiary. I began thinking of a way to buy back Jessica Dee Communications."

Emotional turmoil ensued. "I'd never run a business before, and I really had no idea how to do a buy-back," reflects Tanaka. "It was a little bit of 'I have a barn. Let's put on a show.' I approached all twelve shareholders of the subsidiary and found that six of them felt it was the right thing to do. First, we tried to get a bank loan. We approached six banks and they all said, 'No.' Then, I tried to convince the shareholders to put in their own money. That didn't work either. Finally, on the advice of our lawyer, we convinced Chiat/Day to buy back my 125,000 shares of stock in the company at $5 per share as part of their asking price. My parents gave me a $60,000 loan after taking out a second mortgage on their home, and we then used that as the capital investment to start Patrice Tanaka & Company. Since I'm under five feet tall and our lawyer and banker were both barely over five feet themselves, we jokingly referred to our deal as 'Midgets at the Gate' in allusion to the then hugely bestselling book *Barbarians At The Gate* about the multi-billion dollar RJR Nabisco takeover. All twelve of the shareholders joined in when they realized they wouldn't have to put down a penny of their own money, and the deal was closed in July of 1990."

Although Tanaka's parents have long since been paid back and the company now has a full roster of clients, PT&Co.'s first year was rough going. The recession had seriously trimmed most companies' public relations budgets, and billings dropped by 50 percent. "The typical response for a public relations agency in that situation would be to lay off half of their staff," says Tanaka. "I knew that would be our death knell. I said, 'Look, guys, the only way we can ride this through is to hold on. People won't see us as a viable entity if cut back. All of us will just have to take a salary cut.'"

The shareholders' willingness to hunker down during the tough times paid off. Within a year, the company had fully recovered its losses and began gaining clients. In 1994, billings increased by 25 percent, and the company has plans to relocate their lower Fifth Avenue offices to Manhattan's West Village, doubling the size of their corporate headquarters to more than 10,000 square feet, in a space built to the firm's specification.

"We gravitate to companies that gravitate to agencies like us," she says of her current clients. "We tend to share the same corporate culture and philosophy . . . Our employee ownership is a strong competitive advantage in distinguishing PT&Co. from other PR agencies. It's very powerful for clients to know that their business is being serviced by employee/owners. They know that we will do whatever it takes to deliver results because we understand that their fortunes and our fortunes are inextricably linked. We put a lot of passion and soul into what we do and we want clients who appreciate that kind of work . . .

When we started, we went after large corporate clients that would help to build the PT&Co. brand name. Most important, I always want the freedom to be able to walk away from any account. We work too hard and we're too good to take just any old thing."

Tanaka tries hard to keep the office environment as intimate as possible and her schedule relatively stress-free. She occasionally takes on speaking engagements "to get the PT&Co. name out there," and she sits on the boards of organizations such as Women's Resource Center of New York and 100 Asian/Pacific American Women because, she says, "The more I'm in the business world, the more sensitized I am to the fact that women need to reach out to help other women get ahead."

The rest of her energies are devoted to keeping the company going strong. She has opened offices in Dallas and Los Angeles to provide her clients with coast-to-coast service and has recently joined forces with RJS, a Latin American marketing company, to expand PT&Co.'s global capabilities. Nevertheless, she insists that she has no intention of enlarging her company beyond 40 or 50 employees, or, for that matter, working to increase the company's annual billings beyond $4 or $5 million. That, she says, is the optimum size that will allow her to provide clients with "small agency" care and attention and "big agency" resources and capabilities.

What's more, gone are the fourteen- and sixteen-hour days that were a staple at Jessica Dee Communications. Most nights, Tanaka leaves by 7:00 p.m., either to work out with her personal trainer or to get home in time to have dinner in the Murray Hill apartment she shares with her husband, Assad Hakiek, an artist. In recent years, Hakiek has undergone several operations for a brain tumor, a condition that demands a great deal of Tanaka's support and emotional energy and makes her all the more aware of her need for a closely knit, harmonious community at work.

"Life is short, and I want to spend my time around people who are fun to be around," she says philosophically. "I look for people who will add to the party, people who can create good energy in our workplace community.

"As the owner of a business, I believe that I have the power to create a positive or a negative workplace environment which can send employees — citizens — out into society who will be charged by that positive or negative energy. Thus, I have the power to impact positively or negatively on the world, making it a better or worse place. This, to me, is one of the greatest responsibilities of business ownership. If we as business owners don't understand and exercise this power responsibly, we will squander the real opportunity to help create a brighter future for us all."

"If necessity is the mother of invention,
then boredom is the father."

JOEL GLICKMAN

**Plastics innovator and creator of
the K'NEX connector toy set**

⌒

According to Joel Glickman, "If necessity is the mother of invention, then boredom is the father."

Indeed, for Glickman and his brother and partner Bob, it was boredom — along with a major investment of capital and time — that led to the launching of K'NEX, one of the most successful new products to enter the $13-billion American toy market in 1993.

Joining Lego, Erector Sets, and Lincoln Logs in the construction category of toys, K'NEX is a set of colorful plastic rods, connectors, and pulleys that enables children to build everything from trucks, doll houses, and spaceships to complex carousels and roller coasters that move and spin with the aid of wheels and one large, strong rubber band.

The Glickmans' Connector Set Toy Company, manufacturers of K'NEX, has reaped $23 million in sales since they began national distribution in 1993. And if you ask the Glickman brothers, that's just the beginning.

Media legend has it that Joel invented the toy in 1988 at a cocktail party when, bored by the loud music and the dull conversation, he morosely began fitting plastic straws onto the prongs of a fork to create a three-dimensional construction. But it wasn't quite that spontaneous. "There was no 'Eureka! A toy is born!'" admits Joel. "Invention is a complex process that involves understanding a problem and then using intelligence or intuition or a combination of both to solve [it].

Usually that leads to a new problem, which requires a different solution, and so on until the process is complete."

And what really began this maze-like process was, quite simply, boredom. For almost 30 years, Joel, now 52, had successfully run the family-owned Rodon Group, one of the largest privately held businesses specializing in what he describes as "injection molding of small component parts in high volume." What that means is just one word — plastics. In an immaculate and expansive fully automated factory housing 100 highly sophisticated molding presses, the Rodon Group had been churning out hundreds of such small plastic necessities as shower curtain rings, bottle caps, eyeglass case clips, pegboard hooks, and the like.

"Bob and I were running our operation so smoothly," recalls Joel with candid good humor, "that we had virtually delegated our jobs out of existence. Between us I think we worked half a day each week, and we spent the rest of our time playing golf and tennis, riding bikes, and most of all, thinking about what to do next.

"We were looking for a new product that we could design [to take advantage of] our world-class expertise in mold-making and manufacturing. Up until this point we were contract manufacturers. Companies called us up and asked us to come up with the best solution to their particular company's plastic needs. Although we had several patents on component parts of various products, we had never actually produced our own complete product. I knew we had the talent pool — the designers, tool makers, and engineers — to create something new.

"So the question became: 'What are we going to do?' We certainly didn't know gene-splicing. But we did know how to play with toys. As manufacturers, we wanted to choose a toy that would be a staple and not a passing fad. Barbie and G.I. Joe were already taken. Construction seemed the obvious choice."

Both Joel and Bob readily agree that Joel is the creative force behind K'NEX. Although he earned only average grades in high school in Philadelphia and "crayoned his way" through college studying graphic arts at Syracuse University, he did have a strong visual sense and a unique natural talent for geometry. This innate ability to grasp the three-dimensionality of concepts proved essential in the designing of K'NEX.

As the Rodon Group continued its manufacture of small component parts, Joel spent the better part of 1991 and 1992 coming up with prototypes for a toy. He used flexible plastic straws and connectors until he realized that the concept couldn't work unless he created rods and connectors that would remain stable during construction. He then spent hours snapping and unsnapping rods and connectors to determine the most logical lengths, sizes, and designs for his toy.

"It took weeks, if not months, to get the molds built. I was impatient, but not frustrated. I am very determined — like him," says Joel, pointing to the sculpture of a marble bison, horns bowed and ready to ram, that stands behind his desk. "My wife bought that for me because she said it reflects my personality. Once I had the first rod and connector right, I was sure we had it. And then I couldn't let go until I finished it."

"My brother is unbelievably focused," said Bob, who left his own Philadelphia law practice to join Rodon in 1978, adding that he and his brother have always been very close. "Joel does not like to think about things like administrative details. For instance, he can understand the problems involved in very sophisticated molds, but he can't figure out how our phone system works. But I've watched Joel focus in on a problem and virtually tune out everyone and everything going on around him. I often have to apologize to his employees and tell them, 'He's not ignoring you. He's just lost in his own world.' Nothing distracts him once he gets going, and no problem scares him off."

"I just worked on until I got it right," says Joel. "I played with the parts until I knew that they were technically perfect and distilled down to the minimum number that would be necessary to give consumers the greatest value."

Thus, by 1992, having spent tens of millions of dollars on new machinery and a 123,000-square foot plant in Hatfield,

Pennsylvania, K'NEX was ready for the public. The initial straw-like prototypes had given way to 22 bright, color-coded, solid, high-quality plastic parts — seven grooved rods ranging in length from 11/16" to 7-1/2", ten straight to 360-degree connectors, three tires, two pulleys, and a rubber band.

"I asked myself 'What would I want in a toy?' and then cut no corners," explains Joel. "I had to be satisfied that it was the best thing I could make. If my name was going to be on it, only I could determine what was right or wrong. We never once focused on the money. We only knew we had to make a superb toy. I'm convinced that if you focus and do whatever you do in the best possible manner and follow only the most basic business rules, then the finances will take care of themselves . . . I'm not always right, but I'm always sure. I was sure it would make a worthwhile business."

Fortunately for the Glickmans, America's four major toy companies didn't agree. The original plan was for Rodon to manufacture the construction sets and for one of the big-name toy companies to handle the packaging, distribution, and sales.

"All we got were rejection letters," recalls Joel. "The toy business is tough. No one wants to talk to amateurs. For one thing, there are a million kooks out there that think they have invented the best toy in the world, and the big guys just don't have the time to talk to everyone. But, more importantly, they want to protect themselves from lawsuits. Their big fear is that they may already be working on a toy that a new designer will later claim is his. So, pretty much, they look at nothing and talk to nobody. We sent letters and proposals and even with the connections we had, all we got back were form letters. They flat out said, 'No!' "

So the bison dug in his heels and rammed harder. Using his excellent design sense, Joel came up with a heavy-duty plastic carrying case and attractive packaging and contracted out for their production; he sought out a public relations firm to help market the toy; and he began raising capital to finance the venture himself.

"We simply rethought the whole project," he recalls. "I figured we could do it in a small way and own the company 100 percent or we could raise some money and play in the big leagues. I was always a competitive guy. In college, I was too short to play competitive basketball and not good enough to play competitive baseball so I became a really good pole vaulter. This was kind of the same problem. One way or another, we were going to play big and win."

In no time, the Glickmans' experience, integrity, and creativity — and the superior quality of their new toy — attracted more limited partners than they knew what to do with. They raised in excess of $10 million in venture capital from over 100 partners and were forced to turn many people away.

Joel's marketing philosophy was backed by the same determination that had brought K'NEX this far. The toy was tested in relatively few focus groups before the finishing touches were applied and the product was brought to the public. Some decisions required more thought than others. For example, experts told them the toy needed to be pink and purple to sell to girls. The brothers didn't agree; instead they called their plastic suppliers and picked the brightest colors that were readily available — yellow, green, red, blue, orange, purple, gray, and white. "We knew that if kids got their hands on the product they would buy it," Joel said with his characteristic confidence. And he was right.

The big day came on October 16, 1992. Hatfield Township was celebrating its 250th anniversary and the local Chamber of Commerce asked the Glickmans to set up a K'NEX booth to show the locals that these days, even toys were being manufactured in their largely agrarian town.

"It was incredible," recalls Bob. "We set up a booth and brought along some toys just for display. In no time, there must have been 1,000 people lined up around that booth, six and seven deep, and all of them wanted to buy our toy...People in the toy business told us to get our toy out to a critical mass. If it's a quality toy, they said, then the people will buy it. After that town fair, we knew we had to take K'NEX on the road."

Later that year the Glickmans assembled as many family members, Rodon employees, and friends as possible and began demonstrating K'NEX in local Toys R Us and K-Mart stores. They set up displays that demonstrated the versatility of the toy and made three different sets — Basic, which retails for $34.95, Intermediate at $59.95, and Giant at $99.95 — available. They worked every weekend, covering about 25 stores in the local Philadelphia area. "The kids loved us and the media picked up on our 'David and Goliath' story," recalls Bob. "Before long, Toys R Us stores across the country were calling us to do demonstrations for them." By the time the annual New York Toy Fair rolled around in February of 1993, both big chain stores and mom-and-pop stores across the country were interested in distributing the toy they heard had sold so well at Toys R Us.

This hands-on marketing approach was further supported by the "K'NEX Build-in Circus," an idea devised by the local Philadelphia Elkman Advertising firm. Bob took the show on the road to thirteen cities across the country, setting up a small canopied K'NEX "tent" decorated with an assortment of five- and six-foot lighthouses, grandfather clocks, chairs, juke boxes, and barnyard animals, all cleverly constructed from the brightly colored rods and connectors.

"We mostly set up in local museums," explains Bob. "Kids were invited to come into the K'NEX tent. Our theme was: If you built something and left it, there was no charge. If you built something and wanted to keep it, then we would weight it, charge a certain amount of money per pound, and then donate all proceeds either to the museum's scholarship foundation or to children's charities such as the Make a Wish Foundation, which supports kids with terminal illnesses. The museums and the charities supplied the volunteers to work the circus, and we developed a great reputation."

Along with the "Circus" tour, they presented demonstrations at county fairs across the country. For instance, for the 1994 Sonoma County Fair, which was organized to celebrate the 100th anniversary of the Ferris wheel, they displayed an eight-foot Ferris wheel built entirely of K'NEX.

"As my brother is fond of saying, 'What we don't know about the toy business could fill volumes,'" quips Bob, "but our reaction time was very fast. We did anything that seemed rational at the moment. And we did our best to provide a product we would be proud of. K'NEX is not expensive when you realize how many models can be built from just one kit, and when you consider that it comes with its own carrying case, the value is incredible. We advertised our toy as something that would encourage kids to think and we never pandered to any kind of violence. To this day, we offer no instructions for building war toys such as tanks."

Their instincts paid off. During its first year on the market, K'NEX won fifteen major toy awards, including the National Parenting Publication Awards Gold Seal, *Time*'s "Best Products of 1993," and "Toy of the Year" awards from *Family Fun*, *Parenting*, *Parents*, and *Parents Digest*. The Glickmans expect sales to double shortly, with the introduction of several new sets, including the Roller Coaster, a model that runs cars made of K'NEX and draws power from either a hand crank made from the set or from a separate 12-volt K'NEX motor pack.

What does Joel have to say now to the toy companies that turned them down? "Thank you!" he says with a big grin. In fact, the Connector Toy Company is now in discussion with some of those same big leaguers about a joint venture to go international with K'NEX. They have already begun some distribution in Great Britain and in Australia, and studies reveal that children's taste in construction toys is the same around the world. What's more, the K'NEX color-coded instruction manual uses computer-generated photographs and very few words, making it an obvious choice for the overseas market.

"The toy industry is a lot like show business," says Joel. "In our Rodon business, no one paid much attention to our success or failure. But the toy business is like Hollywood. You're only as good as your last toy. You put yourself on the line with a toy, and the success or failure is public.

"Everybody thinks it's romantic to be a toy maker. We get lots of people calling us up to say they think they have a great idea for a toy. We tell them, 'Don't kid yourself. You have to be prepared to put everything you have behind it. You have to throw your whole self into a toy.'"

In the meantime, for Joel and Bob, the risk has definitely paid off. The Glickmans are quite clearly having a good time with K'NEX. On most days, the brothers' attire rarely gets more formal than jeans and a sweater, and their expansive and tastefully decorated modern offices are comfortable and artfully appointed and clearly reflect Joel's background in graphic design. "I'm happy to say, 'This is my product!'" says Joel. "We couldn't be world champion bike riders or basketball players but, at 52 and 48 years old, we can be the best in the world at making toys."

Joel and his brother are never bored now. "In fact," says Joel, "We're growing so fast and have to make so many decisions so quickly that we rarely have any time off. It often feels as if we have to make a critical decision every fifteen minutes, and we're just going by instinct. There is no time to reflect. Most days, we work till we drop. If we worked half a day per week between us before, we work 24 hours a day between us now. At this point, all we want to do is bring in enough people so that Bob and I can have a weekend again."

"There is a Navajo poem that goes like this:
'I seem to be working and thinking, but
I am really running through a meadow.'
That poem sums up my life because I love
what I do and where I live."

R.C. GORMAN

Native American painter, sculptor, printmaker, and gallery owner

R. C. Gorman thinks of himself as a "simple" man. "To me, a visionary is someone who perceives where he would like to be years from now. More often than not, if he thinks he can do that, then he's just plain full of himself," he explains. "I don't find myself unique. I am rather ordinary. It's other people who create you as a legend."

There's no doubt about the fact that thousands of art collectors, gallery owners, and museum curators around the world, not to mention an astounding assortment of first-time art buyers and tourists seeking souvenirs from the American Southwest — an area whose Native American culture has been *en vogue* for several years now — have helped to turn the 62-year-old Navajo artist into a legend in his own time. During the last three decades, Gorman's posters, lithographs, drawings, and sculptures depicting serene Navajo women draped in woven blankets have earned him the moniker "the Picasso of American Indian artists." Moreover, his use of spare yet suggestive lines, brilliant colors, and finely detailed Native American landscapes and artifacts have inspired enough imitators to create a whole new school of contemporary Indian art.

But by any standards, "simple" seems something of an understatement when it comes to Rudolph Carl Gorman. There are, after all, few Navajos who tool around Taos, New Mexico, in a big mauve Mercedes, habitually set off their headbands and turquoise jewelry with specially ordered, extravagantly patterned Hawaiian silk shirts, or reside in a four-building adobe compound at the foothills of the Sangre de Cristo mountains, complete with a Japanese-style sculpture garden, an Olympic-sized indoor swimming pool, an electronic security gate, and a spectacular art collection that includes paintings by Picasso, Matisse, and Miró.

And perhaps no other American Indian — a term Gorman prefers over the more politically correct "Native American" — has the artistic talent as well as the flamboyant charm to garner regular appearances on national television and radio programs, be presented with keys to the cities of San Francisco, Palm Springs, Scottsdale, Houston, and San Antonio, and inspire profiles in most of the major newspapers and magazines in the country. Certainly, few of us would consider it "ordinary" to dine in the best restaurants every night, play host to the likes of Elizabeth Taylor, Arnold Schwarzenegger, and Jackie Onassis, and regularly turn over our homes to host extravagant fund-raising benefits for myriad local causes. But R.C. Gorman does all of these things and enough more to inspire one person who knows him to liken him to "a combination of P.T. Barnum, Florenz Ziegfeld, Cecil B. DeMille, Mike Todd, and Joseph Papp."

But "R.C." or just plain "Gorman," as he likes to be called, manages to make his well-publicized lifestyle and astronomical success in the art world seem as natural as eating or drinking — both of which he does with sophisticated taste, in great quantities, and as often as possible.

"There is a Navajo poem that goes like this: 'I seem to be working and thinking, but I am really running through a meadow.' That poem sums up my life because I love what I do and where I live," Gorman writes in *The Radiance of My People*, his recent art-book-sized autobiography which features over a hundred illustrations of his work. "I'm quite happy with the work I do. I've been drawing since age three and I'm too lazy to do anything else. I know what I do best and simply keep doing it."

As with just about everything Gorman says, there is an earnest candor to his understatement. He is aware of the patent absurdity of describing himself as ordinary or lazy, but he means what he says. He makes no bones about enjoying the trappings of material success—fine wine, gourmet food, marble floors and etched glass windows in his home—but he does not take these creature comforts as proof that he possesses great character or a deep soul.

His understatement does, however, sometimes go too far. One could hardly regard as "lazy" someone who in the last three decades has been the author, subject, or sole illustrator of seven books, including three editions of *Nudes and Foods*, a book featuring examples of his work along with a collection of some of his favorite recipes. He has also opened two very successful art galleries in Albuquerque and Taos, that sell only his work, purchased a ceramics studio that produces only Gorman vases and plaques, and produced hundreds of works of art in a wide range of media. But Gorman genuinely perceives his journey from poverty on a Navajo reservation in Chinle, Arizona to fame and fortune within the international art community as "a run through a meadow." What emerges from conversations with the artist is his conviction that his commercial success has, in fact, been the result of nothing more than steady work, choosing the right people to help him organize his business, and a childlike need to do what he likes to do best — create art.

"I've always liked what I'm doing and I'm trained for little else," he explains, quite clearly uncomfortable trying to translate his needs and motivations into words. "I always knew I was an artist, and I've never really tried to do anything else."

Gorman was born on a Navajo reservation in northeast Arizona within the fertile cradle of Canyon de Chelly, an area plentiful in corn, beans, pumpkins, and peaches before being taken over and virtually destroyed by the U.S. Cavalry under Colonel Kit Carson in 1863. Gorman was born in 1932 and raised during the Depression. Although as a child he lacked most material comforts, he remembers that his family "always had enough to eat" and says that he never perceived himself as poor.

What he lacked in physical comforts was made up for by a rich cultural heritage. His ancestors were sand painters, silversmiths, weavers, chanters, and holy men. His father, Carl, who is still alive and working as an artist in Ft. Defiance, Arizona, is a painter and a respected authority on Navajo legend.

"I was the oldest of a family of five children, and it was my job to take care of my brothers and sisters," he recalls. "We used to swim in the Chinle Wash. We thought nothing of being naked and playing in the mud . . . When the water floods out of the canyon at Chinle and then recedes, it leaves the most beautiful muddy places. As a small boy, I used to draw pictures in the mud with my fingers or with a stick . . . The Navajo child has to make his own toys, so the creative approach becomes natural to him. After a flood I would model animals and toys out of the clay, sitting in the Wash, caked with mud. I did my little Mickey Mice and automobiles, the only cultural expressions of the Anglo that filtered to me, and those were my first sculptures."

Gorman's father spent much of his son's childhood overseas as a Navajo code-talker during World War II. He divorced his wife and left home when R.C. was twelve, leaving the boy to be raised almost entirely by his mother, grandmother, and aunts. Gorman concedes that his being raised by several strong Navajo women is largely responsible for the images of women that pervade his work today.

"Navajos always had respect for strong, powerful women who would go out and chop wood, herd sheep, have babies in the field. My Indian woman isn't glamorous but she is beautiful," he says, explaining that his works are always created from live models. "My models may be Asian or white or Indian but what they all have in common is that they are solid and earthy. I paint the common woman who smells of the fields and maize. She is earthy and nurturing and has big hands and strong feet. The feet are particularly important to me because the Navajo people needed good strong feet to survive. I like big, fat feet! Sometimes I do a whole drawing just to comple-ment one lovely foot.

"I don't draw the 'ideal' woman who would fit into Playboy-bunny underwear. I draw beautiful women who are sometimes fat and have calluses on their feet. My women are soft and strong like my grandmother and like my aunt Mary, who used to make clay sculptures with me when we [were] out in the field herding sheep. But they are also remote, with-drawn in their silence. They don't look out, but glance inward in the Indian way. They do not reveal whether they are look-ing at us or not . . . I guess my paintings are my way of saying 'thank you' to the women who raised me."

Gorman's mother was quite pragmatic and taught her children English before Navajo. She also worked in the field to pay for Gorman to attend St. Michael's, a Catholic boarding school on the Navajo reservation near the eastern border of Arizona. "The teachers were very strict and I was punished for speaking Navajo," Gorman recalls. "We were also punished for speaking to girls and forced to shovel coal all day on Saturdays. The experience left me with very little enthusiasm for Catholi-cism for a long time."

A year later, in 1944, Gorman was enrolled in the more progressive Ganado Presbyterian Mission School and baptized as a Protestant. "The Presbyterians encouraged us to speak the native language so that the gospel could be carried to the non-English speaking people," he continues. "My art instruc-tor there was Jenny Louis Lind. She was a volunteer and she encouraged me to paint in my own style. She introduced me to art books full of the works of other artists in other lands . . . Where I was raised we didn't have museums, so the only in-fluence I had in my early years came from books. I knew some Indian artists — Harrison Begay, Andy Tsinajinnie, and Beatien Yazz — and I tried painting like them. But Jenny Lind never insisted that I paint that way or any other way. She encouraged me to try everything. She taught me how to work in different media like oil paintings, watercolors, and pen and ink."

Gorman's schooling did not so much separate him from his Navajo heritage as create a unique blend of Anglo culture and Indian attitudes and beliefs. Though the images of his childhood landscapes and the women who raised him continue to suffuse his work and many art critics credit him for furthering a positive image of American Indians, he claims to have no particular political commitment to Native American causes, and these days is, in fact, a practicing Catholic. "I understand very little of Navajo ways," he has told the press when asked about his "Indianness." "However, I do respect much of what they do and their outlook, so in that regard they do have an impact on me. As an example, I made sure that my house was blessed by a Navajo medicine man. That's traditional. But then, I turned right around and had this priest come in and give his blessing. I'm waiting for the right rabbi to do the same thing! I make sure I'm safe."

In conversation, he neither romanticizes his roots nor ignores them. "It's obvious I'm not white, black, or Oriental. I am Indian and I am an artist," he insists. A large man with strong features, a ruddy complexion and shoulder-length black hair held in place by a headband, he is every Anglo's storybook-formed image of an American Indian. "I don't get offended when people call me an 'Indian artist.' A lot of artists who are described that way get uptight about it. I was painting a long time before it was the vogue to be an Indian artist . . . The reservation is my source of inspiration for what I paint or draw, but I never realize this until I find myself in some far-flung place. Perhaps when I stay on the reservation I take too much of what it has to offer for granted. While there, I paint or draw very little, [but when I'm] off the reservation, it is my [idea] of reality.

"Though I no longer live like most Navajos, I can't escape my roots. I have to relate to what I know best. I still have Indian attitudes. My Aunt Mary visited me a while back, and I saw her sitting on an old stool out there in the driveway. She'd dug a little pit and started a fire and she was cooking sheep intestines over the fire. That was her gift to me. The cars, my swimming pool—those things don't mean anything to her. She was bringing me a part of my home country, to keep me in my place, so to speak."

Gorman moved closer to assimilation when he enlisted in the Navy after graduating high school at the Ganado Mission School. It was in the Navy that he acquired the nickname R.C., which was printed on his shirt pocket. He was stationed in Guam and developed a taste for travel and for the cosmopolitan delights of Anglo culture. At the same time, he continued his "art education," supplementing his income by charging officers $7 and his fellow recruits $2 for portraits of their girlfriends. Most of the time, he would draw the faces from head-and-shoulders photographs and further illustrate them with voluptuous bodies in the style of Vargas or Petty.

After being transferred to Moffett Field near San Jose, California, Gorman visited San Francisco and became enamored of the city. "It had everything I love," he says, "great food, a cosmopolitan culture, beautiful architecture, and interesting people." Following his discharge from the Navy, he enrolled at Northern Arizona University, where he majored in American literature and minored in art. He continued to draw and paint and supported himself with odd jobs, including one at Disneyland, where he spent one summer paddling a canoe dressed as an Indian.

In 1958, discouraged with academia and more interested than ever in pursuing his art, Gorman moved to San Francisco. Then a friend from the University of California at Berkeley took him on a trip to Mexico. "We went to Guadalajara and Mexico City," he recalls. "We visited an orphanage in Guadalajara that had some huge, overpowering murals by Orozco on the walls.

"I cannot forget the moment I first saw those murals. They depicted, in monumental scale, the sweeping history of the Mexican people and it took my breath away. It got me to realize my own background, and I decided I could do the same thing with my own people. So I started being directed toward representing my own background. Until that time, I was trying to paint like a European. After studying the works of Rivera, Siqueiros, and Tamayo, I started to paint like a Mexican, except that I was using the Navajos for my subject matter." That same year he received a grant from the Navajo Tribal Council and was awarded a scholarship to study at Mexico City College. "I developed my technique for drawing my pictures of women during my classes there," he continues.

Never a disciplined student, Gorman returned to San Francisco after three months and worked as an artist's model at schools around the city. Modeling in art school, he says, not only earned him enough money to support his painting but allowed him to pick up some formal training by listening to the class lessons being taught around him. "I'm not big on academic training," he insists, although he is the recipient of honorary degrees from the College of Ganado in Arizona, Eastern New Mexico University in Portales, and Northern Arizona University, and, in 1986, of Harvard University's Humanities Award. "It can be very constraining because teachers often want you to paint in a certain way. I think [academic training] is best for artists who want to become teachers." It was during these early years in San Francisco that Gorman's career really took off. He began selling paintings and drawings to galleries around the Bay area and soon was discovered by Suzanne Brown, who with Elaine Horwich owned a successful gallery in Scottsdale, Arizona.

Brown, who Gorman calls "my Jewish mother," encouraged him to return to Mexico. He was invited to study lithography with Mexican artist Raul Anguiano, and he did his first lithograph with Jose Sanchez, a lithographer who worked with Tamayo, Orozco, and most of the other well-known Mexican artists. "Jose Sanchez didn't speak a word of English and I didn't speak a word of Spanish," Gorman recalls. "But it didn't matter. We managed to create some beautiful work together and all of it by using sign language."

Lithography is a technique that involves drawing on stone with a greasy pencil or brush; the stone is then etched with acid, inked, and printed. The method attracted Gorman because of its spontaneity and speed and because he was able to make hundreds of salable pictures from a single drawing.

"I owe my graphics to Dr. Byron Butler, whom I met at one of my art exhibitions," Gorman continues. "He immediately suggested sponsorship of my lithos at Albuquerque's Tamarind Institute." Before long, Gorman was producing complex prints that represented a big step forward in quality and technical expertise and selling them almost as fast as he was turning them out. His subjects — almost exclusively Navajo women — were tremendously well received in Scottsdale, where the market had already focused on Indian art. "My best things just seem to happen," Gorman says, explaining that many of his lithographs take between five minutes and two hours to create. "I always find it irritating to hear an artist say that he worked hours and hours on a piece. It's so easy to overwork something."

In the early 1960s a Gorman lithograph sold for $150. Today a lithograph brings in anywhere from $1,000 to $2,500, with original drawings bringing in as much as $4,000 to $5,000 and sculptures and ceramics upwards from there. Although critics and gallery owners have suggested that he is flooding the market with his work, and thereby reducing its value, Gorman produces 225 lithographs of each drawing that he makes and feels comfortable with this number. He is quick to add that he is not responsible for many of the ubiquitous Gorman images on postcards and ceramic tiles that are now being sold in souvenir shops across the country. "I don't receive a penny for them," he insists. "But I let whomever's making them go ahead and sell them anyway because I figure it's good publicity for me.

"I don't see why art should only be available to a select few who can afford it," he adds. "My work is priced so that just about anyone who wants to can afford a poster for $50, and many can move up to a lithograph. There are a lot of people out there, and every minute somebody's being born who is going to be a Gorman collector." If so, he or she would be joining the likes of Gregory Peck, Elizabeth Taylor, and

Arnold Schwarzenegger, as well as Barry Goldwater, former President George Bush, and former Vice-President Walter Mondale, to name only a few of the better-known Gorman fans. Art dealers who handle Gorman in their galleries insist that a Gorman lithograph is not only a good investment but is priced to be virtually recession-proof. While other artists' works were dropping in value in the early 1990s, the sale of Gorman's works has remained all but constant.

In fact, Gorman's work is probably handled by more galleries than that of any other artist in this country. He brags that his gallery coverage is so extensive that he no longer offers exclusive deals and proudly announces that his art is handled in every state of the Union and sold in just about every airport in America. He is full of tales of wandering to a remote restaurant in Thailand or an art gallery in India and being delighted to find one of his lithographs hanging on the wall. His biggest sales, however, come from his own Navajo Galleries in Taos and Albuquerque.

Gorman traveled to Taos as a tourist in the mid-1960s and instantly fell in love with the place. "When I first visited, I was struck by the incredible beauty of Taos — the mystery, the open space, and the clean air. New Mexico is so vast and unrestricted, you can't help but feel free. The light and color continually stimulate me. As the aspens turn in the fall, they cover the mountains in mottled patches of dull greens and bright yellows. The summers are a rich green, and the winters are white."

When in Taos for the first time, Gorman met art gallery owner John Manchester, who saw slides of his work and immediately offered him a show. "My successful show at the Manchester Gallery confirmed what I already knew instinctively — that Taos was where I belonged and needed to be to accomplish my work," he reflects. In 1968, Manchester put his gallery up for sale and Gorman borrowed money from his father to buy the place and open the Navajo Gallery, making him the first American Indian to ever own and operate his own fine arts gallery. Never a good businessman, he relied on friends and patrons to help him get established. "I started with 55 artists," he recalls, "but none of them sold except me so I cut it down to myself."

Throughout the 1970s Gorman lived and worked at the gallery. "I would get up in the morning and work with a live model in the living room of the gallery. If anyone came in to look around and perhaps buy a drawing or a painting, I would simply invite them into the room where I was doing a drawing and let them meet me and the model and whomever else was there."

In 1970, an elementary schoolteacher named Virginia Dooley moved to Taos, and she and Gorman hit it off instantly. By 1972 she was the Director of the Navajo Gallery, where she still works today. "People always ask me how I can be an artist and such a good businessman," Gorman says with an impish grin. "The artist part is easy to explain. When I produce something well, I sell it. That is my only pride. I don't sell anything and everything. I throw away about thirty percent of what I do. I've been inspired by many artists. In fact, Picasso is my hero. He has a certain childlike implication in some of his work that is similar to how I worked at one time. But my biggest influence has been myself. I truly haven't patterned myself after any trend, or teacher, or artist, or parent. People will be surprised to hear it, but even my father has been no great influence on me. I am a self-made artist. I got a lot of help and encouragement from teachers, but what I have done I have manipulated myself.

"I must admit, though, that I am the worst businessman in the world! So I have surrounded myself with good lawyers and good accountants, a good foundry and good printing companies, and people like Virginia who know how to do what I can't do. I think I just lucked out. The people around me, like Virginia, were there from the beginning. I owe a lot of my success to her . . . Maybe my gift is knowing who are the best people to rely on. All the people who work for me — my housekeeper Rose Roybal, Virginia Dooley, Barbara Castner-Smith, who runs my other Navajo Gallery in Albuquerque, even my models and the people who take care of my home — have been with me for years and years. My staff never leaves me! Maybe it's because I'm the kind of boss who lets other people be bosses. Rose runs the house; Virginia and Barbara run the galleries."

These days, Gorman spends most of his time experimenting with ceramics, cast paper, and other new media, most of which he learns by teaching himself. He still travels to his regularly scheduled openings in Paris, London, and in galleries around the United States, where he frequently dons Native American garb, and as he puts it, "dresses the part." Though he thinks of himself as a private man, he enjoys the hectic schedule that suits his taste for travel and for sampling the cuisine offered in the world's best restaurants. Claiming that "devoting time to myself was responsibility enough," he never married, but he rarely wants for companionship. In fact, he often invites Virginia or Rose or other friends along on his trips around the United States and to Europe and Asia to share his gourmet dinners and to accompany him on visits to local museums, galleries, and theaters.

Even when he's home in Taos, Gorman rarely dines alone. Rose cooks up a grand luncheon every midday for guests who range from close friends to Taos's society ladies to the many celebrities who have come to Taos and looked him up over the years. Gorman delights in relating stories about visiting luminaries, such as the time Jackie Onassis came to his home and spent hours chatting in the kitchen with Rose or the afternoon that baseball star Jim Palmer simply drove up to his house and rang the bell and said into the intercom: "My name is Jim Palmer, and I'd like to meet R.C. Gorman."

In fact, Gorman, an unabashed star-gazer, has probably met more celebrities than he has painted pictures, and he loves to tell the stories, complete with dramatic illustrations. He does a mean imitation of Salvatore Dali, whom he encountered in the elevator of a New York hotel, and his Bette Davis isn't half bad either. He has also devoted one whole room of his home to autographed photographs and memorabilia from some of those encounters. "I miss your kisses sweeter than wine," says a framed note from Elizabeth Taylor. Along with signed photographs from Mae West, John Travolta, and Dennis Hopper are also a framed invitation to the wedding reception of Arnold Schwarzenneger and Maria Shriver and two silk-screened portraits of Gorman in profile by Andy Warhol.

"I used to be a bit of a madcap," he says as he walks past a wall of photographs of himself kissing or toasting or bear-hugging a mind-boggling array of well-known faces. "Now I think of myself as a simple man. I don't work on such a rigid schedule anymore and I don't go out partying very much either. I spend much more time at home. I still have a number of regular deadlines for gallery shows that I have to meet, and for the rest, surround myself with the people who are important to me and take pleasure in offering my house for causes. I have a big place that's perfect for a large bunch of people."

The four-building complex just a mile outside of Taos is indeed perfect for entertaining. Overlooking a spectacular view of the mountains, the house has so many art works both inside and out that tourists frequently confuse it with the nearby Millicent Rogers Museum. In the gravel-raked yard outside Gorman's front door stand two Gorman masterpieces, a pair of almost life-sized bronze sculptures of serene Navajo women, entitled Natoma II and Nellie Begay II. In addition to an Armand Lara fountain in which water flows mysteriously from a suspended rock, there are also several metal, rock, and wood sculptures, including a brilliantly colored totem pole by Joseph Sparks and Doug Coffin. Within the house hangs a collection of early Gormans, including his first drawings done as a boy of three, and wall-to-wall displays of the mostly local, Mexican, and Asian art works that the artist has collected over the years. "If I like something, I buy it. I don't hold back. There is no one artist or trend that I'm interested in. I never bought something because it was an investment, although many of my purchases — the Tamayo, the Miró, the Picasso, the Chagall, for instance — turned out to be good investments," he says when asked to define the philosophy behind his collection.

"I've gotten everything I have without being greedy," he says, with the same modesty. "Some people who have struggled to the top have shuffled people aside to get there. But they ended just like the rest of us — they died . . . I've always felt successful. Even when I wasn't making any money, I just knew it was all there. I always believed in myself. I knew I had talent; there was just no doubt about it. Throughout my career, I always worked. I worked to support my art and I worked at my art. I just didn't give up. That's the single biggest piece of advice I could give to anyone starting out now. There's nothing good about being a starving artist. People who are starving can't make art. You've got to work to support your art until your art starts rewarding you.

"As for success . . . well, anyone who says he doesn't like recognition I don't believe. But if I lost my popularity, one thing's for sure, I wouldn't jump out of a window. I had nothing to begin with and I could go back there quite easily."

"In general, women think that they've got better people skills than men. They don't. Women tend to bring a lot of trivia to the job and personalize too much. They've got to unlearn a lot and become more objective."

BETTYE MARTIN MUSHAM

**Founder and CEO of Gear Holdings Inc., marketers
of well-designed, affordable home furnishings**

B ettye Martin Musham likes to think of herself as "the Norman Vincent Peale of Home Furnishing."

"If we can help people create an attractive place to live, then we can help them have self-esteem and a sense of worth," says the 62-year-old CEO of Gear Holdings, Inc. "We give Americans a way to furnish their homes. Most people wake up every morning knowing how to dress themselves without even thinking about it. But the average American decorates a home twice in a lifetime and has no idea how to do it. The home is very important today. What it looks like affects the way people feel. We came up with a way to give people the confidence to decorate."

Musham's innovative idea to create a line of fully coordinated home furnishings formed the basis of Gear Holdings, Inc., the company she founded in 1978. Until that time, decorating a home stylishly often meant spending long hours wandering through department stores in an attempt to find furniture and accessories that would complement one another, more often than not with disastrous — and costly — results.

For many Americans, the only alternative to this confusing process, which often led to the frustrating sensation of having no taste, was to put the job in the hands of a high-priced decorator who would do the job for them — but leave them feeling just as confused and lacking in taste. Gear ended this misery by designing, licensing, and marketing an extensive and modestly priced line of coordinated wall-coverings, fabrics, and furniture, as well as framed art and accessories that would all work together to create a tasteful and well-decorated home.

In the fourth-floor Manhattan loft that serves as the Gear showroom, bolts of fabric printed with cabbage roses, rococo paisleys, and patchwork patterns hang like elegant tapestries along exposed brick walls. The wide-planked pine floors afford only narrow paths between a clutter of canopied four-poster beds, wicker armchairs, scrubbed pine chests, and breakfronts filled with color-coordinated vases and lamps. Mirrors framed with folk art lean against country pine tables heaped with tasseled pillows, flowered quilts, and multi-colored woven chenille throws. More like the living room in a chic, renovated barn than an office space, the loft is comfort-able and cozy — and the effect is distinctly American.

"Gear was the pioneer in creating American country deco-rating," marketing manager Marcy Matthews tells a class of students from the nearby Parsons School of Design as she leads them on a tour of the company's offices on downtown 7th Avenue. "You see this style everywhere now, and you think it's been around forever. But Gear created it fifteen years ago, and we're the only ones [who produce as] many things that all work together in one collection." In fact, the Gear collection includes 46 categories of furnishings for the home.

"When I first began I had no particular interest in home decorating," says Musham, sitting down on a high pine stool at a worktable in the back of the Gear loft and pushing away the stationery and journals whose covers repeat the same folk art patterns embossed on the surrounding artwork, lamps, pillows, and blankets. "But I am a marketer by background, and I felt that what I had to do was look for a niche in which there weren't any players yet.

"In the late 1970's, I walked around the department stores and saw that the only things designers got involved in were sheets. Bill Blass did them. So did Geoffrey Beene and Halston. But absolutely no one thought of having other home products that worked together. Home furnishings seemed the obvious choice. I may have been innovative, but more than anything, I was analytical. I asked myself, 'O.K. Now what's the next biggest market?' and then I went for it."

Musham's confidence in her own vision and her ability to market that vision have their roots in childhood. She grew up with her parents, two sisters, and a brother on a farm in a small Quaker community in Guilford, North Carolina. When her brother was eight, he developed meningitis, a disease that left the handsome, athletic child permanently mentally retarded. Musham's father, devastated by the damage to his only son, enrolled him in a private school for mentally retarded children and forced Bettye, who was only two years older and exceptionally bright for her age, to attend the same school to look after him.

"Fortunately, that only lasted for a few months before the school made my parents put me in public school," recalls a still incredulous Musham. Nonetheless, her father never quite allowed his eldest daughter to pursue her own pleasures. "I always had a good report card, but he wasn't interested. I remember wanting to play the piano and his not letting me because my brother would never be able to play . . . But my mother helped me a great deal. She was a typical Southern woman. She knew nothing about money or how to run a business, but she was very good at coping with life. She was very reassuring to me. She explained my father's hurt and disappointment and taught me to accept the reality that people don't always deal with things the way they should. That was a big help to me later when I had to manage people in business."

Musham's father died the night she graduated from high school, leaving behind neither plans nor means for financing Bettye's college education. With characteristic initiative, Musham solved the problem herself by using the same methods she still uses in business today. "When you don't know how to do something, go to the best person you can find and ask them how to do it," she insists. "There's nothing wrong with asking for help." She went directly to the president of Duke University and asked him how to get into his school. He told her she could have a scholarship as long as she enrolled in and graduated from Duke's nursing school.

"When you're young, you don't think [about the difficulties]," says Musham about her first year at Duke — a year she spent commuting between school and her family's farm, where she helped raise her brothers and sisters and nursed her mother, who had been diagnosed with cancer shortly after her husband's death. She died after Musham's first year at Duke. "It was certainly a hard year," Musham concedes.

"I never really wanted to be a nurse, but I enjoyed nursing school. I enrolled in whatever classes I liked and picked the courses I thought would be most interesting. In psychiatry classes, I learned how to question people in ways that would give me answers. That was a lot of fun. I liked to write, and I told myself I would collect stories in the hospital and write about them later on.

"I learned another important principle that year: whatever you are doing, do a real good job and keep your eyes open. You can only grow if you keep your eyes open and look for opportunities. Most work is repetitive and dull. But you realize there are certain things you have to do to get to the fun part."

After graduating from Duke in 1955, Musham earned a scholarship to study midwifery in Hammersmith, England. She never planned on becoming a midwife, but the scholarship included room and board and a motorcycle, and she thought the international experience would be worthwhile. After graduating, she moved to New York, where she briefly worked as a nurse at New York Hospital. In New York she met her first husband, an intern at Bellevue Hospital, and married him in 1957. "I liked nursing all right, but I couldn't earn a living at it. I think I got paid $48 a week," recalls Musham. "But nursing taught me how to deal with crises. If you work in an emergency room, you get perspective. This was a big help later on when I started running a business."

It wasn't long before Musham began taking odd jobs, including a well-paid job as an assistant to a commercial photographer's agent. She enjoyed this work well enough to start her own business, Bettye Martin, Inc., an agency that represented photographers such as Guy Bourdin, Saul Leiter, Deborah Turbeville, and Harold Becker. From there, she moved naturally into the world of advertising, working first for N. W. Ayer, organizing photo shoots and managing the campaigns of clients like Sealtest, AT&T, and De Beers Diamonds. She later moved to the Carl Ally agency, where she launched campaigns for large corporate clients such as Federal Express.

Always on the look-out for a new challenge, Musham next responded to a headhunter's search for a U.S. manager for Louis Vuitton, the prestigious French luggage company. Her job was to manage production and oversee product development. "I did things like visiting factories and discovering they were operating on one shift. I'd put on a second shift — simple things like that," she recalls. "I also wanted to expand — get into clothing, jewelry, perfume — but they didn't want to." Again relying on her own initiative, she decided to take her marketing ideas and do it herself.

In 1977, Musham and a Vuitton co-worker, designer Raymond Waites, started Gear as a design and marketing firm for soft-sided luggage. "We decided to stay in licensing since we had no idea how to run a factory, and we thought we'd do an American version of soft luggage," says Musham. "We did a lot of red, white, and blue ticking."

By 1980, Musham, and Waites knew there was a bigger market out there and began to work on their home furnishings collection. Two years later, they had signed a licensing deal with a firm in Japan. Following her own principle of seeking help from "the best person you can find," Musham simply called ex-Senator Mike Mansfield, then U.S. ambassador to Japan, and asked him how to do business in Asia. Senator Mansfield gave her two staff people to work with, and in short order, Musham set up an agreement with the Isetan Company.

Building on their success, in 1983, Musham and Waites established Gear Kids, the first fully coordinated kids furniture line, soon followed by Gear Kids lines of ready-to-wear, books, toys, and stationery. Shortly thereafter, they set up an exclusive licensing agreement in Great Britain for Gear Kids with The Boots Company PLC.

Today, Gear does more than $300 million in sales annually, and Musham is enjoying national recognition. In 1992 she was named one of the eight most powerful women business owners by *Entrepreneurial* magazine; in 1994 she received the Outstanding Entrepreneur Award from the National Association of Women Business owners; and she has been named one of America's Top 50 Women Business Owners by *Working Woman* magazine for the past three years in a row.

As in many success stories, however, the road to recognition and financial gain was not smooth.

For instance, Musham divorced her first husband, who left medicine to study philosophy in Oxford, England, in 1967. She was still single when she founded Gear in 1977 and had a difficult time securing financing for the company. "At that time, any woman going to the bank to borrow money to start a business was [treated like] a second-class citizen. In fact, if you're a woman and an entrepreneur, you *still* can't count on getting money from the bank." Undaunted, she overcame that problem by obtaining all of her financing from friends and business associates.

Then, between 1981 and 1986, Musham and Waites decided to open two retail stores in Manhattan to further their marketing concept. Like the present Gear showroom, the stores displayed all of the Gear furnishings and accessories in a country antique setting.

"[Opening] the retail stores was a terrific bomb," admits Musham, shrugging. "We were running the stores [by] committee, and none of us agreed. I thought they should be used as focus groups to develop our product; others thought of them as antiques stores . . . Rents were expensive in New York; it cost a lot of money to hire the top people to run the stores; and there was a lot of theft, even from our own employees.

"But we learned a lot . . . You have to take these experiences as part of the whole process. In general, women tend to become more emotionally involved in their businesses and their jobs, and that's a drawback. You have to have a passion for what you are doing, but as Rodin said, 'You can't become a tyrant to your own emotions.'

"You have to be willing to take risks and you have to know when to cut your losses. We may do retail stores again, but next time we'll go in with someone who already knows how to run a store."

Looking back on her career thus far, Musham cites several people whom she thinks of as "mentors," people who "had my best interests at heart and who taught me new ways to look at myself and what I was doing." These friends include the two women who helped her raise her only daughter Claudia, an actress, painter, and musician born in 1961. Though Claudia leads a very different life and wants no part of her mother's business, the two remain close.

Musham is particularly grateful to Tom Meloy, a friend of the family who lived next door to her uncle's farm in Virginia. Meloy had a daughter Musham's age and understood her drive to succeed. He became an initial investor in Gear. "Tom helped me think about things in big scale," Musham reflects. "He taught me the questions to ask and how to fit opportunities into my game plan."

Then there was Egon Hood, one of the artists she represented through Bettye Martin, Inc. in the late 1950s and early 1960s. "People need friends to talk to when they are building a big business. Egon convinced me to get out of the advertising business where I was in the daily firing line of managing people on shoots. He helped me get the perspective to go out on my own and [he] helped me learn how to deal with people.

"Over the years I've learned that being a good manager depends upon your ability to deal with people. In general, women think that they've got better people skills than men. They don't. Women tend to bring a lot of trivia to the job and personalize too much. They've got to unlearn a lot and become more objective.

"I don't think women are really more nurturing than men, either. Men and women both need to learn that nurturing is not patting on the back; it's helping people improve and get perspective. You [develop] a very tough skin running a company, and you have to help people learn the difference between perception and reality. I don't try to nurture. I try to challenge people. You have to tell people what you expect of them and when you expect it. That's what helps them."

Indeed, Musham is sensitive to the role of women in the marketplace, a situation she has called "the pink [collar] ghetto." She is a member of the Committee of 200, a group that consults with women starting out in business, and she has started internship programs between Gear and a number of colleges and universities. The programs are designed to help demystify small to mid-sized businesses for students preparing to enter the work force. In addition, she is a trustee of Marymount Manhattan College, a member of the Business Council of the United Nations, and on the Advisory Board of Duke University's School of the Environment.

"You have to give women the opportunity to excel," she says. "In the current business environment, women are still not promoted as men are. What's worse, I think women are less encouraging to other women than we admit. I don't think women are team players. They want to get to the top and will sabotage other women to do it. Men do it, too, but women are more overt about it. The issue, I believe, is self-respect and self-esteem. Without it, there is a lot of egotism, anger, and pride."

Over the years, Musham has worked to create an environment that will be supportive of her fifteen to twenty employees, many of them women. "For one thing, I don't have a big ego. And in the creative world, the risk-reward system is so high that it really doesn't matter what gender you are as long as you deliver . . . When I hire people, I look for curiosity. I ask how many jobs they've held previously and how long they've held them. I ask for writing samples, listen to their language, and look at how they present themselves. If they do well, we have a profit-sharing plan that allows them to buy into the company."

Undoubtedly, affirms Musham, the biggest influence on her life has been her current husband, Bill Musham. The retired Vice Chairman of the Board of ITE Imperial, a $2 billion electrical firm, Bill became the Chairman of Gear Holdings, Inc. in 1978. Today, the couple share a townhouse on Manhattan's Upper East Side and a country home in Bucks County, Pennsylvania. The 1870s stone house was formerly owned by writers S.J. Perelman and Nathaniel West. A barn on the property has been renovated and serves as a guest house for her daughter and Bill's three children, one of whom now works for Gear.

"Bill taught me that if women are going to have any say in life, they are going to have to be in the same positions as men, where they can get the same perspective. Bill encouraged me to get on the board of directors of big companies so I would get that perspective. It is very difficult for a woman to get on a board of directors, but I have recently joined the board of the Brunswick Corporation, a $2 billion sailboat and marine company, and I'm looking to join another.

"Bill also taught me to look and see what's ahead in my own development." With her husband's encouragement, Musham decided to run for Pennsylvania State Senate in 1993. Although she withdrew from the race, deciding she would rather put the time into building Gear worldwide, she doesn't rule out a political post in the future.

"It's never been money that drives me," Musham reflects with the same introspection and intelligence that illuminate almost everything she says. "In order to succeed, you have to have a clear vision and you have to be willing to wear blinders to get it accomplished. Many business people aren't very interesting because they stick to what they're doing and don't pay attention to anything else.

"I'm a little different. I like to work and I like to create jobs and product. But it's the challenge and the stimulation of being part of whatever is going on out there that moves me."

In the past year, Gear has signed a new deal with Lane Furniture that will increase their distribution throughout the United States, as well as a new exclusive licensing arrangement in Great Britain with Ametex, U.K. And plans are underway to expand Gear operations in China and South Africa.

"We're always looking ahead to new venues where there are licensees and manufacturers with whom to create co-ventures. Right now, the U. S. is the only country where people can go to school for continuing education, but things are changing quickly. We won't recognize the world in five years. Things will get better and better and I want to be part of it."

"I've been around a long time and I've seen everything written about me — good and bad. But if there's one thing I know I'm good for, it's living proof that you can still do it in America. It may not be easy, but, hell, what is?"

J.R. SIMPLOT

**Billionaire Founder of J.R. Simplot
Company, an agri-business conglomerate**

Never mind that he's 85 years old; J.R. Simplot is literally bounding through the halls of the Micron Semiconductor plant in Boise, Idaho, spryly taking the stairs two at a time. This is a routine visit, but he's eager to show off one of his favorite investments. Just over twenty years ago, he put $1 million worth of venture capital into Micron, and today he owns a sizable percent of the company, now worth over $100 million. He struts past the sealed windows overlooking the static-free electronic wafer assembly process that manufactures over 13,000 wafers each week. He is quite clearly pleased as punch.

Dressed in a blue suit and a tie printed with a red, white, and blue cartoon cow, Simplot looks a lot like a contemporary Daddy Warbucks. "Heck, I'm a cow man," he replies to repeated compliments on this snappy accessory, and he tips his fedora to each and every employee he passes. "How're we doin', son?" he says heartily to one man. To almost all the women he says, "I'm Mr. Simplot. How long have you been here, pretty ladies?" Everyone grins in obvious appreciation of his sheer energy and offers a cheerful, "Howdy, J.R.!" in return.

"Can you believe it? We're building quarter microns now," he says, bursting with pride. "Well, I don't know what a micron is, but it's awful damn' small and that's a quarter of one!" It doesn't bother J.R. that he knows so little about the

technology behind semiconductors. In fact, he has never ques-
tioned expanding into the esoteric world of high technology
after a lifelong career in agriculture.

"I predict that we're going to educate the world in digits,"
he says, quaintly using the word "digits" to describe anything
to do with computer technology. "You'll be able to dig a degree
out of a computer. It's awesome . . . This was absolutely foreign
to me when my son first suggested I get into this business. As
soon as I saw the 64-megabyte chip these boys were building
in the basement of a dental office downtown, it looked like it
had some merit to me. I bought up 40 percent of the company. Most of my life I have gotten into businesses I knew
nothing about. I like to bet my judgment. I'm a gambler and
I've been a gambler all my life. J.R. Simplot is a $2 billion
company now, and, honey, that's just the beginning."

There's no question that betting his judgment has paid off
for John Richard Simplot. After dropping out of high school
at age fourteen, he spent the first three-quarters of this century
building one of America's largest privately held agribusiness
corporations. He is best known as "Idaho's potato king" and
drives a cream-colored Lincoln Towncar with the license plate
"Mr. Spud" to confirm it.

And we're not talking small potatoes. The J.R. Simplot
Company produces 1 billion, 900 million pounds of potatoes
per year and owns five plants that process them in almost every
conceivable form. In fact, J.R.'s company has been credited
with inventing the frozen French fry and supplies 80 percent
of McDonald's franchises worldwide with their trademark
shoestrings. Then, of course, there are the spuds and curlicues,
the crinkle cuts and steak fries in all the national supermarket
chains and fast-food restaurants that serve them up to the
consumer. Chances are, those were Simplot potatoes you were
dipping in ketchup the last time you went to McDonald's,
Wendy's, Burger King, Dairy Queen, or Taco Time, to name
just a few of the outlets for Simplot spuds.

And potatoes are only a part of the menu. The company is
a major producer of meat and dairy products and processed

fruits and vegetables. Simplot plants process broccoli, carrots, corn, peas, asparagus, avocados, cauliflower, and strawberries. The J.R. Simplot Company grows beans and tomatoes and makes over 30 varieties of natural cheese products. The Simplot cattle-feeding business, based on an innovative way to process waste generated by the Simplot potato-processing plants, is one of the top ten suppliers of cattle in the United States, producing over 390,000 head annually.

As if that weren't enough, the Simplot Minerals and Chemical Group is a major phosphate fertilizer company, with facilities in thirteen states as well as in Canada and Mexico. Although the group's core business is agricultural fertilizer, it is also a key supplier of specialty fertilizers for consumer markets, as well as industrial chemicals, animal-feed phosphates, and silica sand. The group owns two phosphate mines in Idaho and shares ownership of a third in Utah, plus the nation's largest deposit of high-grade silica sand in a mine in Nevada and natural gas reserves in Canada.

Although most Simplot agricultural products are marketed on a wholesale basis, the company also runs a network of over 100 Simplot Soilbuilders retail farm supply and service stores throughout the U.S. and Canada. Over 50 different products packaged under the BEST brand are also available at local garden centers for consumer use on lawns and gardens. And to transport the wide range of Simplot products, J.R. started Simplot Transportation Operations — a bulk trucking fleet of over 150 tractors and 200 trailers, a fleet of over 150 rail cars employing innovative refrigeration techniques, and Simplot Aviation, an in-house airline service.

Then, of course, there's the venture capital Simplot supplies for computer hardware and a host of real estate projects, including Brundage Mountain Ski Resort, 100 miles north in McCall, Idaho, and Columbia Village, Boise's largest planned community. Simplot set up a partnership along with his son, Don, and a local promoter named Al Marsden to finance the development of 1,000 acres of land — a tract large enough to incorporate 1,800 homes, two swimming pools, 200 acres of park, 20 soccer fields, twelve baseball diamonds, and a 170-acre golf course, picnic area, and football field. And that's just the first stage of plans. If J.R. has his way, over the next 20 years, there will be 8,500 homes on the miles of land that he owns surrounding Columbia Village. "By God, that's a biggie!" J.R. says, using a constant Simplot refrain.

In short, name a business and J.R. has had a stake in it at one time or another. And it all belongs to J.R. Simplot, his sons, his daughter, and his grandchildren. "I built this company with my own guts and my own judgment," says J.R., explaining his choice not to bring his company public. "I wouldn't be where I am today without doing it myself and there was no way I was going to sell my stock and let a bunch of goddamn' yahoos tell me what to do."

From the giant picture window in his wood-paneled office on the 13th floor of the J.R. Simplot building in Boise, J.R. can see most of the city's downtown area and several thousand of the millions of acres of land he owns throughout the Northwest. He also has a fine view of the castle, complete with equestrian trails, man-made waterfalls, and ponds that he and his wife Esther built fourteen years ago on a 60-acre hilltop towering above downtown Boise.

Everyone in Idaho knows the Simplot house. For one thing, it's the only one with a 65 by 30 foot American flag flying out front. The way J.R. tells it — in typical J.R. fashion, it sounds more like a folk legend than a simple story — he bought the biggest flag he could find to express his patriotism for the country that has been so good to him. The only problem he says, was that the neighbors complained about the flag's flapping on windy days. "I was in violation of the compliance laws governing flags," he says, with his usual impatience for government agencies that wield "the power of God" and "create a lot of red tape." The Simplot solution? Build a higher flagpole — 160 feet high, to be exact.

"I'm not a dreamer. I'm a facts man," he says, drumming his fingers impatiently on the arms of his chair and chomping on a toothpick like a squirrel working an acorn. "And I don't put much stake in religion. My mother was a Methodist and went to church; my dad never saw the inside of one. My mother made sure me and my two older sisters got religion, but I remember listening to those hellfire and damnation speeches the [minister] made and thinking [that] the way they see it, you run out of facts pretty damn quickly.

"I got this thing figured out my way and nobody's going to sell me a bill of goods. No hocus-pocus for me! But I do have a vision. I had the vision to see that someday a good piece of land with water on it would be worth something." In fact, J.R. has no idea just how many acres of land he owns today. When asked, he dismisses the question with a casual wave as if to say "far, far too many to count."

"I'm scattered clear across America. I got started early when there were assets. There were phosphates in the ground and land to be homesteaded and timber to be claimed . . . I've made some bad bets once in a while. But, hell, if you're gonna get rich, you gotta get out there. There are no cinches. It's a rough, tough world. But the way I see it, 99 percent of the people get rich and then spend the rest of their time trying to stay on top. I believe you gotta keep pumpin' your assets back into your business. If you don't stick your neck out, you're not going to get anywhere."

Simplot has stuck his neck out from the beginning. Born in 1909, he was raised on his father's 80-acre homestead near Declo, Iowa, and then moved with his family to Burley, Idaho. There the Simplots operated a subsistence-level farm; for a time, the entire family — J.R., his parents, and his brother and four sisters — lived in a one-room log cabin with a dirt floor. Meanwhile, his restless father aggressively expanded his farming operation, buying up several neighboring homesteads, and he expected his son Jack to help run it.

"My dad taught me everything," he recalls. "He was a very principled man. When he married my mother, her old man, an Iowa farmer, gave them $20,000 to get started. Dad wouldn't touch that money. He kept it until the day he died.

"He drove me hard. You ran home from school; you

didn't walk. You didn't go to dances; you worked. I worked until dark every evening and then woke at dawn to milk the family's 30-cow dairy herd. One day I told my dad that I wanted to practice some basketball. He said 'No.' So I got my shoes and I left."

On his own at fourteen, with only an eighth-grade education, Simplot learned how to exploit opportunities and began the career that is still growing. Armed only with $80 he had earned by raising and selling "bum" (orphan) lambs with the help of his mother, he headed back to Declo, paying $1 a day for room and board. He then moved back to Idaho, supporting himself by sorting potatoes and "rip-rapping" — digging out irrigation canals with volcanic rock. The Idaho farm economy was depressed, and he was able to purchase 500 head of "weaner and feeder" hogs at the low price of $1 a head with the money he'd saved. By the time he was seventeen, J.R. had earned close to $8,000 fattening hogs on a low-cost stew he devised from the "cull" potatoes routinely discarded at potato cellars. With the help of a hired man, he worked "like a damn' slave" locating, preparing, loading, and unloading tons of hog feed for his stock. Then, anxious to make it on his own, he sunk his earnings into draft horses, farm machinery, a car, and seed potatoes. In 1926, he rented 120 acres of land and went into the potato business.

Shortly thereafter, J.R. joined forces with an older farmer, and the two invested $254 in an electric potato-sorter, a relatively new invention that made sorting potatoes far faster than had previously been possible. J.R. quickly figured out that it would be good business to move the sorter and crew to the potato cellars of other farmers. He began sorting their potatoes too, putting several friends out of business in the process. Then Simplot and his partner argued over the business and decided to part company. They flipped a silver dollar for the sorter; J.R. won the toss, and the Simplot potato packing business was solidly launched. By the late 1930s, J.R. was operating 32 packing warehouses and had become the largest single shipper of Idaho potatoes in the country.

"Now we ship out over 250,000 10-pound bags of potatoes every day and employ over 9,000 people," says J.R., continuing his story as he, his daughter Gay, a Simplot Company vice-president, and Simplot president Steven Beebe, drive his Lincoln out to one of the potato processing plants in Caldwell, Idaho. The purpose of the trip is a meeting with executives from Tyson — "the chicken people," puts in J.R. — to discuss a joint international distribution deal.

J.R. points out all of the farmland he owns along the way. "By God, this is a biggie," he says with childish delight. "See that truck on the road? That's a Simplot truck . . . See that acreage over there? That's mine . . . See that big field over there? That's the site of the new Micron plant for building computers . . . We're building that, too. Ooh. It's a biggie." His pleasure is palpable as he tots up his successes.

As his potato business grew, Simplot moved into onions. When a California customer, a vegetable dryer, failed to make an $8,500 payment in the late 1930s, Simplot went to the man's Berkeley office to collect. There he met a customer who was buying dried onions to make onion powder. Simplot liked the sound of the drying business and made a deal with the onion powder dealer on the spot. The two wrote their contract on the back of an envelope. Simplot collected his debt before the vegetable dryer "found out I'd taken his business" and returned to Idaho to pump his assets into building his own drying plant.

"The plant cost $100,000 in borrowed cash," explains Simplot. "We netted $600,000 the first year." The story, now a Simplot legend, has all the elements of a Simplot deal. He overcame a problem by seeking to collect his debt in person, then took advantage of an available opportunity — even though he knew absolutely nothing about the business at hand. He gambled his assets on a deal with a stranger because he had a hunch he could make some money — and made a fortune.

It was World War II, however, that sealed J.R.'s fortune. Answering the country's call, he expanded existing plants and built new ones, ultimately supplying one-third of the dried potatoes and onions used to feed the U.S. military forces overseas. In four years, he sold the government more than 33 million pounds of potatoes and five million pounds of onions.

Many businessman would have been content to rest on their laurels. Not J.R. Always a long-range planner, he anticipated that the end of the war would also mean an end to government contracts. He decided that he needed a new potato product to meet the next market. Ray Dunlap, a Simplot Company chemist, came up with the solution.

"Ray told me to buy him an icebox and he would come up with a frozen product that would sell. I told him, 'Hell, you can't do that. Freeze a potato, and it'll turn to mush.'" Dunlap solved the problem by frying the potatoes for two minutes at almost 400 degrees and then freezing them. The result was a French fry that, when reheated, was crispy on the outside and chewy on the inside. That was in 1944. By 1953, frozen French fries were a staple of the American diet.

"I've always believed that you should hire good, honest, hardworking people, turn them loose, and let them use their initiative," Simplot says. "I like to let people use their judgment. That's what this country is built on." J.R. expects his employees to devote themselves to the company. "I think of myself as a builder and I like my employees to be the same way. I want them to be enthusiastic and to want to build on what they are already doing."

Though J.R. himself would never use these words, the Simplot Company became what one of his employees calls "a vertically integrated agribusiness" — a company that re-uses as much of its own waste as possible and expands its businesses to further its self-sufficiency. For example, since potato-processing creates a lot of organic waste that can be used as feed, Simplot buys as many as 100,000 to 200,000 cattle a year to fatten and then slaughter. The remaining waste is converted into starch for bookbinding and for the manufacture of fuel-quality ethanol.

As his potato business grew, J.R. worked closely with the company's farmers and suppliers to furnish fertilizers designed to produce potatoes that met Simplot Company specifications. This eventually lead to the farming products chain called Soil-builder Service Centers and the acquisition of phosphate mines for producing fertilizer. His first mine, named for his daughter, Gay, opened in 1946 on the Fort Hall Indian Reservation near Pocatello, Idaho; the purchase of three more mines has made the Simplot Company the leader in fertilizer in western America.

Indeed, self-sufficiency has driven most of J.R.'s enterprises. When he needed packing crates for his products, he purchased a sawmill to make them; when he needed to transport his potatoes, he manufactured the rail cars and purchased the trucks to haul them; when he needed fruits and vegetables, meat or dairy products, he supplied the farmers with the land, the fertilizer, and the farming products to grow them. In nine out of ten cases, he knew almost nothing about these businesses before he got into them. He simply saw an opportunity and moved quickly, figuring he'd learn what he needed along the way.

Of course, not all of his ventures were absolutely successful. Over the years, J.R. experimented with raising chickens but found it "impossible to make a buck." He purchased several gold and silver mines in the Dominican Republic, only to have them confiscated by the local government after a hurricane devastated nearly every other enterprise in the country. Bunker Hill, one of his domestic mining ventures, was closed by the U.S. government for environmental code violations. Not too long ago, he plunked $25-30 million into a fish plant just outside of Boise. But plant managers were unable to control the nitrogen levels adequately in the man-made breeding ponds and the fish died.

"We just replaced the ponds with tomato and bean fields," J.R. says with a shrug. "These kinds of things don't bother me. You just take your bumps and move on. It's part of the business."

Several of those bumps earned him significant negative publicity. In 1977, for instance, the Internal Revenue Service claimed that he and two of his companies were guilty of income tax evasion to the tune of $1.3 million. In 1978, in another heavily publicized incident, the New York Mercantile Exchange alleged that Simplot had tried to manipulate the price of Maine potato futures. During a period of rapidly increasing potato prices, he and several others promised to produce millions of pounds of potatoes on contract and then failed to deliver them when the contracts were called, resulting in a collapse of the market.

Both of these issues were settled out of court. The Commodities Futures Trading Commission fined Simplot $1.4 million and banned him from trading on the Exchange for six years. After extensive investigations, he agreed to pay the IRS the disputed taxes, plus assessed fines, penalties, and interest. With characteristic bravado, however, Simplot has denied any wrongdoing in either of these instances.

Of course, some bumps are harder to take than others. When J.R. was 22, he married Ruby, his first wife, with whom he had three sons and a daughter. They remained married for almost 25 years until Ruby, as J.R. puts it, "got tired of being Mrs. Idaho." Unwilling to stand the strain of J.R.'s highly public lifestyle and frequent business trips away, Ruby left J.R. and married her best friend's husband. It was eleven years before J.R. married Esther, an opera singer from Wisconsin. "She was singing at Carnegie Hall when I met her," J.R. recalls. "She was working as a secretary for the Phipps estate and was singing whenever she had the chance. I was there to borrow $10 million from her boss when I met her. It worked out. We got married and I paid Phipps back double."

Today he and Esther share two homes — the castle on the hilltop in Boise and a country retreat surrounded by riding trails and pine trees. The house is situated on an exquisite peninsula jutting into Payette Lake in McCall, just outside the Simplot ski resort on Brundage Mountain.

Eight hours into his workday, J.R. is still going strong. After traveling well over 50 miles and visiting many of his holdings, he is still fresh enough for eighteen holes of golf. He has worked a twelve-hour day for most of his 85 years and sees no reason to stop now. "I can still go all day and much of the night," he booms, looking no wearier than he did at ten that morning. He concedes that he gave up jogging and horseback riding when he was 75 and relinquished the big-game hunting he loved in favor of the less strenuous sport of shooting waterfowl, but he still takes a daily morning walk with Esther, swims regularly in his heated pool along Payette Lake, and skis all winter long.

Only recently, J.R. decided to step down officially as CEO of the Simplot Company and hand over the day-to-day running of the divisions to his sons, daughter, and a handful of non-family members. "When I'm needed I'll be there, but I told them [that] one of them has to take over," he says. "The company will certainly stay in the family. I've got my grandchildren starting at the bottom and working their way up."

He and his wife remain very active in philanthropic circles in the Boise community, giving away millions of dollars to hospitals, schools, and cultural institutions. Esther is responsible for the Esther Simplot Performing Arts Academy, which brings the Philharmonic, the opera, and, as J.R. puts it, "the toe dancers," to Boise.

"I don't give to churches because the way I see it, if the people who built 'em can't support 'em, then you don't need 'em," J.R. adds. "But before I die, I want to build a big museum. It's going to have a big endowment so that it can do whatever it wants. I just want it to be the biggest and the best because I don't know a better place to put the money."

In the meantime, J.R. has funded construction of the Simplot/Micron Instructional Technology Center and the Morrison Center on the campus of Boise State University. For twelve years he sat on the board of trustees for Albertson College of Idaho and has made large contributions there and to the University of Idaho and Idaho State University.

"I got my education the hard way," J.R. reflects. "It's our job to propel the next generation. I believe in education. The smarter you are, the better able you will be to enjoy the world. If this democracy is to continue to thrive, we've got to see the same initiative that built my company.

"It's all here in America, but if you're going to amount to anything in this world, you have to have the desire. You have to make it yourself because no one will do it for you. The potato business was run by a bunch of gamblers and I taught 'em all. I used to sit on a plow and cover eight or nine acres a day. The horses would get so tired I'd have to change teams halfway through. Today, I've got the equipment to plow 300 acres a day. That's because I was a long-range thinker. You have to be. You have to wonder where everybody's going to go and what everybody's going to do when they get there. And you have to be willing to risk all you've got on what you think will work.

"It's not easy today to get the kind of assets it takes to build a company like mine. Hell, if you're smart enough to get the assets, then you're smart enough to gamble with them and win. I've been offered a lot of money for my divisions. I've seen just about all of my competitors sell out to bigger companies. I've been tempted, but then I've thought, 'Hell, if I sell, then the government will get half my profits.' Besides, what would I do if I sold out? The only smart thing I really did — and it was an accident, but I'll take credit for it — was to hang on.

"I've been around a long time and I've seen everything written about me — good and bad. But if there's one thing I know I'm good for, it's living proof that you can still do it in America. It may not be easy, but, hell, what is?"

Post Script: In March of 1995, Micron Technology Inc. announced that it would build a $1.3 billion semiconductor plant in Utah, ending a nationwide search for a new manufacturing operation. The new plant will employ 3,500 people and will be part of Micron's plans to double its semiconductor manufacturing capacity over the next four years.

"I'm big on envisioning. I like to figure out where I want to get to before it even starts, and I always have an exit strategy."

MANNY JACKSON

Owner of Harlem Globetrotters and
Senior Vice-president of Honeywell Inc.

~

Ask Manny Jackson what motivates him and the answer you'll get is immediate and unqualified. "Fear," says the former basketball star and one of the most successful African-American entrepreneurs in the country today. "I'm always feeling that the ground will fall out from under me, and I don't want to go back to what I left behind."

Jackson was born in a Cotton Belt Railroad boxcar in Illmo, Missouri and spent the first five years of his life sharing the cramped quarters of his birthplace with his mother and father, a sister, and ten aunts, uncles, and cousins. "That boxcar got pretty crowded," he quips. "Poverty and racism were like a prison, and I've spent most of my life in pursuit of freedom from that prison."

Jackson's pursuit has included a stint as a college basketball star, a number of years traveling around the world as a member of the legendary Harlem Globetrotters basketball team, and a 25-year climb up the corporate ladder of the Minneapolis-based Honeywell, Inc., where he is currently a corporate officer and senior vice president at the world's largest manufacturer of thermostats and other controls for industrial energy and environmental systems.

On top of his typically twelve- to eighteen-hour workday at Honeywell, he is also involved in a number of sideline ventures, which includes a chain of health clubs in Minneapolis called The Firm, a publishing company that he set up and sold at a profit, and, most recently, in the fulfillment of a lifelong dream — attaining majority ownership in the team for which he once played, the Harlem Globetrotters. If Jackson continues to have his way with an aggressive new management and marketing plan, the Harlem Globetrotters will soon trade their current sagging status for one more commensurate with their upbeat new moniker, "The World's Greatest Basketball Show." Jackson wants the Globetrotters to be an international team, showcasing impeccable technical basketball skills in a comic entertainment format. Better still, hopes Jackson, the team will become "a force for social change."

"I'm big on envisioning," says Jackson, whose trim, six foot, two inch frame is fashionably hung with a black dress shirt and tweed sport jacket. His hip threads and smooth, handsome face make him look every inch the basketball star and impossibly youthful for his 55 years. "I like to figure out where I want to get to before [I] even start, and I always have an exit strategy. I believe that when people get into something, they should see the end game right away because it will set up everything that comes before it. If you've got a viable end game strategy, then you can develop a viable process plan."

Jackson believes envisioning the future is particularly important for black Americans who are setting out in business. To communicate the lessons of his experience in corporate America, he became a founding member and is past president of the seven-year-old Executive Leadership Council, an influential business and social network of senior black executives from top companies. "We want to lead by example," he explains. "It was important to me to demonstrate to young people [something] about personal freedom and risk-taking. The end-all is not in working for someone else. We did that on the plantations in the South. It just wasn't in the black worker's software to seize his own options and pursue them. Though it's important for everyone, it's particularly important for black Americans [to learn this]."

A networking resource for successful African Americans,

the Executive Leadership Council is a non-profit group that advises black executives on how to be more powerful, more positive, and more effective within their companies and in society in general. The council provides lectures, seminars, and mentoring programs for executives not yet senior enough to be members as well as for students in business schools and universities. Above all, they believe in what they call "economic empowerment" and work to give black business executives networking opportunities that will lead to lucrative business deals. They also create forums to advise black executives on national policy issues such as whether corporations should deal with investments in South Africa. "Companies tended to hire black executives who were very conservative. They choose careful, non-invasive people," says Jackson. "We want to train our people to be more risk-oriented, to make waves. Our goal is to teach the next generation of black Americans how to ask for and get more power within their companies.

Although Jackson has not always been politically active about the problems confronting blacks in American society, issues of race are at the center of most of his childhood memories.

He thinks of himself as the offspring of an interracial marriage, even though both of his parents were black. "My father was a light-complexed, somewhat elitist [black] who could easily pass for white. He came from and associated with families of doctors and lawyers, schoolteachers and engineers," says Manny, whose name is neither a nickname nor an abbreviation. "My mother, on the other hand, was a very dark, very beautiful, soulful woman with movie star-like African features. Her father was a railroad worker and a jazz musician, a two-fisted drinker who led a crew of railroad workers and owned a baseball team. Their marriage caused considerable consternation in both families, and I was the product of that tension . . . I was attracted to both sides. My father's parents were warm and loving and had a strong sense of values and ethics and that felt important to me. But my mother's father was a real 'man's man.' He was tough and romantic and adventurous."

His father's father, distraught at the squalor of the Jackson family's boxcar existence, moved them to Edwardsville, Illinois, a nearly all-white bedroom community of St. Louis that gradually was integrated with domestic workers and other blacks who obtained jobs in neighboring factories. He got Manny's father a job as a supervisor at a parts distribution warehouse and enrolled five-year-old Manny in the Lincoln School, where his step-grandmother was his teacher and Manny became an instant teacher's pet. "I was very bright," he reminisces. "My grandmother used to drag the high school kids to my class and say, 'See here, my little five-year-old can read better than you.'"

All went well until 1952, when integration of America's public schools became the significant political and social issue of the day. Manny's father became an activist for the cause and engaged in marches and demonstrations to demand that more blacks be permitted to attend the predominantly white public school. Although his fight for integration of Edwardsville's schools was successful, Manny's father lost his home and his job in the process. The angered white community in Edwardsville pulled the loans from his home, and his boss, then the head of the school board, fired him. Manny's father moved to Chicago for the next two years, and Manny, his sister, and his mother were forced to move into a low-income housing project in Madison, Illinois. "That was very tough," Manny adds. "There was a lot of crime and a lot of drugs. My mother was a domestic and my father had run through a series of jobs as a postal worker, production welder, and plant supervisor. But until that time I thought of my family as well-off. Life in the public projects was a rude awakening."

A serious student, Manny, driven by his mother, continued to commute to the nearly all-white Edwardsville School almost 40 miles away for the remainder of his junior high and high school days, a place with what he calls "an apartheid mentality" that left him virtually friendless. "The only place I really felt safe was in my own family, but a lot of white grownups kind of adopted me," he says. "I was a hardworking student and an aspiring athlete. We had a fantastic basketball team and upon graduation I was offered literally hundreds of scholarships." Perhaps his saving grace, however, the first of what he has come to think of as "guiding lights and safety nets," was his best buddy, Govonor Vaughn. "We were both recognized basketball players and every Saturday and Sunday we'd put on exhibitions. People came from miles around to watch us ... He was truly a safety net for me. I always felt he would be there if I needed him and vice versa, and we stuck together." At that time, Jackson was recruited by the Harlem Globetrotters, then based in Chicago, but decided to finish school instead.

The two friends accepted scholarships to the University of Illinois, where they both enjoyed All-American careers as the first blacks to play on the university's basketball team. At that time, Jackson, who later became team captain, met a fellow student who was to be another of the influential guiding lights in his life — Jesse Jackson. "Jesse has always awakened me to political reality," Manny says now. "He's been a kind of wake-up call for me. To this day, whenever I have to make a decision, I ask myself 'What would Jesse do?'"

At the University of Illinois, the Globetrotters' coach and founder, Abe Saperstein, once again paid young Manny a visit. Although he wanted him for the team, he insisted that Jackson finish college first. "Abe kept his eye on me. He was my friend," Jackson recalls. "He did me a great favor by insisting that I finish college and [he] told me he'd have a job for me when I was through."

Although Jackson hoped to join the National Basketball Association upon graduation, he says that the league's stringent quota on black players made that all but an impossibility for a player of his level. Instead, he and Govonor Vaughn moved to New York City, and Jackson took a job at the Technical Tape Corporation of New Rochelle, a manufacturer of cellophane, masking, and other industrial tapes.

"The president of Technical was a guy named Paul Cohen," continues Manny. "He became the next of my guiding lights ...

When I applied for the job, he was impressed, and instead of sending me to the factory where most of the black guys —even those with a college degree — worked, he gave me an office job as a customer service clerk. Paul was a wealthy, powerful leader, and he was very helpful to me. He gave me training classes in sales and marketing and awakened my interest in business.

"I have always made myself accessible and vulnerable to certain people throughout my life, and I've almost never regretted it," he adds. "Of course, I always worked hard in return for the faith they put in me. That's what makes the game work."

In 1961, after Jackson had spent a year at Technical Tape, friend and mentor Abe Saperstein returned again, this time convincing Jackson to leave his job and join the Globetrotters. "I was very conflicted at the time," he says. "My dad told me to stick with business and build a career, but I couldn't turn down a chance to travel around the world . . . And as it turned out, we went to 50 countries in Europe, Asia, the Middle East, and Africa. I met the Pope, and I met Khrushchev. Abe really took me under his wing. He used to say to me, 'You're not like the rest of these Oscars.' By that I think he meant that I had an unusual combination of basketball skills, a strong work ethic, and presence. Abe would say I was articulate and assertive and that made me different from lots of the others. He used to bring me along to all the public relations events and I would try to explain the civil rights movement to people overseas [who] really had very little idea of what was going on between the races in America.

"We traveled to Austria and Poland together and Abe showed me the concentration camps where his family and friends had been killed during the Holocaust. He took me with him to meetings with all the promoters and I got the chance to listen to the negotiations. I learned a ton from him . . . Joining the Globetrotters turned out to be the best decision I ever made."

Jackson traveled with the Globetrotters until 1963 and then joined the American Basketball League, the creatively marketed organization that had been founded by Saperstein to rival the NBA, and drew its strength from top-rated black players. Jackson played first for the league's Chicago team, then for Pittsburgh, and quit organized basketball in 1966, just a year before that league folded altogether.

"I'd had enough of playing," he recalls. "I was ready to go back to business." He entered the University of Detroit to earn a master's degree in marketing and economics and began investing some of the money he had earned as a professional basketball player in a variety of businesses that included a fight promotion company and a small fast food business. "I would ask myself, 'Am I interested in this?' 'Is it fun?' 'Can I add value?' If the answer was yes to all three, then I'd try it." Those are the same questions Jackson asks today.

He took a job as a labor relations conciliator for General Motors' Cadillac division in Detroit in 1967, the same year that the city was rocked by civil rights disturbances. "That was a crucial time for me," Jackson reflects. "I realized that I had been straddling two societies — black and white — for all this time. My grand plan to succeed in corporate life, which was clearly dominated by whites, was being disrupted by racial tension and I was mad and resentful."

He even considered leaving the country and moving in with a friend who was living in Stockholm. Instead, he moved to Minneapolis after being invited to Minneapolis to give a talk about the Detroit riots to a management group. It was there that he met Ed Spencer, then president of Honeywell's U.S. operations and soon to be chairman of the board. Jackson's next guiding light took him under his wing.

"Ed never offered a job, but I applied for one and got it, with his help. He offered me a way to look at my career," Jackson says. "I was doing okay. I had money in the bank, a brand-new home, and two Cadillacs ... But Ed encouraged me to commit myself to a job and to grow with it. I learned to be technically competent but I also learned a value system. I learned that what counts is integrity and [the ability] to make customers and employees trust us. In a short time I was learning how to work."

Jackson rose to become Honeywell's director of labor relations before being sent to Boston in the mid-1970s to join a team to oversee the $1 billion merger of Honeywell's computer operations with those it had acquired from the General Electric Company. He went on to manage the company's new-ventures program, including seven acquisitions and the formation of a telecommunications partnership with L. M. Ericsson of Sweden. In addition, he continued the job he still does today, overseeing marketing, employee relations, government affairs, and other administration functions. "During all that time I gave up on basketball entirely," he says. "I chose not to be associated with being a jock. I felt that made it too easy for people to pigeonhole me."

It wasn't until 1986 that he felt ready to return to sports. "I met an executive with Northern Telcom who also owned the Milwaukee Braves [and] that impressed me. I guess in my own mind I finally felt comfortable that I'd gone beyond being a gimmick," Jackson says. "I had learned a lot about process — how to manage people and resources and think strategically. I was good at building a team. I had traveled all over the world to talk about individual freedoms in the workplace and about how individuals could be powerful in the context of a team ... I was a founding member of the Executive Leadership Council and decided it was time for me to go public and become a role model for black youths. During the 1980s, television and merchandising made the sports industry very powerful in America. There were no black team owners, only players. I saw a potential business situation for myself and an opportunity to make an impact on society."

In 1989, he attempted to win an NBA franchise in San Diego with a group of partners, but ten months and several hundred thousand dollars of his own money later, the project fell apart. "I picked bad partners," he says, reluctant to name names or offer details. "Let's just say that ultimately my partners and I weren't in agreement with what would be best for San Diego, for the team, and so, as the newspapers reported it, 'we made a decision for the greater good' to give it up ...

It was very difficult for me. I felt I had put a lot of people on the line. People had bought season tickets in advance. I made a public apology in the local newspaper and rather than get trapped, just moved on."

In 1991, he and Dennis Mathisen, a friend he met through charitable work to save the Minneapolis Children's Theatre, heard that the International Broadcasting Corporation was declaring bankruptcy and selling off their various holdings, including the Harlem Globetrotters. "We shared the feeling that we wanted to build companies that would be profitable and socially relevant," Jackson explains. They found financial backers in Ed Spencer, Jackson's mentor at Honeywell, Dr. Jack Jones, an executive with Jostens and fellow E.L.C. member, and National Westminster Bank USA, which controlled the team after the bankruptcy of International Broadcasting. Together they bought the Globetrotters in 1993 for roughly $6 million.

After only one year under their new ownership, the Globetrotters have grown nearly seventy percent in revenue and expanded their annual game season to over 200 games in nearly 30 countries. Jackson has moved quickly to upgrade the team's skills, to create a second Globetrotters team, to arrange promotions with a range of sponsors, and to establish a strong social image through youth clinics and charity work. The team's grinning portrait now graces the cover of Target store shopping bags and seven million Wheaties boxes, and the faces of the team members will soon be merchandized on t-shirts, dolls, and a host of souvenirs. A feature film dramatizing the team's history is currently in negotiations, and says Jackson, will probably bring in between $5 and $7 million upon release from licensing and merchandising royalties.

Jackson says there is very little difference between marketing a basketball team and marketing any other product. "We use the same three principles," he insists. "First, we believe in continuous improvement. We don't believe in maintaining the status quo, and the team holds regular meetings to screen films of their plays and review training procedures. Next, we want our audience to be delighted. Our players are told that they should play and behave as if their own parents and children are in the audience, [that they should] always give the crowd more than they expect. Finally, we tell them that they have to be concerned about the public good. What goes on in society has to matter. They have to know their community and be involved. My partners and I feel if these are the things that drive you, then your job will become something you simply love to do. Then it's not a job anymore. If you do something because you love it, then you are more likely to be successful at it.

"There's just so much money in sports," he adds, avoiding any current estimate of the team's worth. "Let's just say the athletes are paid well and we've figured out a way to make money . . . In the meantime, we've signed a national partnership with United Way's Success By Six program, a comprehensive program for city children, and we've committed $250,000 to the United Negro College Fund. The membership of E.L.C. and their companies sent millions of fundraising dollars to South Africa to help elect Nelson Mandela and I have a priority to support my friend Jesse Jackson's Rainbow Coalition Fairness in Sports program.

"I like others to think of the Globetrotters as the world's greatest basketball show and the true ambassadors of good will, the best example of concern for human values and sportsmanship. Our goal is to entertain and make adults and children laugh and feel good in the most positive environment. We have the unique ability to cross borders, generations, racial, religious and ethnic groups . . . We are in the rare position in the multi-billion dollar business of sports of serving social responsibility. That's the dream. That's where the pleasure is."

When he's not working a long day, Jackson tries to find time to play golf. He and his wife Cathy and their two teenage daughters share a Victorian home in the fashionable Kenwood section of Minneapolis. But even now, his eyes are focused on the future.

"As business continues to go global, I would personally like to focus more on the public policy issues: that alone makes someone a global player. For example, if work ethics are culture-driven, then what values should companies take abroad when they decide to go international? I want to spend more time studying how to get countries and people to work together. The body behaves as the brain directs it. In the global marketplace, public policy is often the brain. That's where the future lies.

"Through Honeywell and through the Globetrotters I have the opportunity to meet with leaders all over the world and create an atmosphere of tolerance. I like what I've done and I want to hold on to it. I want to make it work for my family, for all the people and mentors who have taken care of me along the way, and for the greater good of society."

"You need deep pockets and a strong stomach and I have both. On top of that, I have the conviction that an entrepreneur needs. I know I am right."

MICHAEL BLOOMBERG

Founder and CEO of Bloomberg Financial Markets

M ike Bloomberg doesn't own a personal computer. He doesn't see the need for one since he can't type and prefers organizing his thoughts on yellow legal pads to hunt-and-pecking on a keyboard. Luckily for Mike, however, more than 35,000 people feel differently, and "The Bloomberg," the computer model named for its less-than-modest creator, graces the desks of offices in almost every capitalist country in North and South America, Europe, and Asia.

Since 1982, Bloomberg Financial Markets has been peddling "The Bloomberg," a terminal and software system that transmits quotes on stocks, bonds, currencies, and other securities, as well as an incredible assortment of historical and current financial data that tells institutional investors and traders just what to buy and what to sell to turn the biggest profit. It can do everything from calculating the future value of a bond to evaluating a portfolio under various interest rates to displaying the price history of a stock. Given the current volatility of interest rates and currencies, every second counts for traders in the global financial markets, and quick access to the latest rumor, news event, or price change is absolutely essential.

Much of the information provided on the Bloomberg screen comes from 650 researchers and data-entry workers housed in a fully Bloomberg-occupied office building in Princeton, New Jersey. The researchers there peruse thousands of prospectuses and financial statements daily to provide information for Bloomberg's service.

Of course, Bloomberg is not the only provider of this kind of information. Reuters, Telerate, Quotron, and Dow Jones's information services group, to name a few, have been doing similar things for much larger audiences, and in some cases, for a much longer time. The success of the system is all the more impressive when you consider that the Bloomberg software runs only on Bloomberg hardware and is compatible with no other computer system. "Successful media companies have to have two things," Mike is fond of telling the press. "They have to control their own distribution and they have to have their own programming. People who don't have both either have to rectify that or go out of business."

But, claim Bloomberg's salespeople, few financial services offer so much information in so user-friendly a fashion. For example, unlike their competitors, who offer only the price and volume of various offerings, "The Bloomberg" provides simple, descriptive information such as the name, business, and address of a company, its total capitalization, the call dates for its bonds, the frequency of interest payments, and so on. Wrap that up in a nifty bit of hardware that provides lots of full-color diagrams and enough flashing lights to rival a Sega Genesis game, and you've got some happy customers. All it takes is the push of the "Go" button — and $1,100 per month to lease the equipment — and a wealth of financial information is at a user's fingertips.

What does that mean for Mike Bloomberg? "You do the math; I can't be bothered," says Mike, with a gleam in his eye and the kind of modesty that's so patently false it's practically an out-and-out boast. "That's $1,100 per month × twelve months × 35,000 customers."

These days, Mike, as he's known to friends and employees alike, has plenty to brag about. Since 1990, Bloomberg Financial Markets has become Bloomberg Financial Markets, Commodities News L.P., incrementally picking up steam by adding *Bloomberg*, a monthly magazine for Bloomberg's clients; WBBR 1130 AM, an all-business-news New York radio station; a global radio network broadcast through Bloomberg computer terminals; and a 15-minute television news program for business professionals, co-produced with Maryland Public Television and distributed to public television stations nationwide. Thanks to a hook-up with GM Hughes Electronics' satellite-to-home broadcasting service, an audio channel carrying WBBR will soon be added to the list. A subscriber to the satellite service will be able to hear the radio station 24 hours a day through a television set broadcasting a blank screen.

In the last four years, Bloomberg has set up domestic news bureaus throughout the United States in addition to overseas bureaus in London, Tokyo, and Singapore. Bloomberg's staff of almost 200 reporters publish more than 2,500 stories daily, feeding 70 of the world's major newspapers. The operation is headed by Matt Winkler, a former *Wall Street Journal* reporter who met Bloomberg while writing a profile on him and stayed to become the editor in chief of Bloomberg Business News. With several Pulitzer Prize-winning writers on staff and many reporters wooed from the *Wall Street Journal*, the *New York Times*, *BusinessWeek*, *Fortune* and *Forbes*, Bloomberg Business News has already won several awards for in-depth coverage of emerging events. Most recently, the company has added *Bloomberg Personal*, a Sunday magazine supplement about managing personal finances for newspapers across the country, to the mix.

In addition, Bloomberg offers a host of new services to "The Bloomberg" each month, at no added cost. Although services like Telerate have long carried a few light features — sports scores, weather forecasts, and movie reviews, for example — Bloomberg offers a whole lot more. In the past year alone, horoscopes, sports results, ski reports, airline schedules, and classified ads for jobs, boats, racehorses, and airplanes have been added. Now, there is even an on-line shopping network available. Want to buy a car, order some new dress shirts, check *Consumer Reports* for advice on the best word processor? Do it all through the Bloomberg.

With added information features come improved equipment. The latest generation of terminals can display still-picture videos with audio so that major WBBR news stories can be called up with an accompanying image. In coming months, Bloomberg plans to build up an entrepreneurial picture directory so that users can check out a particular stock and call up a picture of the company's CEO at the same time.

"I remember telling my people four years ago, 'We're going into the news business.' They didn't say anything, but I knew they were thinking. 'How the f____ are we gonna do that?'" Mike recalls with his near-legendary profanity. "Well, nobody questions it anymore."

Indeed, Bloomberg's penchant for pithy parables and bawdy, irreverent humor, coupled with his volatile temper and vociferous, blatantly politically incorrect appreciation of the opposite sex — and his innovative communication systems — have made the 52-year-old a darling of the press. He claims he drinks as many as 30 cups of coffee a day and favors cheese as the perfect "balanced" food because "the cholesterol in it clogs the arteries while the high-salt content creates the blood pressure to open them up." Whether it's due to the caffeine or the high blood pressure, Mike Bloomberg is a blur of motion, even when he's sitting down to talk.

What he says his former wife couldn't stand — his near 24-hour obsession with his business and his inability to confide his biggest fears — has made him a far more charming companion for the media. He has been likened to everything from an improbable heir to Joseph Pulitzer to a latter-day Henry Ford to an electronic Horace Greeley to a Wall Street version of the Terminator.

For Mike, the secret to success is fairly simple: "I can't imagine not loving what I do for a living. After all, work is where most people spend most of their time. If you like what you do, you do more of it. If you do more of it, you get better at it. If you get really good at it, you become successful . . . You need deep pockets and a strong stomach and I have both. On top of that, I have the conviction that an entrepreneur needs. I *know* I am right.

"I don't confide; I run," he continues, moving through these verbal reveries at break-neck speed. "Most mornings, I get up around 5:15 and go running in Central Park, and every morning I talk through all of my worries and all of my concerns with the one person I trust. You know who that one person is? The same person I see in the mirror when I shave."

The origins of Mike's drive are not so easy to discern. He had what he describes as a "blue-collar" childhood in Medford, Massachusetts. Though his father, a bookkeeper for a local dairy, worked hard, there was "never any pressure" for Mike or his sister, two years younger and now a geriatrics specialist, to achieve. And he has no particular memory of wanting the kind of material success he now enjoys. "Now that I can have it, it's great," he says of his current lifestyle, which includes a townhouse on Manhattan's Upper East Side, a condominium for ski vacations in Vail, and a large house in Westchester county, not to mention horses for his two equestrian daughters and the private airplane he likes to pilot. [But] "I didn't think about things like that when I was younger."

His fondest childhood memories are of being a Boy Scout — "an invaluable experience for learning how to deal with peers" — and of being taken by his parents to the Museum of Science every Saturday morning, an experience that first got him interested in "using the scientific method as a way of understanding things."

By Bloomberg's perhaps exaggeratedly understated reckoning — part of the "ordinary guy" persona he is fond of creating for himself — he received "straight C's" in high school and "straight C's" as a physics and engineering major at Johns Hopkins University. "I managed to get straight A's one semester," he recalls, "so that I could get into Harvard Business School, and then I got straight C's at Harvard."

He put himself through college with a little help from his parents and a number of government-sponsored student loans. Living expenses were covered by a $35-per week night job guarding the parking lot of the Johns Hopkins Faculty Club from parking violators.

He decided to become a physics and engineering major simply because he was "interested in how things work," but realized before graduating there was little future for him as a physicist. "I was never going to be a Nobel Prize-winner, so I thought I'd try going into a business that would use my science background," he recalls. As things turned out, that never quite happened but, he adds, being a physics major taught him "how to use the scientific method and test things to see if they would stand up," a method that he still holds to today, frequently writing out his newest schemes on yellow legal pads "so that I can see where the holes are."

Harvard eventually led him, in 1966, to a job as a clerk earning $9,500 a year at Salomon Brothers, the high-powered Wall Street securities firm then run by John Gutfreund. Bloomberg spent the next fifteen years politicking his way up and down the corporate ladder at Salomon.

"I used to get in at seven a.m.," recalls Bloomberg. "I was the only one in the trading room other than Billy Salomon and we would chitchat. I would stay until seven at night, and after six the only other person in the room was John Gutfreund and he'd give me a ride uptown. Both of these men were very smart in their own ways. Billy was a great manager and good with people; John was great with numbers. They were more or less my rabbis."

He went on to become the head of equity trading at the firm in the 1970s and integrated his training in computers with his trading experience to develop an information system that could analyze securities information. Says Mike: "There might be better traders than me and there might be people who know more about computers, but there's nobody who knows more about both."

After getting caught up in one too many corporate in-fights, he was demoted to the back office and placed in charge of Salomon's computer systems. On Gutfreund's advice, he quit in 1981, staying just long enough to collect somewhere between $10 and $25 million in company shares ("depending upon how you calculate all the tax bonuses and stock values") when Salomon went public in a merger with Philbro. To this day, says Mike, John Gutfreund enjoys all of the services provided by "The Bloomberg" free of charge.

"He hired me; he fired me," says Mike. "His timing was impeccable on both."

After leaving Salomon, Bloomberg rented an office where he spent several months "reading the newspaper and getting coffee and buying another newspaper and drinking some more coffee" while he tried to figure out what to do next. Even in retrospect, he doesn't really look at that difficult time in his career as a "turning point." Relying on his bullish self-confidence, he more or less forced back any fears, then bought his wife a sable jacket so that she would feel comfortable that his success was continuing, and pressed on. "I figured I might as well start my own business. Then I would have no one else to blame."

Having gained experience in building a computerized information, analytics, and bookkeeping system at Salomon, he pitched a similar system for U.S. government bonds to Merrill Lynch. "I was down there every day," recalls Bloomberg. "Every morning I would buy six cups of coffee and tea and give them out to whomever would listen to me as I lobbied for my system."

Finally, he came before an informal committee. Merrill's computer experts said they would need six months to study the practical possibilities for such a system and Bloomberg simply said, "I'll deliver a finished system in six months, and if you don't like it, you don't have to pay for it." Six months later, the system was more or less complete. Shortly thereafter, Merrill put $30 million into Bloomberg's company in return for 30 percent interest. Their investment is now worth well over ten times that.

Playing a cross between a serious entrepreneur with a vision to share and a cocksure adolescent spouting truisms to test just how seriously he might be taken, Bloomberg offers his philosophy: "First of all, nobody likes paranoids, and just because you're paranoid doesn't mean anybody's really out to get you. Everyday you should look at what your company's dependencies are and try to make them fewer by developing back-up plans.

"Second, long-range planning is a waste of time. Worry about the things that you can do something about now. It's ridiculous to start out with a game plan — a five-year plan or a ten-year plan. The future is so imprecise that it's virtually useless to try and predict it. You are better off trying to set a direction and do a lot of small things that will lead you that way.

"Third, learn to delegate. The difference between the successful and the less successful is in delegating. The successful people grit their teeth and give up some power."

Bloomberg L.P. is, in fact, a study in shared managerial responsibility. Nobody in the expansive glass-enclosed offices occupying five floors of a skyscraper on Park Avenue and 59th Street has a private office, not even Mike. Nobody has a title on his or her business card, not even Mike. And for that matter, nobody has his or her own secretary, not even Mike. Under the theory that no one knows exactly why a new customer decides to lease a Bloomberg, salespeople are not paid a commission. Employees are paid a salary, and most are rewarded with "certificates of participation" that entitle them to share in the firm's revenue growth over the following two years. The bonus, paid annually, can equal anywhere from 25 percent to 100 percent of their salary.

The boss is known for his extravagant company parties, which include an annual family picnic, complete with petting zoo, pony rides, and carnival games at his home in Armonk, New York. Several thousand employees and their families are bused and flown in at company expense from as far away as Asia to spend the afternoon amidst clowns, magicians, and barbecue smoke. He also prides himself for his general accessibility to his employees. There's even a miniature deli in the center of his Park Avenue offices, where employees can go for free coffee, soda, fruit, cereal, assorted junk food, and a quick "schmooze."

The boss is also known for his hot temper. But "I'm consistent so they know where they stand with me," says Mike, rattling off a list of rules that includes: "Don't consume liquor to excess — you represent your company even when you are off duty; don't travel or entertain extravagantly so as to give customers the impression that we are too successful; don't brag about our success; and don't withhold from your firm anything you learn inside or outside that is important . . . I may yell and scream, but I am open to hearing what my employees have to say. You don't have to be a rocket scientist to realize that if you say to me, 'You're the boss and whatever you say, goes,' I'm more than willing to listen." And everybody who works for Mike Bloomberg knows who's boss.

"I expect absolute loyalty from my employees," he insists with pride. "No one who leaves the company is ever allowed to come back. If you leave, I will not wish you the best. I will not go to a farewell party for you. You're a traitor . . . But I tell [employees] the rules in advance and why I adopted them, and then I bend the rules if I think it will make a difference." It is this clarity, combined with his high-voltage energy, that inspires most employees to a devotion bordering on fanaticism.

"The whole ethic of the company," offers Mike as a partial explanation for the loyalty of his employees, "is to take kids just out of school and let them work their way up the ladder. I do my best to tell them what they need to do to succeed . . . I tell them there is no free lunch. The best they can do is to work hard, work for the best company they can find, and pay their dues.

"There's no percentage in being overambitious and trying to rise to the top of the company too quickly. The thing to do is to work your ass off and say 'Thank you' for the opportunity. It's not so much a question of learning technical skills. You can give me a liberal arts major and I can teach him or her to run a computer. The real important thing is to learn to analyze, to put things in perspective, and to acquire interpersonal skills."

Though Matt Winkler is responsible for hiring most of the new reporters — more than a few of whom were lured away from competing newspapers and magazines as much by the idea of being involved in an innovative form of journalism as by the competitive salaries — Mike has the last word on who gets hired. A sense of their loyalty is as important as any skills;

half of one floor of Bloomberg's Park Avenue offices is devoted to a "training" room, complete with easels, video monitors, and a scheduled series of seminars in how the Bloomberg technology works and which are the best ways to sell it.

"The odds are that many of my people are smarter than I am. But somebody's got to get it going. That's where I come in. I'm willing to take the blame and give the credit to whomever deserves it. Finally, I give the authority along with the responsibility."

These days, Mike Bloomberg looks to be a happy man. He is delighted with the divorce settlement he made with his wife of eighteen years; they still share their weekend house in Westchester, and he sees his two daughters often. Best of all, he can spend as much time as he likes doing what he likes most — meeting people, schmoozing, getting involved in philanthropic activities, and doing business in the office, where he can make casual patter with his employees, admire the pretty ones from what he insists, with the look of a cat with feathers stuck to the corners of its mouth, is a "safe" distance, and come up with new ways to expand Bloomberg L.P.

He practically struts around the open spaces, drinking coffee from "Bloomberg"-embossed paper cups, proudly surveying all that he has wrought. Billboards bearing his name are prominently displayed at bus stops and train terminals throughout Manhattan, and one is strategically placed along the Henry Hudson Parkway where Mike can see it when he drives to his weekend home. Daily newspapers in the closer suburbs are delivered with protective plastic bearing the legend "WBBR News Radio" wrapped around them, and his name is heard regularly on the radio and on television. Bloomberg says that marketing strategy, rather than ego, is behind the ubiquitous use of his name. "It's all part of a piece," he shrugs. "We're in the information business and there's a cohesive theme and everything feeds back." He nonetheless admits to getting a real charge out of seeing his name everywhere.

Time was when Mike was fond of talking about his "inferiority complex," saying that such feelings drive all successful people. Not anymore. "I live by the sword and I'll die by the sword," he announces with bravado and perhaps the remains of a nagging fear. "There's no question that successful people get a thrill when they accomplish something. But the older I get, the more I realize that although it's nice to be the center of attention, in the real world there are both ups and downs. You do what you gotta do.

"My standard of ethics is that I can always go home at night and describe to my daughters everything I did that day and feel good about it."

For the rest, Mike makes a point of having no long-range plans for Bloomberg L.P., besides having better trained people, better data to offer on his equipment, and better equipment. "If you gave me a crystal ball, and it showed me doing the same thing in ten years, I'd be happy," says Mike, eyes wide with sincerity. "On the other hand, if it showed me doing something different, that would be good, too. You can only keep the status quo by moving forward. To stand still is to slide backward . . . I only know if we keep plowing money into R & D and work hard, we'll get a lot done. I don't know what the specifics will be, but we'll get a lot done." The way Mike sees things, it's almost impossible to lose.

"It never even occurred to me to feel daunted by being a woman or by being a foreigner. In fact, I felt that being a woman and being an Asian were clearly my best assets."

JOSIE NATORI

**Founder and CEO of Natori Company,
makers of exquisitely designed lingerie**

The showroom of the Natori Company on East 34th Street in Manhattan looks like the walk-in closet for a sensuous, multi-cultural harem. Floor-length velvet kimonos, elaborately embroidered with exotic birds and oriental flowers, hang beside paisley silk dressing gowns belted with tasseled, golden cords and a rainbow of slinky, floor-length, satin gowns in forest green, claret, and vermillion, delicate pink, pale mauve, and subtle lavender. The shoes are the stuff of fairy tales. Cinderella-style velvet slippers adorned with ribbons and ostrich feathers share the shelves with backless mules that sparkle with bugle beads and gold-threaded embroidery. And then there are the bras and panties, the camisoles and bustiers — carefully draped rows of multi-hued silk and satin, black lace and gauzy leopard prints.

"It's all part of my vision, a concept that appeals to the emotions and the senses," says Josie Natori, the woman behind the fashion empire that helped to redefine the boundaries between underwear — what she calls "innerwear" — and outerwear. "People ask me if I have some sort of fetish for sexy underwear. I don't have a fetish. I am simply drawn to the emotional quality of beautiful things. We design clothes that make women feel good about themselves. Our things are meant to appeal to something deep inside a woman." Their appeal is not lost on men, either.

As president of the Natori Company for the last seventeen years, Josie Natori has built a $40 million worldwide industry of exquisitely designed lingerie that caters to everyone from Madonna to corporate CEOs. Her three subsidiary companies — Eve Stillman, Josie, and Natori — offer everything from moderately priced sleepwear and daywear to haute couture eveningwear and "at-home wear" based on a vision that challenges pre-conceived fashion norms by offering lingerie so beautifully functional it can be worn as regular clothing.

She has won numerous awards for her role in revolutionizing the fashion industry, including the New York City Asian-American Award and the Philippine-American Foundation Friendship Award, and has displayed her designs at New York's Metropolitan Museum of Art. She is also an active member of the Committee of 200, a group of women entrepreneurs who head multimillion-dollar companies. Most recently, President Clinton appointed her to the White House Conference on Small Business, an eleven-member presidential advisory council to help small businesses.

"What drives me," says Natori, a petite woman whose delicate, Filipino features are enhanced by her perfectly fitted designer suits, bright red lipstick and fingernails, and sleek, bobbed hair, "is that I don't believe in playing by rules written in concrete. I'm a gambler at heart. I always take risks. If you don't take risks, you don't move ahead. I always ask the question, 'Why not?' That's what made our company distinctive and has made my vision consistent."

Natori came from a background that helped to build her tenacity in questioning and challenging traditions. The oldest of six children born to an aristocratic Filipino family, Josefina Cruz grew up in Manila, surrounded by entrepreneurs. Her father, a self-made man, built his own construction business with the help of her mother, nicknamed "the Commander in Chief." She confides that her real mentor, however, was her maternal grandmother, "the Supreme Commander in Chief," who ran several businesses, including coconut and sisal plantations, with a tough managerial style.

Though she showed a gift for playing the piano at an early age, a talent that led to a solo concert with the Manila Philharmonic Orchestra when she was only nine, Natori always knew she wanted to be a businesswoman. Her family encouraged her decision to go to New York in 1964, at age seventeen, to study economics at Manhattanville College. "The whole idea was to graduate and come right back home," recalls Natori, who takes great pride in her cultural heritage. "But after two years in New York, I realized I would never leave."

After graduating with straight A's in 1968, Natori became a stockbroker in the corporate finance department at Bache Securities, where she was responsible for setting up the Manila office for the firm. Natori's success on Wall Street was immediate. By 1971, she had moved to Merrill Lynch, where she became an investment banker in the considerably less glamorous public utilities department. She soon met her future husband, Ken Natori, a third generation Japanese-American who was a stockbroker at the rival firm of Smith Barney Harris Upham. They married a year later.

By 1975, Natori had become the first woman vice-president of Merrill Lynch. But, shortly after the birth of the Natoris' first and only child, Kenneth, Jr. in 1976, Natori was ready for a change.

"I was bored. It all came too easy," she recalls, her emphatic hand gestures keeping pace with her high-speed banter. "I'm the ultimate JAP," she quips about her ability to speak a rapid blend of English and Yiddish with a Filipino accent. "I was making tons of money, I had risen very quickly and received recognition for my work, but the novelty had begun to wear off. I just wasn't challenged anymore.

"I knew there must be something else, and Ken and I had already decided to run our own business one day . . . It never even occurred to me to feel daunted by being a woman or by being a foreigner. In fact, I felt that being a woman and being an Asian were clearly my best assets." Working as an investment banker, Natori came across a lot of business possibilities. She briefly considered a McDonald's franchise, then a Bun 'N'

Burger, a car wash, and even a fertilizer company. None of these ventures felt right. "I felt I had to find something that I could relate to, something that would satisfy [both] my deal-making side and my aesthetic side. But more importantly, I wanted to do something that would connect with my heritage. Not only am I deeply patriotic, but I knew that my heritage was my strength. It was what would set me apart from everyone else."

She returned to her homeland in search of products she could import to the United States. She tried her hand at a variety of local Filipino products, from wicker baskets to reproduction Queen Anne furniture, only to find herself beset by a host of manufacturing and shipping problems.

Always willing to push on, she next considered a children's clothing store. Then an old friend from high school sent her some samples of hand-made Filipino children's clothing, including a few hand-embroidered and appliquéd adult blouses in the shipment. These were the shirts that would later launch thousands of ships and a $40-million industry.

"I wouldn't have been caught dead in those blouses," recalls Natori. "Even though the craftsmanship was beautiful, they seemed too old-fashioned and provincial for me. But the peasant look was popular in Paris at the time, and I thought someone might go for their ethnic look. I showed the blouses to everyone I knew and someone told me to go see a particular buyer at Bloomingdale's. At the time I didn't even know that she was a lingerie buyer. Well, she took one look at the embroidery and said, 'Make the shirt longer and we'll call it a nightshirt and sell it as lingerie.'"

Natori gave up her six-figure salary at Merrill Lynch, and while Kenneth, Jr. napped in his crib, began selling her new lingerie line out of the living room of her East Side apartment. Without any background in designing or marketing apparel, she relied on retailers for product ideas and began to add her own touches, venturing into bold colors and patterns for nightgowns instead of sticking to the more traditional pink, white, and blue, which struck her as dull.

Three months later, she had $150,000 worth of orders from such major department stores as Saks Fifth Avenue and Neiman Marcus. She and her husband invested $200,000 to lease a small showroom on East 34th Street. Less than a year later, the Natori Company expanded to an 11,000-square foot loft in the same building and added a sample and design workspace in another building around the corner shortly thereafter.

In 1985, Ken Natori left his job as a managing director at Shearson Lehman and joined the company full-time as chairman, overseeing the finance, distribution, and administration of the company. Today, the Natoris employ more than 100 workers in New York and some 900 local craftsmen in the Philippines.

"I think what made us successful was that I had a vision and we stuck to that vision," reflects Natori. "In all of our clothing, there is an East-meets-West feeling. We try to have no particular nationality but rather a global appeal. We are sold in over 40 countries. Our line is not only popular in the United States, but in Canada, Italy, and Japan. We even have a boutique in Paris, in the country that supposedly defined lingerie."

If France defined lingerie, then Natori may have redefined it. "We recognized that women enjoy beautiful lingerie and are willing to spend as much as fifteen hundred dollars for themselves rather than wait for a man to buy it for them." Although she was raised by nuns and was taught that it was sinful to talk about sex, she quickly overcame her inhibitions, and now speaks boldly about women's interest in buying clothes that make them feel sexy.

In 1990, she introduced Josie Natori Couture, a very high-ticket lingerie line that was marketed as evening wear to up-scale stores like Martha International and Bergdorf Goodman. Although the exquisite gowns that cost well over $1,000 have never been the biggest money-maker for the company, the line still serves, says Natori, "as a laboratory. The design ideas flow through it and are used or licensed elsewhere.

"From the beginning, I wasn't consciously trying to challenge the established ideas of lingerie. I simply followed my instincts. I had no preconceived ideas and asked questions that forced buyers to reconsider what [a garment] should be used for. I naturally asked questions like, 'Why can't a nightgown look like an evening gown?' or 'Who says you can't wear these slippers with that dress?' Everything evolves. Why not lingerie? I learned on the job. What I knew for sure was that since we didn't know the slick business moves, the product would have to make our name."

And there were plenty of stumbling blocks along the way. "I had no experience with manufacturers and had no idea that we could send defective goods back. I didn't know, for example, what a reject was. We once got an order from Horchow's for a thousand scalloped-neck nightshirts and they came from Manila without scallops. [My mother and] I stayed up all night cutting them ourselves." Natori ameliorated that problem in 1980 by having her father, Felipe Cruz, design and build her a $500,000 factory in Manila.

"I was accustomed to Wall Street ethics and I was unprepared for the rag trade," she continues. "We once got a $25,000 order from a big New York store and after everything was made, they canceled it. On Wall Street, you cement a deal over the phone. In fashion, you can sign in blood and it doesn't mean a thing.

"Another near-disaster was in 1983 when Mrs. Aquino's husband Benigno was shot. All shipping came to a halt and we had to cancel almost all of our orders. I thought we were dead for sure. I had to write formal apologies to all of our clients."

And, of course, satisfying the demanding tastes of New York's fashion industry was not always easy. "I had ideas that bombed. I was certainly not always right. Some years we couldn't meet the demands; other years no one bought. But they came to expect us to innovate, and we did. That is now part of our identity."

Now Natori is bringing what she has come to call her "lifestyle concept," a vision that includes items that appeal to a woman's need to express her sensual side, to new products. "I just love accessories," she once told the press. "My mother could never have enough jewelry and neither can I. It's the same with handbags, scarves, and shawls. Maybe it's a Filipino thing — like Imelda Marcos's shoes."

For several years, she has included slippers, sachets, lingerie, and evening bags in her collection, but she has recently begun to step up efforts in that direction. In the Fall of 1993, she introduced an upscale costume jewelry collection under a worldwide licensing agreement. In 1994, she launched the Natori shoe collection and began her latest international venture, a collection of fragrance, bath, and boudoir products licensed by Avon Products, Inc. The typical licensing deal nets Natori a royalty of between five and ten percent of the retail price of the items. Natori comes up with the design, and the manufacturer takes care of the rest, including marketing. Her sights are set on a Natori cosmetics line in the near future.

Though she and her husband Ken share a spacious, walnut-paneled office in the 34th Street showroom, Natori sees their jobs as very different. Ken, she says, deals with "the outside," hunting potential licensees and tracking orders and inventory, while she takes care of "the inside" of the company, incubating new ideas and products and overseeing their production. The couple divide their time between their East Side Manhattan apartment, their country retreat in Pound Ridge, New York, and their apartment in Paris.

Josie exercises with a private trainer three days a week and spends any remaining free time devoted to her "only hobby" — shopping. "I'm a shop-a-holic, and Paris is my booze," she announces proudly. "My life and work are very intermingled. Even when I'm shopping in a flea market, I am searching for inspiration. But like most women, I love indulging myself, pleasing myself, not just a man."

These days, Natori never feels the kind of boredom wrought by her success on Wall Street. "Holy Macaroni!" she yelps, a refreshing enthusiasm shining through her sophisticated exterior. "I'm never bored because I'm always on to the next thing. I play many roles. As head of the Natori Company, I work with the designers, the salespeople, and the manufacturers. But I'm also a wife, a daughter with family obligations, and a mother. And I am dedicated to my country. I want to make a difference in the Philippines and give back to the country that gave me so much. I'm involved with many charities, and I am interested in helping to develop the fashion business there and elevating the perception of what Filipinos can do. It is very important to me to raise the awareness of talent there."

Working up a head of steam, she waxes effusive. "I love New York and I love my country. If you ask me if this is what I'm going to do for the rest of my life, I'll say 'No!' But helping an industry along is exciting. I feel as if I am making a difference.

"I think we've done a lot to uplift the image of the fashion industry. It used to be a very sleepy industry and now all the fashion news has focused on this play of inner and outerwear and we had a lot to do with it . . . I never sit back and say, 'Everything is just fine.' You can never be totally okay. But I always believe if something doesn't work, you should just go on to the next thing. Everything happens for a good reason. I never regret anything. If I have a bad year or a product doesn't take off, I simply pick up the pieces and find the strength to move on."

"I feel very lucky. I've had extraordinary things happen to me so far. I move in a great variety of circles. I meet with science advisors at the White House; I play jazz with Ornette Coleman; I consult with Japanese businessmen. Thus far, I've had a good tour."

JARON LANIER

Coined the term "virtual reality" to describe his
visionary work with interactive computer technologies

I t's hard to miss Jaron Lanier on the street. Perhaps it's the
three-foot curtain of blond, waist-length dreadlocks that
falls to his rotund middle and releases a mist of fine golden
coils around his face, making him look like some wacked-
out, Rastafarian Apollo. Or it may be his wide-eyed, almost
cherubic expression, an improbable mix of intellectual intensity
and child-like glee, like the wise and benign smile of a
"Wookie" escapee from a Star Wars set.

But if Jaron Lanier's ideas about the future applications of
media technology are right, the Sun God may get some help
enlightening the world. At the very least, Lanier's work in
"virtual reality," a term he coined to describe his work with
interactive computers, has created enough new approaches to
exercising our imaginations to give George Lucas food for
thought.

Thanks to Lanier's efforts throughout the past decade,
anyone with access to the right equipment—a head mount
display containing a small TV screen eyepiece and a wired
"DataGlove" for manipulating objects in a computer-generated
"cyberspace"—can use computers to gain access to a seem-
ingly infinite range of artificial yet so-real-they-are-"virtually
real" environments and interact with as many objects or crea-
tures as can be found there. Without ever leaving home, a
user can virtually "hang glide" through the Grand Canyon,

"swim" through the human circulatory system, or "walk through" a multi-leveled mall, complete with fully stocked shops.

"I view the world we live in as a puzzle," says Lanier, whose long-range perceptions often suggest experience beyond his 33 years. "The puzzle is not only how we can survive, but also how we can have a life that's as fully realized as possible. I'm trying to find a culturally and spiritually valuable mode of creating things for other people. At the same time, I'm trying to find out what makes a good goal. It just so happens that technology is a kind of talisman for our culture. Since the media are immensely powerful, I tried to figure out what the ultimate wonderful medium would be.

"My goal was not merely to make media, but to change the structure of media as it exists today to communicate with people. I studied [Marshall] McLuhan and the other critics of the media and came to the idea that to have a better world in the future, you would have to invent a new medium with an eye towards esthetics and community."

Lanier is no "outsider" or "seer" espousing incomprehensible systems without practical applications. He is very careful to make his oftentimes complex theories as accessible to the uninitiated as possible. He attributes his odd appearance to pure convenience (his hair, he says, is "hard to brush") and thinks of himself as very much an "insider." He has presented his ideas to a wide variety of audiences, including scientists, university professors and students, international CEOs, and U.S. government science committees. Vice-president Al Gore is a friend of Lanier's and frequently invites him to Washington to conduct seminars.

His ground-breaking work with computers, he says, is inspired above all by what he sums up as the "momentum of being." "Humanity is like a bunch of teenage kids. You have to give them something to do or they get in trouble . . . Most of us walk around intensely frustrated because we have very active and complete imaginations, but our day-to-day reality is very limited. That leaves us with two choices — either to be alone with infinity or to be with others in a very limited world. Most children don't want to accept the chasm between these two choices, and most adults grudgingly acquiesce to it. My work bridges that chasm." It offers, he adds, a kind of "technological permission" for the child in each of us to come out and play and, in effect, for us to "create shared dreams."

Although he has no trouble addressing the ways in which children perceive and process the visual world, Lanier's memories of his own childhood are very murky. Much of this he ascribes to the "blackness" that descended in the wake of his mother's death in a car accident when he was nine. The experience left him depressed and withdrawn for much of his teenage years. The details of his childhood, he adds, are "not something I'm particularly interested in."

He was born in Harlem, New York, he says, carefully adding, "that's never been confirmed," but he and his family moved to a small town on the border of Texas and New Mexico when he was less than a year old. His father, a Russian Jewish emigré, was a physiologist, and his mother, interned in an Austrian concentration camp when she was a small child, was a dancer, a pianist, and, says Lanier, "a great entrepreneur who had her own clothing business and loved to play the stock market."

"I'm definitely Jewish," he says of growing up in a part of the Southwest not exactly renowned for its Semitic heritage, "as Jewish as I am male — but I'm not sure what that means."

Shortly after his mother died, he and his father bought an empty piece of land in the New Mexico desert, where they set up tents and spent the better part of the next seven years building a house "filled with crystal shapes and spires that was born of a sixties idealism about experimental building techniques."

He attended high school in Las Cruces, New Mexico, dropped out when he was fifteen, and, with the help of some questionable paper-shifting, was accepted to New Mexico State College as a freshman without ever actually obtaining a high school degree. Many of his biographers describe him as a "mathematical genius," but Lanier shrugs at this characterization. "Each person has his or her own form of genius," he insists. "Society tends to overemphasize certain types of intelligence, which does damage to us all."

At New Mexico State College, Lanier became fascinated with computer science. He was asked to join a team to create interactive programs to teach graduate math. This was the beginning of his work in what he calls "post-symbolic communication," an approach to mathematics that rejects the use of notation, symbols, and syntax in favor of direct manipulation of what a computer does.

"In my teens studying math in high school, I noticed two things," explains Lanier, clearly making an effort to make his abstract work as concrete as possible. "As I learned a particular mathematical theorem, I would feel that it was all incredibly difficult. But once I had finally succeeding in learning it, I would feel that what I thought was so complicated was actually fairly simple, even trivial.

"I wondered why the same material could look so hard on the approach but so unimportant afterward. I figured that, on the whole, the programming being used to teach math was wrong."

"Later on, in college, I began to consider the computer programming that was being used to teach graduate math students. It seemed to me that if we could eliminate all notations, symbols, and syntax and replace them with interactive computer graphics to represent the notation — if we could begin to consider a more interactive approach in which we could directly manipulate the computer without using symbols — then we could create much simpler and more effective programming for learning math."

Does this mean the death of language as we now know it? "No," insists Lanier. "Right now language is lonely. It means language will have a new playmate."

Soon after he began his work in post-symbolic communication, Lanier moved to Santa Cruz, California, to pursue a career in music. Unable to find suitable work or housing, he moved across the mountains to Palo Alto, where he did free-lance work creating video games, including the enormously popular "Moondust," which he designed in 1983 for the Commodore 64 home computer. With the money he made selling video games, he set up a garage workshop where he continued his work in developing an electronic "virtual environment" that would replace ordinary mathematical programming with a "visual programming language."

Lanier is not the first to have toyed with the visual and philosophical applications of computer technology. Computer scientist Ivan Sutherland did some work with computer-simulated images in the early 1960s. Myron Krueger, a Connecticut inventor, performed the world's first experiments with virtual reality under the auspices of the U.S. Air Force in the 1970s, leading to such government-researched applications as flight and combat simulation. Similar work was continued by NASA's Ames Research Center at Moffett Field in California as a means of training astronauts for the rigors of space travel. And now, of course, thanks to much of Lanier's work, virtual reality has become an industry. Automobile companies use it to design better cars; architects and interior designers use it to create the spaces we live in; doctors are beginning to use it to study surgical techniques; and in the most accessible use of the technology, virtual reality centers where children can play a variety of supergraphic, three-dimensional computer games, are cropping up in cities across America. Indeed, entire amusement parks are now being devoted to the new technology.

"So far as I know," he says, "I was the first person to have the idea [of putting] a human body inside a simulation and certainly the first to put more than one person inside a simulation at the same time," Lanier explains.

In 1984, he and several colleagues started a company specifically designed to make this new technology available to the public. Their goal was to start an industry, Lanier told the press, "based on a new experience and a new way of thinking." He collaborated with Tom Zimmerman, an electrical engineer, to create a "DataGlove," a glove equipped with optical sensors which worked as an input device to interact with the images on a screen. He and Zimmerman joined forces with Young Harvil, a painter, computer programmer, and optical engineer, Ann Lasko, a painter and sculptor, Steve Bryson, and Chuck Blanchard, a software engineer, to found VPL (for Visual Programming Language) Research Inc. to develop a headset or "eyephones." The idea was to shoot pulses of visual image independently to the left and right eye; this, in combination with the DataGlove, allows the wearer to generate images according to his head and hand movements.

Word of his experimental work spread, and at the age of 24, Lanier was the subject of the cover story of an issue of *Scientific American*. The way he tells it, "As the story was going to print, the editor called me up and said, 'There's a problem here. We don't have your affiliation.' And I said, 'I'm proud *not* to have one at the present time. I funded this study through a video game.' He said, 'Our editorial policy clearly states that we must have an affiliation following your name.' I said, 'Oh, use VPL — standing for Visual Programming Languages or maybe Virtual Programming Languages' — but mainly it was this spontaneous thing to get this guy off the phone. And then I told him to put a comma and 'Inc.' after it and never gave it a second thought. Then when the issue came out months later, all these people called up wanting to invest."

Within five or six years, the company was generating $6 million worth of business, creating patents, and working with companies as disparate as Mattel Inc. and NASA. For one client, they created a virtual mall, built from an architect's plans. For Matsushita, they created a virtual kitchen in which Japanese shoppers could choose designs, fixtures, and appliances.

Unfortunately, trying to mass produce a virtual reality package with a computer, DataGlove, eyephones with a built-in magnetic headtracking device, three-dimensional audio, and the software to power it, was very expensive. Though VPL Research managed to get a chunk of funding from Thomson CSF Ventures, the venture capital arm of Thomson SA, a largely government-owned French defense contractor, Lanier and his team were not experienced enough in the manufacturing business to pull the project together successfully. The new market for virtual reality was uncertain; the research burned huge amounts of capital; the quality of the equipment package dropped; and VPL began defaulting on its loans from Thomson.

By January of 1993, Thomson had filed a civil suit seeking transfer of title to about 20 of VPL's patents, plus punitive damages and court costs. VPL went into bankruptcy and Lanier was barred from working there any longer. After acquiring the patents, Thomson sued again to force VPL to hand over materials, instruments, and documentation related to the patents — information, some say, worth billions of dollars. No final settlement has yet been made.

Lanier shrugs off these upsets, chalking them up to the inexperience of youth, and is forging ahead with new plans and new applications for virtual reality. "I'm not too worried about it," he told the press in the days after he was debarred from the company. "I will probably end up getting wealthy from the technology in one way or another, but if I don't, I'm prepared for that too . . . I did start an industry, though. Not too many people can say that."

These days, he has plenty of new ventures on his plate, dividing his time between being a musician, a scientist, an artist, an information systems consultant, a software expert, a teacher, and a business consultant. He has a loft in downtown Manhattan and a home in Marin County, California, a place "where if you haven't achieved Nirvana, they revoke your driver's license," he quips when asked about his very vocal concerns about the spiritual aspects of future uses of virtual reality.

Indeed, much of the scientific work he pursues seems clearly inspired by an inner sense of spirituality, even mysticism. "The purpose of science is not to discover truths, but rather to test the falsifiability of things," he explains. "There is territory that can by explored even though it's not falsifiable. The most fundamental things going on are beyond falsifiability. There's only one solution — a somewhat ecstatic feeling of mysticism that is inconsequential to the matters of science. Scientists tend to err in the direction of reductionism; spiritual people tend to err in the direction of superstition. But no scientist need be offended by mysticism. To me, the two are simply different corners of experience . . .

"Since the Renaissance, man's agenda has been to have power over nature. We have already developed enough technology to give us power over nature in most places. There are two places left where nature remains a threat — medicine and natural disaster. Although I've done some work focusing on natural disaster, I've chosen to focus my efforts on medicine."

Through the Company Incubator Program at Dartmouth University, he is helping to start a company called Medical Media Systems, which will develop new ways to use virtual reality to make a better interface with endoscopes, the flexible tubes with mini-cameras doctors use to look inside the human body without surgery. The software will also give doctors greater intuitive control of surgical instruments by creating visualizations of inside the body.

In addition, Lanier has acquired financial backing for a new company called New Leaf Systems in San Carlos, California, which develops virtual reality software. He created New Leaf to "take a crack at developing a new generation of tools to create the content of a virtual world." And he is part of the Global Business Network, an organization that helps growing companies learn the general principles behind the newest computer technology.

At the same time, Lanier continues to spread the word about his work. He teaches students at New York University how to create virtual reality art and is a visiting scholar at Columbia University, where he is doing research in the future of programming languages and in the creation of what he calls a "novel, mathematical model of the brain" that, he insists, "is too complicated to explain unless you've got a few hours."

He is also working on a long-overdue book about virtual reality for Harcourt Brace Publishers and has just released his first record on Polygram Records, *Instruments of Change*. The album reflects Lanier's interest in playing a variety of traditional and arcane instruments from all over the world, including the piano, khaen, shakuhachi, gu zheng, and brass clarinet. Although he has invented "cyber instruments," which can be played inside a virtual reality environment, his album is almost entirely acoustic, "written during the tiny cracks of time left as my life was increasingly consumed by the world's initial interest in virtual reality. They helped me maintain a connection to an inner world under assault."

Despite various upsets in the pursuit of his vision, Lanier's "inner world" has clearly been flourishing. "I feel very lucky," he says with a Wookie-ish grin. "I've had extraordinary things happen to me so far. I move in a great variety of circles. I meet with science advisors at the White House; I play jazz with Ornette Coleman; I consult with Japanese businessmen. Thus far, I've had a good tour."

"I have a lot of respect for people who do what they do well, so it's easy for me to enter into partnership relationships. I have a limited attention span and limited interest in the business part of my life so, it's incumbent upon me to find smart people to work with . . ."

ROD FRIEDMAN

Owner of Rebus Inc., publisher of the *UC Berkeley Wellness Letter* and *Johns Hopkins Medical Letter*

~

When Rod Friedman was growing up in Queens, New York, the center of his life was the magazine rack at the neighborhood candy store. "I fell in love with newspapers and magazines when I was five," he recalls. "I used to go to that candy store every day, drink malteds, and read everything on the rack. I read 60 newspapers and magazines a week."

Though he probably doesn't drink many malteds anymore, the 46 year old Friedman is still surrounding himself with the printed word. Since 1983, when he founded Rebus, Inc., Friedman has been the publisher of health-related books and newsletters that have garnered him a combined readership of well over a million loyal subscribers and a $30 million enterprise. Best known for his *UC Berkeley Wellness Letter* and *The Johns Hopkins Medical Letter,* Friedman has devoted himself to creating a means for helping people find healthier ways to live their lives.

Want to find out if sugar really causes hyperactivity in children, how to sleep with a sore back, whether shrimp are dangerously high in cholesterol, or the best way to make skim milk taste less watery without adding fat? Read it first in the Rebus newsletters. Need a low-fat cookbook, an encyclopedia of medical disorders for people over the age of 50, a book that guides you to lifelong fitness? It's all there in Rebus books — and a whole lot more.

"Our main goal is to empower people to change the way they deal with their own health, to give them enough information to change their lifestyles," says Friedman from the Rebus, Inc. offices in lower Manhattan. For the *Berkeley Wellness Letter*, the audience is anyone who is concerned about health-related issues. "We gear the *Johns Hopkins Letter* to readers over 50 years old who are addressing age-related health issues. Most people feel better when they make their own choices about how to live . . . There is a core of information that we understand, and we try to get it to as many people as we can through as many channels as we can."

Friedman oversees a staff of 40 doctors, nutritionists, medical experts, and writers whose mandate is to find the most current medical evidence regarding a wide range of health-related issues and translate it into accessible stories.

The slant the newsletters take is positive and pushes its readership to take active control over health concerns rather than slink into fear and worry. "Studies suggest," explains Friedman, "that recovery is quicker when a patient has control over the decisions he makes [about his health] . . . We want to set a tone of voice and an attitude on how to think about health. Many of our readers have problems for which the traditional medical community might recommend either medication or surgery. We believe in the power of small changes, and we like to present our audience with a set of options for improving their own health." Recent newsletters have dealt with issues ranging from how to reduce the risk of a heart attack to how to maintain sexual intimacy while undergoing chemotherapy treatment.

"Everything we report on uses the universities' scientific criteria," Friedman notes. "In order to endorse a modality, university scientists must use the scientific method. We stay away from anything we can't prove. We have a well-qualified staff of people, many of whom left the medical profession because many of the reasons [for practicing medicine] just aren't there anymore. Malpractice suits have pushed insurance rates out of control, and the health care system is a mess.

Many of our doctors feel that writing for us is a more constructive way to benefit a lot of people."

Friedman quite clearly practices what he preaches. His office is hardly the ivory tower one might expect of a Manhattan publisher. In fact, with its polished hardwood floors, high ceilings and wall of windows — and stationary bike and Nordic Track — the 15,000-square foot loft in a Greenwich Village cast-iron building strikes the visitor as a cross between a modern gym and an old-fashioned sporting goods store. In addition to the modern exercise and office equipment, the office contains antique cards displaying fishing lures, shelves of sports trophies, and boxes filled with basketballs and baseballs, lacrosse sticks and bats, spare running shoes and in-line roller skates. On this particular day, the boss — tall, slim, and ruddy with good health — is clad in a royal blue nylon and gray cotton fleece warm-up suit and looks like someone who rollerbladed to work. That's probably because he did, commuting from the Soho loft he shares with his wife and two daughters several blocks south.

"I consider myself a happy person," says Friedman, who consistently comes across with an easy blend of earnest intensity, low-key serenity, and mellow optimism much more typical of California than of his native New York. "I'm in good health and I live with very little stress . . . Having children crystallized for me that the reason I could be so happy with what I do is that I have a life outside of work. I think my attitude comes from literally feeling good and also from knowing that, ultimately, my identity isn't wrapped up entirely in my work.

"A lot of businessmen start out with a marketing, production, and business plan. Then they go out to raise capital . . . I've never raised a penny of capital. My vision has been to try and find out what it is that makes me happiest, to find the work that I think is most meaningful."

Indeed, Friedman seems a living advertisement for the policies he preaches in the *Berkeley Wellness Letter* — "Nutrition, Fitness and Stress Management."

He was born in Queens, New York, the son of civil servants who, he insists, "didn't prepare me for a life of entrepreneurship." One of the earliest lessons he learned was how to lose. "My father was a gambler — not a big risk taker, but a gambler nonetheless," he reflects. "We used to go to Las Vegas and watch people play card games. He reminded me that someone always has to lose, but if you hung in long enough and played smart, you could win." The secret, reinforced in countless childhood games of baseball, football, and lacrosse, was not in trying to win but in "just playing the game."

Friedman attended Hobart College as a political philosophy major in the 1960s. He was a student activist who shared the anti-Vietnam War sentiments that swept most of the country's college campuses in those days. Earnestly believing he could find a job that would "make a difference to society," he went on to law school at George Washington University.

Upon graduating, however, he came to the conclusion that joining the law establishment would not help to create broad enough changes in society and decided instead to become a political consultant. Knowing nothing about the advertising business and even less about political consulting, he set up his own ad agency in Washington, D.C. to represent clients with causes. He had business cards printed up at a local off-set printing shop and went to work. "I helped anyone who wanted to get a message across," he recalls. "I believed that if I could get the facts straight and present them in a clear and non-hysterical way, I could get things done. I felt that I could break through narrow-mindedness and ignorance if I presented information clearly. In fact, that is something that still drives me."

For a short time, Friedman handled such clients as Democratic presidential candidate George McGovern, consumer advocate Ralph Nader, Madison Avenue Against the Vietnam War, and a series of anti-smoking campaigns. "I decided fairly quickly," he admits, "that although I loved causes, I didn't love the cause people. They seemed to be driven more by the idea of campaigning rather than by the issues themselves . . . I had come out of a long educational process realizing that I hadn't learned very much in school. I didn't have any mentors. I studied the classics and came away with a sense that there are truths that transcend us as individuals and that I am just a small part of a larger continuum. But I also came away with a strong belief that most of what I needed to learn I would have to learn on my own and that any opinions I was going to form would come from me . . . I had always been interested in journalism, so I loaded up my van and returned to New York."

In 1974, Friedman and two friends who were graphic designers opened up an office on Third Avenue and 60th Street and started Tree Communications. The partners worked as free-lance producers of magazines for various venture capitalists, creating *Country Music* and *Lifestyle* magazines as well as a series of books "on any subject that interested us." Some of their products were published by Tree while others shared an imprint with such prestigious magazines as *Time, Better Homes and Gardens,* and *Architectural Digest.* "I would get an idea and just want to do it myself, but realize that we weren't equipped," recalls Friedman. "I have a lot of respect for people who do what they do well, so it's easy for me to enter into partnership relationships. I have a limited attention span and limited interest in the business part of my life, so it's incumbent upon me to find smart people to work with . . .

"But I became totally interested in the process of publishing. I was fascinated by things that were not part of my education and published books on anything that interested me — architecture, antiques, cooking. We did a 24-volume family encyclopedia for Time/Life about various crafts, in which expert craftsmen taught readers everything from pottery to weaving to woodworking. There's no doubt that my curiosity alone took me a long way. But most of all, I learned how to take information and give it back out to readers so that they could understand it. That was totally satisfying to me."

In no time, Tree was employing 20–30 people and turning a significant profit — all of which Friedman pumped right back into the business. "One key decision we made was to move into an inexpensive loft space on Park Avenue South. An architect convinced me that renting raw, expansive space would save us a lot of money, a piece of advice I am still following," he says. "Another key decision involved my willingness not to care at all whether I was personally profiting. In the early days, I probably lived on $3,000 per year; one year I think I lived on $1,300. Most of my friends had gone on to practice law and were already buying second homes. My wife, Janet, is a lawyer and was very supportive of me. Our books were selling well, and I decided to put all of the profits back into the business. That's another philosophy I still follow."

Things changed with the birth of the Friedmans' first child in 1983. At that time, Rod's partners left Tree to go on to other projects. Simultaneously, Friedman's parents announced that they had grown bored with their Florida retirement lifestyle and had decided to return to New York. Friedman promptly took them into the business. After all, he reasoned, his mother had been an accountant for the U.S. government and would make an excellent bookkeeper; his father, a one-time government controller, could help manage the office. Although both of his parents are now deceased, they did have the pleasure of seeing their son's business take off.

"After my daughter was born, I felt I went from being almost totally focused on business to trying to find a better balance between my work life and my private life . . . It was important to me that my children know in their souls what I seem to have always known — that there are no boundaries, no self-imposed or societal limitations. I wanted to do my best to create an environment for them that would help them find their true passions and have as much fun with them as I expect to have with mine. To do so, I realized I had to be incredibly efficient," Friedman explains.

Wanting to invest in a new product, Friedman sought the advice of friends and became interested in the growing opportunities of newsletters. "I shopped around and came up with the idea of a health newsletter. For one thing, I was increasingly responsible for my parents medical health at the time, and I felt it was important for me to have access to the right information to make good decisions for their benefit. As I got more involved with their health issues, I generally felt that doctors were not communicating well with their patients or giving them the information they needed to make their own decisions. I had been interested in health for a long time and decided I could work as a facilitator between the lay public and the medical and health communities . . . I wanted to reach people who would be interested in trying to take responsibility for their own health. Almost immediately, I felt I had come across an editorial product that was me. It was so clearly a reflection of my own interest.

"I simply decided it was going to work. So many people don't see all the possibilities they have. They forget they almost always have choices . . . At the time, there were several medical newsletters out and I wanted to do something different." First, he searched for a university that would lend credibility and expertise to his concept. It wasn't long before the University of California at Berkeley gave him its imprimatur. "I did approach a number of different departments at different universities. Both the University of California and Johns Hopkins had a commitment to teaching patients and providing them with options regarding their health. I told them that we could offer them a unique opportunity to extend their reach far beyond the confines of their institutions, and this appealed to them.

"What's more, we were willing to do all of the hard work necessary to get out a monthly publication, and we would not interfere with any of their primary responsibilities as research institutions. Finally, we promised them a potentially large royalty income from the newsletters, which, in fact, far surpassed their expectations." Once he acquired the names that would lend credence to his publications, he used available direct-marketing techniques to gain subscribers. "I realized that our ideal subscribers would probably be people between 40 and 60 years old, who were not necessarily health fanatics but who would be interested in gaining new perspectives on their health or who might be interested in trying to get some control over a health problem they might currently be suffering. The *Dow Jones Theory Newsletter* provided an ideal list for us." Thanks to word of mouth, the subscriber list grew, and by 1987, had reached about 700,000. It has remained stable ever since.

Within four years, the *Berkeley Wellness Letter* was followed by *The Johns Hopkins Medical Letter* and a host of books that would support the same principles espoused in the newsletters, including *The Wellness Low fat Cookbook, The Wellness Guide to Lifelong Fitness, The Wellness Encyclopedia, The Johns Hopkins Medical Handbook,* and *The Johns Hopkins Handbook of Drugs.* In 1994, Friedman took his cause one step further by opening Virtual Health, a retail store in Santa Monica, California, in partnership with a record producer and a film producer. Virtual Health promotes a more holistic approach to health through the sale of homeopathic medicines and a group of in-store interactive kiosks that teach consumers about health and exercise.

"I still put most of my profits back into the business," says Friedman, whose lifestyle includes a 2,500-square-foot shingle-roofed cabin overlooking thousands of acres of state forest, hiking trails, and trout streams in Carmel, New York. The country home is only about an hour and a half north of Manhattan, an easy commute for weekend trips. He spends his summers there with his family, hiking, and mountain biking and communicating with his office by e-mail as much as possible. "It was important for me to create a lifestyle that works for my family. My daughters attend a school that is near my office so that I can pick them up when school is out. And my wife and I go hiking together every morning when we're in the country. I like to live well, but I don't need the kind of personal security a lot of people do. I choose to invest in myself.

"I would like to reach even more people with the same information we are publishing now. We have a total of 1.5 million customers, and [our newsletters] are doubtless read by many more people. I would love to extend our reach to new people using every new form of media that becomes available."

For Friedman, investing in himself, means investing in the people who work for him as well.

"Success in business is a long process, and you succeed only if you conduct yourself in the highest ethical way that you can," he says. "I try to strike a balance between caring for my product and caring about all the people who work for me because, after all, we are only as good as the people we use. My favorite employees are those who are demanding about their needs, and at the same time, take full responsibility for their jobs." In fact, he encourages his employees to create work schedules that will enhance their creativity. Several of his employees do all of their work from home via e-mail, while many others have created work schedules that maximize time with their families. One employee routinely takes off for several months at a time for adventure trips such as trekking across the Himalayas.

"When you run a business, you are responsible for creating an atmosphere that will allow people to prosper and do well and gain satisfaction. My only real job is to do that. Everyone who works with us is intertwined — the designers, the editors, the photographers, all the people who work on a project. My job is to find people who can do the best possible job, because if the wrong person is there, then I've let the whole group down.

"Whatever the vision is going in, it's usually not the vision that comes out. People get fixated on their ideas and they become so afraid of losing what they want that they don't hear what other people say. In the end, you have to be open to hear what others contribute. I really try to hear what people need and try to come up with something that will satisfy everyone involved."

For anyone starting a new business, Friedman has these words of advice: "First, never make a deal that isn't fair for everybody, and don't treat anybody the way you wouldn't want to be treated." Most importantly, he adds, "You have to feel that the thing you do has merit. Really care about what you do or it's impossible to really succeed at it."

"For me, 'profitable enough' means I have the freedom to do what I want privately and to influence people publicly. That's the point where business becomes a passion and not just dollars and cents."

ROBERT JOHNSON

Founder and CEO of Black Entertainment Television Inc.

⁓

Michelle Curtis, Bob Johnson's secretary and self-described "gatekeeper," is apologizing again for her boss's tardiness. "He means well, but he has so many things to oversee and so many people who corner him," she laments, her neat gray business suit riding up her torso as she flings her arms up in mock despair. "It's almost impossible for him to make it to a meeting on time. I think I had a life before I began working for him ten years ago, but I haven't had much of one since."

But what Johnson, the 46-year-old president and founder of America's first and only black-owned cable network, lacks in time management skills he more than makes up for in clarity of purpose. "Some people have a hunger to be the first person in outer space; some want to be the first to fly across the Atlantic," he says. "For me, it's controlling my own destiny and being in charge. What drives me is a need for the luxury of influencing my own life and having the power to influence the lives of others."

The way to that vision has been a fifteen-year effort to build a premier media empire whose primary mission is to reach the black American consumer market. Through a conglomerate that includes the Black Entertainment Television (BET) cable network, a publishing group that produces *YSB: Young Sisters and Brothers* and *Emerge* magazines, a nationally broadcast radio network, and a skin-care products line, direct-marketed on BET television, Johnson has succeeded in realizing his goal of becoming the largest outlet for advertisers seeking to reach the black consumer. At last count, BET's 24-hour, seven-day-a-week schedule reaches more than 39 million subscribers; the magazine circulation is growing and providing additional advertiser support; and BET Holdings, Inc. is worth over $74 million.

"I said to myself, 'There are more than 30 million black Americans out there who make up a very sizeable consumer market. That's more people than there are in West Germany,'" says Johnson. "There was no one providing programming that would reflect the needs and interests of black America. I knew black folks watch television, and I knew advertisers wanted to reach them. I figured if you put those two facts together, you had a business. I saw so many people starting up cable stations in the 1970s. I figured if they could do it, why not me?"

On this particular morning, Johnson is running late because of an emergency meeting with a team of architects designing a new office space for BET Holdings, Inc. The company is moving from its current headquarters overlooking a quaint brick courtyard in the historic Georgetown section of Washington, D.C., into a 65,000-square foot building next to BET's television studio in northeast Washington. Although Johnson is an hour behind schedule, he is barely ruffled. He enters his inner sanctum, a top-floor office with walnut paneling bathed in sunlight from an overhead skylight, and relaxes into a tall leather chair backed by a wall of contemporary art. Dressed in a dark, conservatively cut suit, he looks like any Washington power-broker, except perhaps for the tie, whose pattern of purple flowers suggests slightly less conservative tastes.

"One of the things I look for in employees is that they are cool under fire," he says, quite obviously cool. "In fact, I look for people who reflect qualities I have . . . They should also be willing to work hard and roll up their sleeves and get dirty; they should be prepared to postpone instant gratification in favor of long-term success; they should be smart and have integrity; and they should be able to read people and situations and size up where the power is. This is something I think is particularly important for black people in America today."

Although Johnson is quite clear on the goals he set for himself, he calls his initial decision to move into cable television the result of "serendipity."

Born to a working-class family in Freeport, Illinois, the oldest of ten children, he learned self-confidence and self-reliance early. The son of a factory worker whose income couldn't provide for a college education for his kids, Johnson worked his way through the University of Illinois and earned a Ford Foundation scholarship that encouraged minority students to enter the Foreign Service. His scholarship took him through the Woodrow Wilson School of Public and International Affairs at Princeton University, where he earned a master's degree in public affairs.

"When you're the first in your family to go to college and the first to get a master's degree and the first to get a serious job, you get a lot of self-confidence to take risks," he says. "Today, I'm most definitely a risk-taker."

College and graduate school fanned his interest in history and diplomacy, and Johnson moved to Washington in 1972, hoping to pursue a career in the diplomatic corps. He failed the notoriously difficult Foreign Service exam, however, and instead went to work for the Washington Urban League, a civil rights organization whose target group was black Americans. From there, he moved to the Corporation for Public Broadcasting. In 1976, he took a job as press secretary for Walter Fauntroy, a Congressional Delegate from the District of Columbia. While working in government affairs, he met a woman at a cocktail party who told him he would be a good lobbyist for the cable industry. "Until that time I had really never been involved in business," Johnson recalls. "I had earned my political stripes as a press secretary and my social-responsibility stripes with the Urban League, and I thought becoming a lobbyist might give me a chance to meet business people and earn my business stripes. I didn't know a lot about business, but I had some background in television, so I went for it."

From 1976 until 1979, Johnson served as Vice President of Government Relations for the National Cable Television Association (NCTA), a trade association representing over 1,500 cable television companies. It was on the board of the NCTA that he met his future mentor, John Malone, the visionary — if sometimes ruthless — CEO of Tele-Communications Inc., the highly successful cable carrier. Malone's well-publicized hardball tactics earned TCI one out of every four cable TV customers in America.

"That was 1979, and the cable television industry was growing like crazy. I had reviewed a proposal for a cable channel aimed at the elderly. I felt I could start a cable network and asked myself, 'What do I know?' Well, I know black culture, and I became convinced that there was room for a cable network devoted exclusively to the black audience. I went to John with the idea," says Johnson. Malone immediately became a 20 percent partner by purchasing $180,000 in BET stock and advancing Johnson a $320,000 loan. "I said to him, 'John, I'm new to this business. What advice can you give me?' He said, 'Get your revenues up and keep your costs down.' At a time when there was a lot of skepticism towards blacks on Wall Street, John stood by me. In fact, fifteen years later, he's still a friend and a member of our board of directors."

Johnson borrowed $15,000 from the bank so he'd "have enough money to pay the rent if the business flopped" and convinced Time Inc. (now Time-Warner Inc.) and Taft Broadcasting Company (now Great American Broadcasting Company) to invest, leaving him with 51 percent of BET stock. E. Thayer Bigelow, Jr., the President and CEO of Time Warner Cable Programming, Inc. is a BET board member to this day.

The early 1980s were lean years. BET began broadcasting two hours a week, gradually building the schedule with inexpensive programming, such as black college football games and music videos, as its staples. The early broadcasts were amateurish and unpolished, but BET attracted growing numbers of subscribers and slowly began expanding by adding old network sitcoms such as *Sanford and Son, Homeroom,*

Sugar and Spice and *New Attitude.* Johnson never lost sight of his vision. He purchased as much inexpensive programming as he could, provided it clearly catered to a black audience. It wasn't long before original programming, such as a half-hour gospel music show and several music and entertainment shows, were added.

To raise more capital, Johnson took Black Entertainment Television Holdings, Inc. public in 1990, listing its stock on the New York Stock Exchange. It became the first black-owned initial public offering in history. The sale of stock raised almost $72 million for the company, and Johnson earned $6 million from the sale of 375,000 of his own shares.

Johnson hit a low point in the months that followed, as the value of BET stock roller coastered when Wall Street analysts became alarmed by a discrepancy between the 27.5 million subscribers BET claimed and the 31.6 million cited by the A.C. Neilson Company. His explanation for the difference was that BET counted only those homes that actually paid for the service, while the Neilsen service counted everyone who received it, including those getting the service on free trial promotions. Nonetheless, many investors were disturbed by the confusing reports and bailed out. It wasn't long before the stock recovered and made up the ground it had lost, however.

Another controversy followed in 1993, when Johnson disclosed that BET was seeking to recover $700,000 in "unauthorized" payments made by company executives, a scandal that temporarily rocked BET's financial department. "That's just business," Johnson says today with a dismissive wave. "I don't let that kind of thing get me down . . . Besides, now the company is in great shape financially."

Indeed, BET is growing by leaps and bounds. In addition to the network's popular music shows — *Video Soul, Video LP, Video Vibration, Rap City,* and *Heart and Soul of R&B* — BET broadcasts *Teen Summit,* a nationally recognized and award-winning teen talk show, *Our Voices,* a talk show that features black celebrities as guests, *For Black Men Only,* a public affairs show, and *Personal Diary,* a one-on-one interview show, as well as public affairs programs, sporting events, news, and gospel, jazz, and comedy showcases. During the middle of the day on Sunday and during the early morning hours after 2 a.m., the network also airs what is known in the business as "paid programming" or "infomercials," which plug, among other things, Color Code, the new BET skin products line. Color Code has been developed especially for the Network's target audience and will only be available from another subsidiary, BET Direct. In 1993, the firm added BET Action Pay-Per-View, a national satellite-delivered pay-per-view movie channel offering black-oriented feature films produced by major studios.

Always thinking of new ways to increase market reach, Johnson established the publishing group in 1991 to produce magazines that cross promote the network. *YSB* focuses on black culture and important issues facing black teenagers, such as education, careers, sex, drugs, and family relationships, as well as articles about popular music, art, movies, and sports. *Emerge* is geared to a more adult audience and features profiles of notable black Americans as well as articles on current social trends, politics, economics, art, and literature. Like most start-up publications, both magazines are still operating in the red, but their circulations have grown annually to about 100,000 each.

"I'd like BET to have the same [profile] in the black community that Disney has in the general community," says Johnson. Future plans include BET on Jazz, a new jazz-oriented programming network that will include live performances, biographical features, coverage of jazz festivals, and concerts and music videos. The company also plans BET International, a subsidiary that will provide programming throughout Africa and other foreign markets; BET Film Productions, a joint partnership with Encore and LIVE Entertainment, formed to fund the production and distribution of black-oriented independent feature films; and BET Pictures, a joint venture with Blockbuster Entertainment Corporation to fund, produce, and distribute black, family-oriented films.

"It takes certain things to succeed," says Johnson. "First, you have to be totally focused and be prepared to put blinders on and go after what you want to the exclusion of just about everything else. Then, you have to have a vision of where you want to go. You have to believe that vision is worthwhile, and you have to be able to articulate that vision to banks and to people who can give you money. More than anything else, you need to have some level of support around you — family or friends you can turn to for advice . . . If you follow those three principles, you'll succeed — assuming, of course, you're not trying to build ships in the desert."

Johnson says BET occupies "all his waking thoughts," adding that John Malone and Sheila, Johnson's wife and executive vice president of corporate affairs, have been his two biggest supporters. Although his wife clearly holds a high-level corporate position, Johnson chooses not to talk about her concrete role in the day-to-day running of the business.

"The first time a business becomes profitable, you have succeeded," says Johnson. "Then the question becomes, 'Now that I have succeeded, just how profitable do I want to be?' For some, $50,000 is enough; for some it takes $50 million. For me, 'profitable enough' means I have the freedom to do what I want privately and to influence people publicly. That's the point where business becomes a passion and not just dollars and cents."

These days, Johnson feels he's got the luxury to "influence his own life" as much as he pleases. He and Sheila and their two children share a home in Washington, D.C. and a beach house on Dewy Beach in Delaware, and he's comfortable enough to take a limousine three short blocks on a warm, sunny day when he's a half-hour behind schedule — so that he won't be five minutes later for his next appointment. "Lots of people — both black and white — are jealous of my success," he says about the downside to his quick rise. He is not particularly daunted, however.

"The rewards have been quite clear," he says. "I have been able to give my family financial security; I have justified John Malone's faith in me; and I have the pleasure to employ 450 folks and give them the opportunity to provide for their families. *That* gives me satisfaction."

"When I visit schools throughout the country and talk with educators, I sense that our schools are preparing kids for a workplace that no longer exists. The majority of our schools are still set up to teach kids how to work in an Industrial Age."

JAN DAVIDSON

Founder and CEO of Davidson and Associates Inc., educational software publishers

J an Davidson is a woman with a mission. "I just want to change the world," says the president and founder of Davidson & Associates, Inc., one of the largest educational software publishers in America today. What Davidson may lack in modesty of ambition, she more than makes up for in experience, determination, and vision.

Over the last twelve years, this former high school and college teacher has built one of the top three American companies to develop, publish, and distribute a wide range of IBM/PC and Macintosh-based educational software products. Using her own teaching experiences as a starting point, Davidson was one of the earliest champions of using computer technology to revolutionize the classroom learning experience.

As with most missionaries, Davidson has spent countless hours spreading the word and looking for converts — in this case, America's educators. But the world has finally caught up with her ideas. Today the educational software industry is taking the country by storm, and Davidson & Associates is at its epicenter. Industry-wide, school sales of educational software reached $585 million in 1991 and are projected to grow to $1.45 billion by 1996. In that same period, home sales of educational software are projected to triple to $300 million. Davidson & Associates is leading the way with a list of more than twenty-five award-winning titles that teach math, reading, and writing skills, as well as history and science, to an audience that ranges from small school children to their parents and teachers.

Davidson's *Math Blaster* learning series, designed to teach math fundamentals to kids age six to twelve, has already sold well over a million copies since it was brought on the market more than a decade ago, and that was just the beginning. Today the company has agreements with such prestigious partners as Simon & Schuster, Addison-Wesley, and Fisher-Price to develop, produce, and distribute multimedia products for the consumer, education, business, entertainment, and reference markets.

"As a nation, we are only as strong as our people," says Davidson. "I believe I can make the nation stronger through education, and technology is one of the best means to achieve this." When she speaks about the future of education, Davidson's hazel eyes flash with a blend of fresh enthusiasm and fierce commitment. The combination is compelling. The petite schoolteacher in the trim red blazer and black slacks metamorphoses into a veritable Joan of Arc, leading her country's schoolchildren to a higher quality of life — life in the Information Age, that is.

"When I visit schools throughout the country and talk with educators," she continues, "I sense that our schools are preparing kids for a workplace that no longer exists. The majority of our schools are still set up to teach kids how to work in an Industrial Age. But the world these kids are going to face is an Information Age — a fast-paced global marketplace where American success cannot be automatically assumed. It's [as foolish as] teaching mileage when all the road signs are in kilometers, or using a map from the 1950s to explain what's going on in Bosnia . . .

"In Information Age classrooms, students will learn to access information and work with what they discover. They will move through the schoolday similar to the way their adult counterparts move through the workday. They will manage their time. They will use tools. They will have teammates. And they will take responsibility for a given task, leverage their skills, ferret out information needed to solve a problem, and work with classmates to get the job done."

The offices of Davidson & Associates in Torrance, California, about a half-hour's drive south of Los Angeles, look like Hollywood's version of the headquarters for an industrial giant. The impressive structure arcs into a majestic glass and stone semicircle supported by elegant, soaring columns, with the name Davidson emblazoned in authoritative letters across its facade. It could be the set for a movie about a country girl from the Midwest who rises to become the president of a $60 million company. If it were, then art would most certainly be imitating life.

Born in Ft. Knox, Kentucky, in 1944, Davidson and her younger brother and sister grew up in Frankfort, Indiana, where their father managed a local dairy. "I learned a lot about business from my parents," recalls Davidson. "They started their own business distributing dairy products to grocery stores and finally opened their own chain of convenience stores. My parents were always resourceful in making ends meet and taught me to do the same . . . They raised me in an environment that made me believe I could do anything I wanted to do. They had a real can-do attitude. No one ever talked about failure, and, as a result, I had incredible self-esteem."

By the time she was thirteen, Davidson was earning money as a tutor in her home. Her interest in teaching never faltered in the years that followed. She was the first in her family to go to college, obtaining her undergraduate degree from nearby Purdue University. It was at Purdue that she met her husband, Bob Davidson, whom she married in 1966, just a week after graduating.

The couple moved three times over the next ten years, living first in Maryland, where Davidson obtained a master's degree in communications and a doctorate in American literature from the University of Maryland, and finally settling into the home they still occupy in Palos Verdes, California, in 1976. "Every time we moved, I got a different teaching job," recalls Davidson. "I think I taught every year between the ages of thirteen and forty."

In 1979, Davidson founded Upward Bound, a non-profit tutoring service in a classroom she leased at Palos Verdes Elementary School. Proposition 13, a tax-cutting measure that led many California school districts to end the schoolday at noon, was instituted at the time, making Davidson's after-school classroom an instant success. "People didn't know what to do with their kids all afternoon, so they brought them to me," recalls Davidson.

She hired several teachers to oversee courses in language skills and remedial math, and the program gradually grew to accommodate students of all ages, from second grade all the way to adult. "The pedagogical [movement] at the time was towards individual instruction," explains Davidson. "We have learned a lot about learning in the last few decades, including the fact that we all learn differently. Traditional schools were focusing primarily on only two learning skills — the verbal and math intelligences — leaving all others, such as creative or analytic skills, basically untapped . . . We could see that the best learning environment was student-centered, allowing each student to learn at his or her own pace and in his or her own style. And we could see that computer technology would allow students to learn in the way that was best for them."

Shortly after starting Upward Bound, Davidson purchased her first Apple II computer, hoping to customize her speed-reading course to accommodate individual students' needs. The effort of computerizing the course led Davidson to meet with a friend who knew enough about programming for the Apple to create *Speed Reader* and then *Word Attack* for teaching vocabulary skills and, later, *Math Blaster*, a game for developing math skills that enabled kids to solve a math problem and shoot a man out of a cannon.

"I knew virtually nothing about technology," adds Davidson with a laugh. "I never had a computer course. I just learned what I needed to do and surrounded myself with people who were smarter than I am. What I *could* see was the incredible potential of technology. It could help educate people and actually improve their quality of life, and I had to convince other educators of that.

"In the early days, people were concerned that computers would dehumanize education. I knew, however, that computers could be a socializing force. For one thing, each of us learns differently and computers enable a teacher to individualize instruction. For another, computers are much more patient than humans are. Finally, a good piece of software — one that has a strong educational foundation and that is engaging and appealing to a child — empowers students to think, analyze, and create."

Speed Reader, Word Attack, and *Math Blaster* were virtually instant successes. Parents began requesting copies to run on their home computers and Davidson and her kids — then eleven, eight, and six — turned their house into a production plant. They took turns copying disks off their home computer and then shrink-wrapping them for shipment to a growing marketplace.

Davidson turned the production business over to Apple in 1983 but a year later decided to get out of the mail-order business and go back to teaching. "I grew up in a time when women were supposed to be wives and mothers," says Davidson. "Bob was working long hours as an executive vice president at Parsons, an international engineering and construction firm in Pasadena, and I already had enough on my plate."

She planned to sell the software she had developed to an outside publisher and arranged a lunch meeting at a local restaurant chain with a small San Diego-based company. As luck would have it, however, the publisher went to the right restaurant in the wrong town and consequently never arrived for their scheduled meeting. Davidson had brought her husband along for the meeting, and as the two waited futilely for their guest to arrive, Bob managed to convince his wife that she would never be happy leaving her product in the hands of someone who cared less about education than she did and that she should do it herself.

Shortly thereafter, the couple borrowed $6,000 from their three children's college funds and started Davidson & Associates, packaging *Speed Reader* in a school notebook-style three-ring binder. Within a year, they sold over 5,400 copies at a net profit of $50 each and used the proceeds to develop new software. The company started with a handful of employees working out of eleven rooms leased out of an abandoned local elementary school. Today, more than 400 employees work for Davidson & Associates in the 44,000 square-foot installation they are now expanding to include a brand-new research and development center and a sound production studio.

"We had a great babysitter. Computers were a novelty and my kids were very interested in them; [and] working with educational software meant I was around schools — and often *their* school — and the kids liked that," says Davidson of her ability to juggle career and family at the time. "Besides, I think I was afraid I might start living vicariously through my children if I didn't go back to work . . .

"But what really drove me was an abiding belief that I could make a difference. There was never any need for me to come to work for the money. In fact, to this day, I argue constantly about my salary with my board of directors. They tell me I need to take a salary. I tell them I do it because I need to teach. I find it invigorating and satisfying. I have always been extremely goal-oriented. I've never managed moderation well. I either do things completely or I don't do them at all."

The company grew by leaps and bounds and Davidson realized she desperately needed a chief executive officer to handle the company's administration. It wasn't until 1989, however, that she managed to recruit her first choice — her husband Bob. "As a lawyer and a business school graduate, and, of course, as my husband and chief supporter, Bob was obviously ideal for the job, but I didn't want to force my dream on him," says Davidson now. "I feel the same way about my kids. My oldest daughter, Elizabeth, now works as an analyst for Smith Barney on Wall Street; my second oldest daughter, Emilie, is a student at Pepperdine; and my son John is entering his first year at El Camino College. Though I couldn't have built this company without them, I would never expect them to follow my dream.

"But Bob was a different story. His dream was to build a family business and to create something from nothing, and this was a perfect opportunity for him. The business works well for us. We have complementary objectives, skills, and styles, and we have the same values. He's more competitive with outside people and companies. I'm more interested in how I am doing against my own internal objectives and goals. You need to be [both] outwardly competitive and inwardly competitive to run a business successfully.

"Bob runs the financial aspects of the business from the second floor. I stay on the first floor, overseeing the creative side — new products, research and development, and production . . . When you care as much about your business as I do, it's a great comfort to have someone you love sharing it with you, and he's certainly having a lot of fun."

When Bob joined the company, he implemented what he called a "studio strategy," similar to the system that evolved out of the movie industry of the 1920s. The key to the success of the studios was to have different sources of product and to build strong channels for distributing the products to the marketplace. Although most small software companies allow others to handle their distribution, Davidson & Associates are determined to own the rights to all of their programs and to deal directly with large consumer accounts like Software Etc.

"In fact, there is no 'typical' Davidson deal," says Jan. "We have no one fixed way of doing anything . . . First, there's our publishing arm, which comprises the vast majority of our business. We design our own product in-house, using our own sound, graphics, and animation facilities. Then we package, market, and distribute it ourselves. Then, there is our affiliated label program, wherein we act as a distributor for other titles which are published by other companies under their own label. These companies come to us for our expertise in marketing, distribution, promotion, and packaging.

"We also have something called 'third party development.' If an individual has developed a product to some extent but does not want to put that product out under their own label, we will work with them and put it out under the Davidson label. Sometimes we have the ideas, and a third party will develop it for us.

"What's more, we have a number of what we call 'strategic alliances.' These are partnerships with companies such as Addison-Wesley, Fisher-Price, and Simon & Schuster, in which we create products together and share in the marketing, distribution, and profit. Simon & Schuster, for example, has over 300,000 book titles in their library from which we will be able to create a range of multi-media products.

"Finally, thanks to Bob's mergers-and-acquisitions experience, we have acquired a number of companies that will help us grow. In 1992, we traded 9 percent of the company's equity for Educational Resources in Elgin, Ill. Educational Resources is the largest reseller of packaged software to schools and offers over 1,200 titles in subjects ranging from algebra to zoology. This gives us a considerable advantage in the school market.

"We also acquired First Byte, which has developed wonderful technologies to convert text into synthesized speech. We have incorporated this into several new Davidson's products, including *Kid Works 2*, a painting and word processing program, and *The Cruncher*, a spreadsheet program for kids."

Their most recent acquisitions are Learningways, an educational software developer in Massachusetts, and Blizzard Entertainment, a leading entertainment software developer known for titles such as *The Lost Vikings, Rock and Roll Racing*, and *The Death and Return of Superman*.

All of this means astronomical growth in three areas: consumer products, educator products, which include software plus a variety of teaching materials, and what Davidson calls, "school-only curriculum systems," which comprise CD ROM software, laser disks, audio cassettes, teachers' guides, and oral and written activities to be used in a classroom setting. It also means astronomical growth within Davidson & Associates.

The company has recently expanded to include a new warehouse the size of three football fields and is now rebuilding their back offices to house a production studio as well as 345 new employees.

"I like to think of the company as a collection of self-directed work teams," says Davidson, who cites Tom Peters' two books, *In Search of Excellence* and *Liberation Management*, as important sources of inspiration in building her company. "We give each team a lot of responsibility and we like to let them plan how best to accomplish their objectives. We think people work harder when they are given a lot of responsibility. They may make mistakes, but that's okay. The way you learn is by making mistakes. I know that; I'm a teacher. We like to grow people and expect them to get better and better, and we try to provide an environment for that growth. I look for people who have a desire to take responsibility and who have a passion for what we do. They have to love kids and love learning. We don't hire people to do a job; we hire them to pursue a mission.

"In *Liberation Management*, Peters also talks about being customer-centered and adapting a company's needs to the customer's, rather than the other way around. In education, the Industrial Age mindset might translate into 'You can have any education as long as you learn with my teaching tools.' A customer-oriented approach would say, simply, 'Learn it your way.'"

Whatever aspect of her business Davidson is discussing, she always comes back to what's most important to her — teaching. Since she began the company twelve years ago, she has traveled the country, teaching educators about the importance of introducing computer technology into the classroom. As one-time president and a member of the board of directors of the Software Publishers Association for the past ten years, she has even founded the Computer Learning Foundation, an organization responsible for encouraging computer use in the classroom through such nation-wide programs as "October is Computer Learning Month." Her efforts have most certainly been rewarded. Today, the company boasts that there's at least one Davidson product in every single school in this country.

And Davidson appears to be enjoying every minute of it. She claims she has "very little time for hobbies," with the exception of a daily regime of exercise that includes an hour of jogging and working out with a personal trainer. Now that her kids are grown, she confesses, she spends most of her time, including lots of weekends, at work. "You shouldn't start a business unless you love what you do and you feel it's important, because you spend an incredible amount of hours doing it," she offers as advice to anyone starting up a new company. "And try not to be too aggressive. Take baby steps, because you're going to have lots of failures and that way you'll never fall too far. Finally, you've got to be willing to take risks. It's less risky than *not* taking any risks. Risk means change and change means growth. I'm a calculated risk-taker. I pride myself on embracing change."

Davidson embraces change not just for herself and her company, but for future generations. "Technology can spark imagination and creativity," Davidson says, concluding with the same intensity with which she began. "I don't ever want to give the impression that teachers will be replaced. They will just have different tools to work with. The feeling of empowerment a child experiences when he or she learns to use a tool on the computer is similar to the feeling of empowerment a child feels when first learning to ride a bicycle. It's exhilarating. And I must admit that creating these tools is also exhilarating . . . Anyone who has seen what a kid can do when let loose on a well-designed computer tool has seen the future."

"The ranch is bigger than life for all of us and longer than life too. It goes backwards in time and, we hope, forwards . . ."

CHASE HIBBARD

**President of Montana-based
Sieben Live Stock Company**

When Chase Hibbard reminisces about his boyhood summers on his great-grandfather's Montana ranch, his blue eyes squint into the nostalgia-clouded distance and soften his weathered features. The denim-shirted, fair-haired cowboy becomes, for that moment, a child in prayer or maybe an adolescent in love.

"When I was fourteen or fifteen, I worked with one of the hands to bale hay. I would wake up every morning, excited about that day's work. I'd bale all day, probably working much too long a day for a child my age, and I'd be so proud because I felt I was doing a man's job," he says, puffing up his chest in dramatic illustration. "When night came, I'd go up to the shower house on the hill and stand under the water, looking out at the rolling hills that stretched as far as I could see in every direction. I felt so good about doing something important for the ranch . . . Something spiritual would happen. I would feel as if I were growing into the ranch and becoming part of it."

Today, Hibbard, 46, is president of the Sieben Live Stock Company and owner, along with his mother, Jane, and his twin brothers, Scott and Whitney, of that same ranch. And he still feels the same way. For more than forty summers of his life, he has worked the land nestled in the Big Belts between the Missouri and Smith Rivers at the foothills of the Rocky Mountains in west central Montana. For the last twenty of those years, he has worked full-time to turn the spread into one of the larger and most profitable sheep and cattle ranches in the state.

"For some people," says Hibbard, "starting from scratch and realizing a goal that creates significant money is success. My great-grandfather Henry Sieben did that when he founded this ranch in 1907. He started with absolutely nothing and built a livestock business out of it. For me, running this place successfully and keeping it alive is the dream. I don't do this because it's a great business; it's not. There's very little return on your land or your capital, and it's hard, hard work. Most ranches can't even break even. If you do, then you are considered successful. I do it because it's a part of me, because it's a part of my heritage, and because I'm in love with the life and the land."

To see the Sieben Live Stock Company Ranch is to get a visceral understanding of Hibbard's love for the land. It is located about 100 miles outside of Helena, in a town some Montana maps still recognize as Adel, even though its post office no longer exists. The ranch stretches for thousands of acres between the Big Belt Mountains and the Jones Hills, where warm Chinook winds sweep eastward from the coast, keeping the area cool in the summer and dusting off most winter snowfalls.

This is indeed — as Montana is known — "Big Sky Country," where golden eagles and red-tailed hawks swoop over snow-packed peaks against an impossibly blue sky and leave shadows on gentle green hills, plush as velvet and threaded with blue and yellow wildflowers and bright pink bitterroot. Fat white woolly sheep and copper and black angus cattle graze in bunches along the hillsides, along with elk, antelope, and whitetail deer; and though rarely seen, an occasional grizzly bear or mountain lion also calls the ranch home. Every breath of mountain air is laced with the scent of ponderosa pine and fir trees and the tart, pungent smell of sagebrush. Over it all hangs an immense silence — a quiet that pays tribute to the sheer vastness and beauty of creation.

According to Chase, asking just how many acres comprise the ranch is tantamount to "asking a man how much money he has in the bank." By most local standards, such a question is considered downright rude. Suffice it to say that Chase speaks of thousand-acre grazing areas as casually as most of us speak of a city block or a suburban backyard. As many as 2,300 cattle and 2,100 sheep move across an expanse so large it sits on parts of four counties and would take close to a week to circle on horseback.

The ranch was founded in 1907 by Chase's great-grandfather, Henry Sieben, a German immigrant who traveled overland with his brother, Jacob, through Lewis and Clark territory from Geneseo, Illinois, in search of gold. Sieben became a part of local history for his encounters with Pawnee Indians and for joining the 100-wagon train led by state hero and explorer John Bozeman in search of the precious metal. But the mining wasn't profitable and Sieben set off to find more stable work.

A consummate risk-taker and hard-working entrepreneur, he traveled throughout Montana, raising and trading livestock. Sieben gradually expanded his holdings, eventually establishing one of the first successful sheep and cattle ranches in Montana. He is also remembered for his innovative ranching techniques. Early newspaper accounts praise him for developing a creative method of feeding bum lambs (those rejected by mothers unable to feed them) — boring holes in a log and inserting reeds equipped with rubber nipples to supply the lambs with milk.

An excellent stockman, Sieben was also active in organizing economic and legislative protection for ranchers. By the time he died in 1937, he had been elected to the National Cowboy Hall of Fame, was a charter member of the International Livestock Exposition of Chicago, and had served as honorary lifetime president of the Montana Wool Growers Association. His wit was as legendary as his business acumen and his work for the livestock industry. In fact, local history recounts that his dying words were: "I don't mind dying at all. I've had a good life and a happy life ... but I just hate to go because I won't know what's going to happen tomorrow."

Henry and his wife Alberta had two daughters, Berneice and Margaret, who eventually assumed ownership of two of the largest ranches in Montana, which had been bequeathed them by their father. Fred Sheriff, the husband of Berneice Sieben, assumed management of the Sieben Ranch Company in Wolf Creek, Montana. This branch of the family still owns that ranch and the Sheriff's grandson, Max Baucus, is today a U.S. Senator from the state.

The other daughter, Margaret, and her husband, A. T. — Chase's grandparents — assumed management of the Sieben Live Stock Company. Chase's father, "Hank" Hibbard, who attended Dartmouth College, receiving a degree from Montana State University and an MBA from Harvard, followed in his father's footsteps and became manager of the Sieben Live Stock Company in 1945. He ran the Sieben Live Stock Ranch until his tragic death in 1976 when the Piper Supercub he was flying over the ranch collided with a power line and crashed.

"I was working for the Crocker Bank in San Francisco at the time," recalls Chase. "I was handling credit analysis and commercial lending and was exposed to a lot of business... Shortly after Dad died, Mom, Whitney, Scott and I had a meeting to decide what to do about the ranch. Neither Scott nor Whitney was prepared to give up the ranch, but neither of them was prepared to run it, either. Scott was doing a lot of writing at the time and felt intimidated by the responsibility of managing ranch business. Whitney was going to graduate school in psychology and counseling and didn't want to return to the ranch.

"So the responsibility really fell to me. At first, I was reluctant to give up my career. And when we met with the accountants and lawyers, they strongly encouraged us to sell out. The ranch was in debt, and business was bad. If anyone else in the family had been willing to take over, I would gladly have let them do it, but no one did.

"But I really didn't have to think about it for very long. Some decisions don't feel like decisions. You simply *know* what to do. And this was one of them. There was simply no way I could let go of the ranch. It was part of my family history and part of me. It would have been like giving up an arm or a leg."

"We all believed fervently that we should keep the ranch," adds Scott. "It was something we all simply felt would always be there for us ... It comes down to something you can't quantify, something that has to do with heritage and lifestyle. But Whit and I were involved in graduate studies and our backgrounds were in liberal arts. Chase was really the only one equipped to run the place."

Chase quit his job with Crocker, moved back to Helena with his new wife, Anne, and decided to take over the running of the ranch — a radical departure from anything his under-graduate years as a political science major at Amherst College during the 1960s or his fast-track career as a banker in San Francisco had prepared him for.

"There was really never any pressure on any of us to go into ranching," says Chase. "Our parents sent all of us to the east coast to get an education and some experience with how the rest of the country lives. This was very unusual for kids from Montana, and it sometimes made us feel a bit like out-siders both at home and at school.

"But a liberal arts education also taught me how to find answers to any questions, concerning ranching or other mat-ters, so it was very useful for me. After awhile, I had fun with the differences. I moved into a different economic strata and a more liberal political attitude. My family were staunch Repub-licans and very conservative. The move to the East helped to change my way of thinking. But the important thing was that I was free to decide what I wanted to do."

"You can't make someone choose to be a rancher," offers Chase's mother, Jane, who still spends a great deal of time on the ranch in a renovated turn-of-the-century wood and stone structure filled with patchwork quilts, bearskin rugs, antique furniture, and old farm tools. Chase and his brothers' boy-hood tent still stands on the property, one wall covered by a collection of their old hats and denim jackets and their well-worn cowboy boots, some of them so well-worked in their time that they are literally held together with masking tape.

"When Hank died, I made it very clear to the boys that they didn't have to take on the ranch. I think it was simply a tremendous love of the place, of how and when it first started, that inspired Chase to take the job. The boys all spent their weekends and summers plucking chickens, cleaning coops, sprouting potatoes, running the machinery, and painting the fences. It was in their blood . . . Scott and Whitney were headed in other directions, but Chase could handle it. It's in his nature to seek stimulation, and I think he found that running the ranch would give him a chance to do some problem-solving. Chase thrives on situations where he can 'move' on his own — be the boss and make things happen. The challenge to sink or swim and the freedom to do so, based on his own decisions, is what motivates him."

"It was the combination of family history and the business challenge that finally hooked me," agrees Chase. "In my years at the bank, I learned a lot about business and economics. The ranch was having problems, and I saw a chance to use my financial skills, my understanding of long-term planning and business management, and my contacts with successful business people. I love the ranch, but I knew I could also run it like a business."

In fact, the ranch was in serious financial trouble when Chase first arrived. His father had begun to make the switch from sheep ranching to cattle ranching in the mid-1960s but had not yet successfully managed the transition. Market prices were down; good labor was difficult to find; and predators, mostly coyote, were killing off much of the livestock. To make matters worse, the ranch's facilities were not geared to maintain the cattle, and establishing an adequate infrastructure was a slow process.

"Everything is different for cattle than it is for sheep," explains Chase. "Dad had to learn new fencing plans, new breeding seasons, new housing facilities, and new marketing techniques. Then he got involved in politics. He ran for the

U.S. Senate and lost; he became president of the Sheep Producers Council . . . It was difficult handling the enormous burdens of the ranch along with all of his other responsibilities.

"I came in with ideas, but with no confidence or experience. I didn't do anything very quickly. I watched the foreman who was in charge of the ranch under my dad and learned everything I could about the operations and management of the ranch. I developed my own management plan, and, after a couple of years, I decided I had to hire a new foreman and start afresh."

He then began a series of innovations that would ultimately return the ranch to a profitable operation. First he hired Neill Windecker, a rancher with lots of experience and the promise of being a fair boss to ranch crews. "Neill works with the crew to develop them," says Chase. "I try real hard to give him his room and let him be in charge."

Hibbard also began a fairly revolutionary employment policy. Instead of hiring the usual itinerant — and often alcoholic — men who typically seek work as ranch hands, he began hiring young, family-oriented couples who saw ranch life as the best possible environment for raising a family. A crew of between ten and fifteen work under Windecker. By offering them good accommodations and a profit-sharing plan as an incentive award for work of exceptional merit, Chase was able to secure steady, reliable labor. Additionally, Chase began the practice of establishing yearly goals and objectives, holding periodic meetings with the crew to track these goals and attach financial rewards to them. "I made a real effort to draw our people into the management process," he says. "Neill holds weekly meetings with the crew to review the goals of the week."

Finally, he built up the ranch's sheep population again, controlling the predator population with dogs and finding good Peruvian sheep herders through the Western Range Association, a California-based group that matches foreign workers with agricultural businesses in the United States. Because of their "dual purpose" — they can be used both for meat and for their wool — sheep are considered by Chase to be a better investment than cattle. "We also use computer technology now to keep better production records," he adds. "For instance, we categorize measurable traits — reproduction data, weights, length of fleece, and weight of fleece — so that we can separate [the influence of] heredity from environment and produce the best quality sheep. Thanks to better management and genetics, we have increased the weaning weights of both our sheep and our cattle as well. In the last few years, our steer calves' weaning weight has increased from 400 pounds to 590 pounds."

Although careful management has brought the ranch out of debt and turned it into a company doing what Chase describes as "well over a million dollars worth of sales," the business is never an easy one. Each year, the Sieben Live Stock Company raises approximately 1,800 calves, keeping a small percentage of females for breeding and selling the rest of them when they are approximately seven months old and weigh 550–600 pounds. The calves are bought by order buyers, who place them in feedlots where they will stay until they reach their slaughter weight of 1,150–1,200 pounds.

The ranch's 1,500 ewes lamb in March and April, are herded all summer, sold in late September at a weight of 90 pounds, and shipped to feeding lots where they will gain another 30 to 50 pounds before slaughter. The breeding sheep are kept for shearing in March, and their wool is shipped to domestic mills throughout the Northeast. A small percentage of these sheep are purebred Targhees, a registered variety developed by the U.S. Sheep Experiment Station to insure a fast-gaining breed with high wool quality, ideal for multiple births and herding. These sheep are maintained and occasionally sold for as much as $3,000 a head as breeding stock and range rams. In recent years, partially because of breeding advances made possibly by careful record keeping, Sieben's Targhees have risen to the top of the market.

All this means dawn-to-dusk days, often with no breaks for weekends or holidays. In the months of February, March, and April, for instance, Hibbard's crew must work around the clock to aid in the practically simultaneous deliveries of hundreds of calves and lambs. Wool handling is another complex process that involves tedious hours of shearing, inspecting, sorting, packaging, and shipping the raw wool. "We use the most innovative wool preparation process available," explains Chase. "We attended several national and state meetings and invited specialists from Australia and New Zealand to teach us the best methods of preparing our wool. To this day, the traditional wool market tells us we're crazy to do it the way we do, but we get a premium [for our animals] and take more pride in our product."

Then, of course, there is branding each of the livestock with Sieben's "flying V" brand, as well as the daily ranch maintenance — building fences, maintaining sprinkler systems, painting buildings, planting and rotating crops, and herding the animals. Add to that uncontrollable market swings, unpredictable weather conditions, livestock disease, and skyrocketing land prices, and you've got a relentless business with little opportunity for big profits.

Getting the ranch out of debt and in a position to operate twelve months a year without borrowing a penny from the bank is, says Chase, "the reward." That, and "improving the cattle, improving the sheep, improving the physical facilities, and taking a good ranch and turning it into a first class-ranch."

He adds: "It would really be a crime to force someone into this who didn't want to do it. Running a ranch requires a commitment. You've got to love it, or it isn't going to work. An epidemic or storm right before shipping can shrink your herd and your profit by fifteen percent overnight. But things like that go with the turf. My grandmother Margaret used to tell me, 'You don't measure your success in ranching year to year. You have to look at this business in ten-year increments.'

"If you've been profitable more years than not, then you're doing a good job. I would not consider myself a risk-taker. Being successful in the ranching business instills a degree of conservatism. You have to have a lot of restraint because there are so many ups and downs. You have to save in the good times to get through the bad times. I'm willing to be innovative and take risks, but not without a lot of analysis and fore-thought. I contemplate very thoroughly before I jump."

These days, Chase divides his time between the ranch and Helena, where he shares a stunning, perfectly appointed Victorian home with his wife Anne and their two sons, Tyler and Marshall. He spends his rare spare time skiing, hunting on the ranch, and studying wine with the same kind of academic discipline that he applies to every task he undertakes.

Like his father, grandfather, and great-grandfather before him, he has political aspirations that require much of his attention. Since 1993, he has been a State Representative for Montana, another responsibility added to a long list that includes being a member of the board of directors for the Montana Power Company, the chairman of the Montana Stock Growers Association Taxation Committee, and a member of the board of the Montana Wool Growers Association. In fact, admits Chase, if anything would ultimately pull him away from life on the ranch, it would be politics on a national level. He ran on the gubernatorial ticket as the lieutenant governor candidate in Montana in 1988 and lost, but may consider a future run for the U.S. Congress.

"Ranching is a very lonely business," says Chase. "You can spend weeks on the ranch and see no one besides your livestock and your crew. I guess I need to be in the flow of humanity, and that drives me to do more than perhaps I should."

That need may be what led Chase to form the Hibbard Management Company in 1984. The company — staffed only by Chase, his secretary Bonnie Ketchum, and his brother Scott — serves as a consulting firm for mostly out-of-state entrepreneurs who are looking to buy or manage Montana ranch land.

"Many people are interested in owning a ranch in Montana because the land is so beautiful and because of the romance associated with ranching," says Chase. "Few realize how hard it is to make a living as a rancher . . . In fact, I think there will be fewer and fewer family ranches in the years to come. First of all, more and more kids are seeing how their parents work their fingers to the bone for so little reward, and they want no part of it. More importantly, families are getting bigger again, and many family ranches end up divided because the siblings can't agree on how to run them."

The Hibbards have devised a corporate structure they hope will prevent any future conflict over the ranch. Chase is the company president; Jane is the vice-president; Scott is the secretary; and Whitney remains a silent partner. Everyone agrees that Chase is best qualified to run the operation for the present, and he is willing to take all the responsibility because he has a clear vision of what kind of management is necessary to keep it running successfully.

Both Scott and Chase have children and Chase is hopeful that a fifth generation of Hibbards will be available to continue the Sieben Live Stock Company. "My sons are thirteen and sixteen years old now, and it's important to me that the ranch stay in the family. Both Scott's boys and mine come out to the ranch on weekends and in the summer, but they're young and it's not clear whether any of them will want to take over. It's too difficult to do unless you really want to do it.

"You don't just see a place like this, you feel it," Chase says, his eyes sweeping the landscape with familiarity, and, quite clearly, devotion. What comes across is an abiding sense that ranching *is* romantic; it is all about love of place, and it's as strong as any love between two people. "This feeling doesn't happen for me in all that many places, but it always happens here. The ranch is bigger than life for all of us, and longer than life too. It goes backwards in time, and, we hope, forwards . . . It was instilled in us early that the ranch is some-how more important than we are. I never ask, 'What can the ranch do for me?' only 'What can I do for the ranch?'"

"I want to help the world because this seems the most truthful thing for me to be doing. When you are truthful, you are beautiful; when you are beautiful, you are loved; and when you are loved, you are happy."

JHOON RHEE

**Founder of Jhoon Rhee Foundation and a
chain of international martial arts schools**

⌒

The Regency ballroom of Washington, D.C.'s cavernous
Omni Shoreham hotel is filled to overflowing with a
multi-cultural crowd. Chic African-American women in
black cocktail dresses and spike heels sit next to blue-
eyed and tow-headed Midwesterners and black-eyed, black
haired Asian-American pre-teens in tank t-shirts and baggy
gym pants. Several Russian adolescents, the sons of diplomats
serving in Washington, slap hands and cheer in a blend of
flawless English and Russian, their happy uproar competing
with the hoots of platinum-blonde women in spangled dresses
and men dressed in natty business suits accessorized with
heavy gold bracelets and cowboy boots. A few U.S. congressmen and a cabinet member or two are also scattered through
the crowd.

Everybody quiets down when a diminutive man in mari-
gold satin karate pajamas and a black belt walks onto the
stage. Despite his 62 years, his walk is lively and erect. He does
a few warm-up stretches, wrapping a belt around his foot and
extending his leg straight up, almost perpendicular to the
floor. Then he balances a tall glass of water on his head, and,
without spilling a drop, performs a series of graceful high
kicks before shattering an inch-thick board with a final thrust
of his foot. Afterwards, he invites the audience to count along
as he does 100 perfect pushups in less than a minute. Cameras

flash around the room like a thousand points of light. In fact, this is the man former President George Bush named the 721st "Daily Point of Light" in recognition of his community service and his willingness to serve others.

Grandmaster Jhoon Rhee takes a deep bow and welcomes everyone to the 1994 Jhoon Rhee International Championship, the annual spectacle that demonstrates the art of Tae Kwon Do, the Korean form of the martial art the Japanese call *karate*. It is also a celebration of Grandmaster Rhee's own invention — "martial arts ballet," which is a demonstration of Eastern martial arts forms performed to Western classical music. For the three-hour extravaganza, Rhee has arranged a series of championship matches and a number of demonstrations that pit several Republican congressmen against their Democratic counterparts. In deference to what he calls "the marriage of East and West," he has also arranged for his Russian students to perform a martial arts ballet to the American national anthem and for his American students to perform a similar set of moves to the Russian national anthem. These ballets, explains Rhee, are meant to serve as the peace-inspiring prelude to a series of sparring matches between the Russian athletes and Americans.

"This is one way of expressing my thanks to America," says Rhee, only slight traces of a Korean accent audible in his speech. "It is my job to elevate the image of martial arts around the world."

Elevate indeed. Rhee has been credited with bringing the now-ubiquitous art of Tae Kwon Do to America when he arrived here 38 years ago and is responsible for opening some 60 schools that teach "the art of the hand and foot" around the United States. In 1989, he did the same in the Soviet Union, presenting a series of lectures and demonstrations that led to the opening of 65 Jhoon Rhee schools that teach Tae Kwon Do in a country that had until then outlawed any teaching of martial arts to anyone but the military.

What's more, he has taught countless U.S. marines and secret service agents and over 100 U.S. congressmen how to kick, instructed Muhammad Ali in the performance of his famous "accupunch," been a Special Advisor to the President's Council on Physical Fitness and Sports and the author of five Tae Kwon Do books, starred in several martial arts feature films, and invented, produced, and distributed the first standard martial arts safety equipment. On top of these accomplishments, he has begun a successful series of three-day inspirational seminars for business executives based on a philosophy he calls "universal common sense." Grandmaster Jhoon Rhee is not just a martial arts expert; he is — for his thousands of students — a way of life.

As Rhee walks through the lobby of the Omni Shoreham Hotel the day after his International Championship, young boys approach him just to say "Hello, Grandmaster" and offer a respectful bow. Teenage girls sidle up to him with a giggle and ask timidly to have their picture taken with him. Rhee takes it all in stride, returning all bows and tossing off jocular quips. "Whatsa matter?" he says to a young girl taking her friend's picture alongside Rhee. "Don't you want to have your picture taken with this ugly old man?" And though his fans treat him like something akin to an earthly deity, he consistently comes across as good-natured, humble, and utterly without pretense. Ask Jhoon Rhee what it means to be a grandmaster and he replies with a shrug, "If you have a fourth-degree black belt or higher, you get the title 'master.' I've been practicing so long, they call me 'grandmaster.'" Ask him what he did to earn his tenth-degree black belt and he waves his hands dismissively. "I was a ninth-degree and nobody wanted to give me a tenth degree so I gave it to myself. That's one of the things a grandmaster can do." It seems clear that he is more interested in spreading his philosophy and teaching discipline and respect for one's self and others than he is in all the hoopla that his teachings have inspired.

"'Knowledge in the mind; Honesty in the heart; and Strength in the body' is my motto," he says. "That and 'Lead by example'." And the man stands by his word. An instinctively self-effacing man, Rhee tries hard to set an example for the thousands of students and adults who are learning the Jhoon Rhee system of Tae Kwon Do. He works out two and a half hours every day, following a gruelling regime that includes "the daily dozens," a series of stretching, breathing, and aerobic exercises, kicking and punching practice, and 1,000 pushups (500 in the morning, 500 at night). "Living by example is the only way to change society," he explains. "This is why I exercise every day. I cannot prove that I have knowledge and honesty, but I can prove that I have strength in the body."

From his home in the Washington suburb of McLean, Virginia, he travels around the country, visiting each of his schools, or *dojangs,* once a month to hand out diplomas and deliver inspirational speeches about the importance of academic, moral, and physical excellence in keeping America strong and the world at peace. Five years ago, with the help of former Secretary of Education William Bennett, he introduced some of the same principles he enforces in his *dojangs* into the Amidon Elementary school, part of Washington's public school system. He created a program he calls "Joy of Discipline," whose goal, he says, "is to make Washington, D.C. a model city for education."

Rhee's program teaches what he calls the "Seven Qualities of a Champion," qualities that represent certain character traits and are shared by martial arts champions: speed (alertness), endurance (perseverance), timing (punctuality), power (knowledge), balance (rationality), flexibility (gentleness), and posture (honesty). He believes that martial arts is 99 percent philosophy and that the application of that philosophy to discipline in the public schools is of the utmost importance. "The solution to crime and other problems in our cities is really education," he says. "Education is the key. No one is going to come down from heaven and save us. Our own consciences will. Education of the conscience will mold our children's lives in a certain direction and at an early age."

In the Amidon School, Rhee teaches what he calls "attitude classes" in the first through sixth grades. Students are taught the concepts of *chario* (attention) and *kyungye* (respect) and are asked to recite four daily affirmations: "I am smart because I always learn something good every day; I am perfect because I never make mistakes knowingly; I like myself because I always take action to make things happen; and I am happy that I am me who always chooses to be happy." The martial arts, Rhee insists, are important because "our physiology dictates our state of mind . . . If we can teach our young children how to pay undivided attention and hold a sense of respect for teachers, almost everybody will make straight A's." In fact, no one can graduate with a black belt from one of Jhoon Rhee's schools unless he or she maintains at least a B average in school.

His pride in his Korean roots and in his native country's cultural heritage notwithstanding, it would be hard to find a prouder American than Jhoon Rhee. He claims he has no particular religion, other than the one he calls "universal common sense," but he is fond of quoting America's founding fathers as his source of inspiration. His role model, he insists, is George Washington. "I believe we have the same magnitude of vision," he explains. "We both believe in America, in the freedom to express ourselves without fear. Washington recognized what he believed to be the dream of his Creator. He believed in his country and did what he could to further its strength. My motives are the same."

What drives Rhee, he says, is a philosophy he calls "happyism," and his logic, though perhaps overly simple, is hard to refute. "The human race will never establish the standard of right and wrong until the global common purpose of life is understood by everyone . . . What then is the universal common purpose of life?" he asks earnestly, sounding more like a grade school teacher than an Eastern philosopher pontificating on the meaning of life. "If there is more pain than pleasure, we avoid it; if there is more pleasure than pain, we seek it. Thomas Jefferson, one of the greatest founding fathers of the modern human race, in his Declaration of Independence, said that 'Men . . . are endowed with certain inalienable rights, that among these are Life, Liberty and the Pursuit of Happiness.' I am confident that the universal common purpose of life is happiness. Everybody lives not just to exist but to be happy.

"Furthermore, it is obvious that the single universal value for happiness is love. Every person wants to be loved and respected by people . . . It is beauty that triggers the love emotion. Everybody is attracted to beautiful things . . . There are dual human beauties — outer, skin beauty, and inner, heart beauty. Skin beauty may be fixed with cosmetics, but the cosmetic that beautifies the human heart universally is living by the truth.

"What motivates me is this same philosophy. I want to help the world because this seems the most truthful thing for me to be doing. When you are truthful, you are beautiful; when you are beautiful, you are loved; and when you are loved, you are happy."

Rhee's path to happiness has not been smooth. He came to America in 1956, when he was 24 years old. His memories of his early childhood in Korea sound a lot like the plot of a film starring his old, close friend, the late Bruce Lee.

Rhee was born in Sanyangri, Asan, Korea in 1932. When his mother first conceived him, she had what Koreans call *taemong*, a conception dream. "She told me the story of her *taemong* with me," he says. "She was in a palace which was surrounded by a high and heavy castle wall, and she heard a roaring sound of a tiger and then woke up. I believe this dream may have symbolized the years I would later spend on my Tae Kwon Do activities, receiving newspaper, radio, and television coverage all over the United States and Korea."

His early years were not what one might expect of a star athlete. When he was an infant, his eleven year old sister accidentally dropped him on a hard floor while she was babysitting. His thigh bone was broken midway between his knee and hip. The same day, his grandfather died of an intestinal problem. Driven by an ancient Korean belief, his mother carried her baby five miles to her dead father's house and used her deceased father's hand to massage Rhee's broken leg. According to Rhee, the break mended quickly, needing only one visit from a doctor. But as a result of this accident, Rhee's parents never really expected their son to excel physically. In fact, he was always the smallest child at school and the slowest runner. "I was very uncoordinated and I realized quite early that I would have to find a way to become strong," Rhee recalls. "There were no Tae Kwon Do studios in my hometown. The only thing I could think of doing was weight-lifting. I lifted weights until I was thirteen when I moved to Seoul."

At a very early age, Rhee was taught to respect his elders, as was the custom in Korea. He was told to address adults as "Sir" or "Ma'am" after every phrase or sentence during conversation and to stand up when an elder came into the room and remain standing until told to sit. "Although my father was only a clerk at a small company, my grandfather was a scholar with a doctor's degree in Confucian literature. He was a man of high character and wisdom, with a loving personality. I learned a great deal from him. He lived to be 92 and I attribute his long healthy life to his stretching exercises, which he practiced religiously for about 30 minutes every morning. I designed my Jhoon Rhee Daily Dozen for my Tae Kwon Do curriculum based on my memories of watching his exercises.

"One day my grandfather caught me in a lie about a schoolbook I had lost but was too afraid to tell him about. I knew that I was wrong and took his spanking without any ill feeling against him. He said to me, 'My child, don't you know that whenever you lie, cheat, or steal, God is watching, and whenever you do good, you are also being watched?' That made one of the greatest impressions in my life. I believe it was the most important moment of my life in building my character."

When Rhee was a teenager, his parents sent him to Seoul to live with his uncle so that he could obtain a modern education at the Dong Sung High School. In Seoul, Rhee was also able to begin taking Tae Kwon Do classes to help build his strength. In those days, Tae Kwon Do was not as popular and accepted as it is today; Rhee's father, who was quite conservative in his thinking, considered it no more than organized street fighting. For three months, Rhee practiced his martial arts in secret until his uncle persuaded his father to give him his consent. Tae Kwon Do helped the small boy at school. After giving a black eye to one of the toughest bullies in his class, he began to feel good about himself. "I personally gained peace through strength," he says. "Tae Kwon Do changed my life."

In the meantime, a flood of American movies entered Korea following the liberation of South Korea from Japan in 1945. "It was illegal for middle or high school students to attend any movie theater at that time, but one day a friend of mine and I sneaked into a theater," Rhee reminisces. "I had never seen so many beautiful girls in my life. That evening, I set [as] my goal that someday I would marry one of those beautiful American blondes. I knew that the only way to achieve that goal was to find a way to go to America. I also had to think about supporting my future family and myself in the U.S. I [decided] I would introduce Tae Kwon Do to America."

Though he never married the blonde — he's been married for 30 years to his Korean wife, Han Soon, whom he later met in Washington — the rest of his dream certainly came true.

Rhee was accepted at Seoul's Dong Kook University for the fall of 1950, but his college plans were interrupted by the unexpected outbreak of the Korean War. Since the Communist Army was drafting every young Korean man into service, Rhee hid in an underground cell for two months to avoid being seen by neighbors who might reveal his presence to the Communists.

His love for the United States grew from his war experiences. "I thank my hero, General Douglas MacArthur, for his successful Inchon landing operation, which brought freedom back to South Korea," he says. "After two months living in the cell, I was finally free. I can't describe the incredible feeling of being free again. To most American people, freedom is invisible because it has always been there."

Inspired by the spirit of the times, he joined the United States 5th Air Force in Osan as an interpreter, an experience which further fueled his desire to come to America. His plans were interrupted, however, when he was drafted into the South Korean military in 1951. After a difficult time in training camp, which included dealing with corrupt military officials and punishing sergeants, and subsistence-level living on three spoons of rice and a couple of sips of salt water soup each day, he enrolled in officer training school. Only weeks before graduation, the truce was signed.

In 1956, Rhee made his way to the United States for a six-month training program in aircraft maintenance at Gary Air Force Base in San Marcos, Texas. He began looking for a sponsor who would enable him to return and live in the U.S. "Many people in San Marcos had never seen an Asian in person, and I began to despair," he continues. "Fortunately, through the minister at the First Methodist Church in San Marcos, I met Reverend Frosty Rich. Frosty was in charge of the Wesley Foundation on the campus of Southwest Texas State Teachers College in San Marcos. He introduced me to Robert Bunting, a local real estate broker, who agreed to sponsor me as a student." After a brief return to Korea to complete his military stint, he returned to the United States in 1957 and enrolled in the Southwest Texas State Teachers College in 1958.

Meanwhile, Rhee continued practicing Tae Kwon Do. "I would work out at the gym near the air force base and many of the guys asked me to teach them what I knew." In 1962, he was invited to Washington to teach these same martial arts skills to members of the Pentagon. Not wanting to forego the opportunity, he moved to Washington, missing the completion of his degree at the University of Texas by one year.

In 1962, Rhee opened his first commercial professional school on K Street in Washington. In the years that followed, he opened 64 more, all with the purpose of elevating the image of martial arts around the world. To this end, in 1965 he began teaching a Tae Kwon Do class for U.S. congressmen three mornings a week in the Congressional Gymnasium. More than 200 senators, representatives, and cabinet members, including former Speaker of the House Tom Foley and former Secretary of Agriculture Mike Espy, have taken advantage of Rhee's free classes. Indeed, many of them have gone on to obtain black belts.

"I wanted to use Tae Kwon Do to make myself happy and the only way I could be happy was to help other people," he says with characteristic sincerity. "I believed I could lay the foundation to create something significant that would keep America strong as a nation, and I felt it was important that the country see that their leaders appreciated the power that stems from the discipline of martial arts.

"I believe in the McDonald hamburger theory. Why open a million places that work imperfectly? First open one, get the formula right, and spread from there. The principle of creation is that you start with one and from one get two, from two get four, and so on. This was the principle I applied."

In 1969, after one of his students broke a cheekbone during a championship competition, Rhee decided to develop martial arts safety equipment. His invention, based on the design of a padded water skiing life jacket, would ultimately change the face of contemporary martial arts practice. "No one used protective equipment before that time," Rhee explains, "and now our patent is universally recognized as the standard design." Rhee's son Jimmy and his cousin Sunny Rhee took over Rheemax Saf-T Equipment in 1985, and the company now does well over $3 million in sales annually. "My son and my cousin like to concentrate on financial success," says Rhee. "I am more philosophically concerned."

His concerns lead him to develop what he calls martial arts ballet in 1970. "When I first began practicing Tae Kwon Do," he says, "no one used music in martial arts. But I asked myself one day, 'Why have I chosen a profession that centers around so much brutality?' I am not happy when I am engaged in violence, but I am happy when I dance. I couldn't change my profession so instead I introduced ballet to the martial arts." His ballets, which involve choreographing martial arts forms to such classic music as the theme from *Exodus* and Beethoven's *Fifth Symphony*, became the basis for "musical forms" competitions, popular events conducted in martial arts tournaments throughout North America and Europe, and most recently, Russia.

In 1989, Rhee was invited to what was then the Soviet Union by one of his black belt students, Charles Sutherland, who was president of the Washington Film Associates, a firm specializing in the export of American films to the USSR. The purpose of the trip was to benefit the Save the Children Foundation, and Rhee took five of his students along to help him demonstrate his techniques and his martial arts ballet. It was at that time that the Soviet government decided to legalize the study of martial arts.

The Soviet audiences were enthusiastic about the demonstrations, as well as about Rhee's philosophy of individual happiness and the fight for a free society. He soon discovered that he had well over 2,000 students training in the Ukraine under the instruction of one of his former exchange students. Shortly thereafter, Rhee led a training seminar for 65 Russians who had started their own schools. All of them subsequently signed up to make their schools members of the Jhoon Rhee Institute of Tae Kwon Do.

During the following two years, Rhee took six trips to what has since become known as the Commonwealth of Independent States (CIS). Because much of the collapse of the Soviet Union was of an economic nature, Rhee brought U.S. businessmen with him as part of his entourage. His hope was that they would be able to exchange technical knowledge as well as financial aid.

"To me, this is America's duty," he says, "because America is economically successful and the CIS is not. I believe the entire globe is *our* country . . . The CIS government is supporting me by publicizing my ideas because they believe I can do something good for young people. We have to start thinking like politicians with universal views. When I talk to the Soviets

I tell them, 'Don't look at me as a Korean-American. I am a person of this universe; so are you.' "

In 1991, to solidify his work encouraging world peace, Rhee staged "Tae Kwon Do for World Peace — An Evening with Master Jhoon Rhee." The show marked the first opening of the Soviet Embassy compound in Washington to the American public and featured American students performing the Tae Kwon Do form *Soryun* to the national anthem of the Soviet Union, Soviet students performing *Meegook* to the American national anthem, and Rhee, a Russian student, and an American student performing *Hangook* to the Korean national anthem.

Rhee is the first to admit he is not a businessman. Driven to spread the word about the value of his martial arts philosophy in helping the world, he was well over $1 million in debt in 1983, when he became National Chairman of the Nation's 4th of July Birthday Celebration in Washington. Over the decade that followed, he gradually sold each of his *dojangs* to the instructors who ran them, preferring instead to take a fee for monthly graduation visits and a $7,500 fee for the three-day seminars he offers several times a month. The seminars offer Rhee's philosophy and show how it can be applied to teaching and to managing business.

Does he feel he's the right person to teach business skills? "I always tell my students, 'There is no such thing as advanced techniques; there are only basic skills,' " he offers in explanation. "Advanced techniques means only combining two or more basic skills with speed and accuracy . . . I teach that the purpose of knowledge is to take action, and action must be developed into a habit or skill that comes automatically." This, he adds, will contribute to leading a healthy, happy, and successful life.

Thinking of himself as "62 years young," Rhee plans to spend the rest of his life opening more Tae Kwon Do Studios, perhaps with the help of his daughter Mimi, now 26, and his other son Chun, now 27. Chun works as a tournament coordinator for the Jhoon Rhee foundation. Mimi, who received her black belt at thirteen, is considering starting her own business since knee injuries have prevented the further study of martial arts. Rhee's other daughter Joanne, 39, has chosen not to pursue a career in her family's business.

"When I first started my institute," says Rhee, "I took the phone number 202-USA-1000. That's because I planned to open 1,000 schools in the U.S.A." Does he think there are any obstacles in his way? "Only me," he philosophizes. "Compared to most people, I am very diligent. But I, too, put things off ... The purpose of knowledge is action, but timing is important ... One can only act when wisdom and character are perfectly balanced ... Great ideas are like precious metals. They can't be found on the surface. They are hidden deep and take time to dig out and develop.

"I decided many years ago, after watching a *60 Minutes* program about the long lives of people that live in Georgia, Russia, that I would live to be 136. Even though I move slowly, I may have enough time yet."

The Grandmaster offers an open invitation to his 100th birthday party in the year 2032, during which he promises to do 100 pushups in one minute for the crowd. "Tickets are $1,000," he says with a big grin. "But for you, free."

"It takes one generation to build your company and another generation to be recognized worldwide for your accomplishments. If you're going to produce an item that's going to change the world, it takes time."

ROBERT MONDAVI

Founder and Chairman of
Robert Mondavi Winery

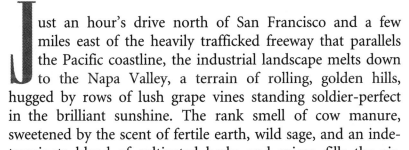

Just an hour's drive north of San Francisco and a few
miles east of the heavily trafficked freeway that parallels
the Pacific coastline, the industrial landscape melts down
to the Napa Valley, a terrain of rolling, golden hills,
hugged by rows of lush grape vines standing soldier-perfect
in the brilliant sunshine. The rank smell of cow manure,
sweetened by the scent of fertile earth, wild sage, and an inde-
terminate blend of cultivated herbs and spices, fills the air,
and the cloudless, powder-blue sky looks less real than a
child's crayon drawing.

This is America's foremost wine-producing region, and
the landscape is interrupted every few miles by glittering billboards exhorting tourists to visit the hundreds of wineries that
have established themselves in Napa and parts north over the
last three decades. Though many vintners have taken advantage of the area's ideal soil and climate to produce a dizzying
array of Cabernets, Chardonnays, Pinot Noirs, and more, the
Robert Mondavi Winery was one of the prime movers in the
industry. The company can lay claim to virtually revolutionizing the American palate for wine by creating a variety of
premium wines and then teaching the public how, when,
where, and why they should drink them.

At 81, wine maker Robert Mondavi is living proof of the
axiom needlepointed on a throw pillow on his office couch:

"Age does not matter unless you are wine." He has the sex appeal of a man half his age — a European *je-ne-sais-quois* communicated by twinkling hazel eyes, sleeked-back gray hair just long enough to curl over the back collar of his sport shirt, and the appraising smile of a connoisseur of the good life and everything it entails. The man is downright debonair. He is the chairman of what may well be the most enduring and best-known wine empire in the country, and he shows no signs of letting up on his mission to make Napa Valley wines the finest in the world. When he speaks about the business of wine, what could sound pompous or pretentious never does. Appealing and articulate, he shares his beliefs with enthusiasm and clarity, candor and humor.

"When you start a business, you should have an established objective and goal which is just a bit beyond your reach," reflects Mondavi, looking back over his almost 60 years in the wine business. "And when you hit that goal — which you will if you have the faith and confidence in yourself to go forward — then [you] establish another goal. You will be amazed how far you can go."

There's no telling how far Mondavi will ultimately go, but today the Mondavi winery is a $168-million family-owned and -operated business that encompasses five separate wineries, employs 500 people, and stretches nearly 300 miles from Oakville, California to Santa Barbara. And if you ask Robert Mondavi, he's only begun to fight.

"A long time ago, the wine experts of Europe told us it was impossible to produce wines that belonged in the company of the great wines of the world. I challenged myself to do that and, sure enough, our wines can now outdo the greatest Bordeaux and Burgundies," he says with a confidence that never seems overbearing. "It takes one generation to build your company and another generation to be recognized worldwide for your accomplishments. If you're going to produce an item that's going to change the world, it takes time."

You might say Mondavi's mission began when he was three years old and first learned to drink wine with his meals.

The son of Italian immigrants who came from the Marche region of Italy and settled in Virginia, Minnesota, early in the century, Mondavi learned to make wine when he was just a small child. "My mother ran a boarding house for local iron ore miners, and she had to feed fifteen to twenty people every night," he reminisces. "We used to put on rubber boots to stamp the grapes, and we'd make a perfectly good wine — what we used to call 'Dago Red' — and store it in the cellar. We served wine with most meals and we learned early that wine serves a lot of purposes. Not only does it taste good, but it enhances your food and digestion and it relaxes you.

"Cooking was my mother's passion, and she was very competitive. If she found a recipe that was good, she had to improve upon it until it was the best. Only much later, when I invited three-star chefs to our winery, did I realize just how good her cooking was. In an Italian family, the mother raises the children. I learned from her to be very competitive and to appreciate the best of everything."

When he was ten, Mondavi, his brother, and two sisters moved with their parents to Lodi, California, where his father set up a firm to ship California wine grapes to fellow Italian emigrés in the East and Midwest for use in home wine making. "From the time I was thirteen until I went to college, I worked nailing boxes to ship the grapes in," he says. "My competitive spirit drove me even then. Whether I was playing marbles or swimming, I always wanted to win. The same was true of my job.

"Even when we bought a machine that would nail the boxes, I would race the machine to nail them faster. It got to the point where I would make 200 boxes in a ten-hour day." His father paid him $1.25 a box and he ultimately saved $20,000, enough to put him through his first year at Stanford University. "I barely made the grades for Stanford," he says with a grin. "But I always wanted the best — and that meant the best school, too."

Mondavi's father agreed to pay for the remainder of his undergraduate education, and in 1935, a year before he graduated with a degree in economics, Mondavi decided to go into the wine business. "At first I considered becoming a lawyer," he recalls. "But it was only a year or two after Prohibition was repealed, and my dad said to me, 'Why not wine?' I figured wine was an industry that was young and growing and I said, 'Why not!'"

The summer before his senior year, Mondavi found a professor at the University of California at Berkeley who could tutor him in enology and spent several months studying the principles of wine making, the philosophy of wine, and the fundamentals for running wine analyses. He followed up with a chemistry course in his senior year, bought a copy of *The Principles and Practices of Winemaking,* and studied it religiously.

In 1936, Mondavi's father bought the Sunnyhill Winery in St. Helena, California, a bulk winery that sold wine in tank cars to distributors in the East, who then bottled it under their own labels. Believing wine had a future in America, he staffed Sunnyhill with Robert and two cellarmen. It was there that Mondavi learned production and marketing and developed his own convictions about the potential of Napa Valley wines.

"My tutoring taught me that wine was a living thing, a necessary part of living the good life," he adds. "At the time, there were only four big California vineyards — Larkmead, Beaulieu, Inglenook, and Beringer. I held them in great regard and used to bow my head in respect every time we passed them. But I believed our wine could be better, and I established my own lab and began running analyses of the bulk wine we were making at Sunnyhill. The more I experimented, the more I wanted to go into the fine wine business. My competitive spirit was up. I wanted to excel." As American interest in wine grew over the next decade, production at Sunnyhill soared from 33,000 cases to 400,000 cases per year.

When the Charles Krug Winery was offered for sale in 1943, Robert knew the facility could accommodate his ambitious plans, and he convinced his father to purchase it for $75,000. "My dad, my brother, and I went to look at the winery," he continues. "There were almost 150 acres of vineyards, two homes and a farmhouse, an old stable and workmen's quarters . . . We bought it almost immediately. I was so excited, it took me two months to calm down." In the first year of business, the family grossed $77,000.

For the next few years, the Mondavi brothers, and their father gradually converted the Krug's bulk winery into a sleeker operation. They replaced the dirt floors with cement, got rid of the old cooperage, and revamped the dilapidated stable into a modern aging room. Realizing that marketing strategy was as crucial as wine making expertise, Robert suggested they produce the jug wine under the "CK" label and gradually begin releasing premium bottles under the "Charles Krug" label. In 1946, he made Krug's first Vintage Selection Cabernet, a wine that still garners the compliments of wine tasters around the world.

"I was continually challenging myself to create a better wine," says Mondavi. "I learned how to improve our techniques by exchanging ideas with other vintners. I visited all of the wineries in the state, took a few courses at the University of California, Davis, and studied the books. I believed it was possible to learn everything necessary to make a truly great wine . . . I saw many people who double-talked when it came to discussing wine, but I believed you could make a great wine as long as you were completely sincere, honest, and completely involved in what you are doing."

Throughout the 1950s and 60s, after many experiments, Mondavi introduced a number of innovations at Charles Krug. He was the first California vintner to use cold fermentation exclusively, leading to fresher, fruitier-tasting wines; he introduced new vine trellising systems; and he popularized several new styles of wine, which he introduced in innovative packaging. For example, he changed the fermentation of White Pinot, a not particularly well-regarded variety, and created a slightly sweeter new variety he called Chenin Blanc. Sales quintupled within a year. Similarly, he revamped the fermentation of Sauvignon Blanc and created a drier wine he named Fumé Blanc. It, too, was an instant success.

In 1962, he made his first trip to Europe and became convinced that the great French wines were his primary competition. "I knew we had the soil, the vines, and the climate to produce the finest wines in the world," he says. "I was appalled when the Europeans said we couldn't produce fine wines in our country, and I challenged myself to do it. I finally determined that the only way to find out what we were missing was to go to the source and study their techniques. I traveled through all of the wine-growing regions of Europe. I went to France, Italy, Spain, Germany, Switzerland, Russia, Yugoslavia, and Hungary." He introduced a number of methods based on his travels overseas. He was, for instance, among the first California vintners to age his red wines in French oak barrels.

More importantly, he introduced blind tastings to the Napa Valley, allowing both consumers and members of the wine trade to discriminate between and evaluate differing wine qualities. The tastings also proved to be excellent publicity. To this day, in fact, Mondavi has never formally introduced an advertising campaign for any of his wine. "Mass advertising for fine wines isn't the best way to sell it," he explains. "Making good wine and letting people taste it is what will sell wine."

As Mondavi's innovative techniques gradually increased America's knowledge of wine, they also led to a family rift that ultimately caused him to leave Charles Krug. Under their father's supervision, Robert and his brother Peter had divided their responsibilities. Peter oversaw the wine making while Robert was in charge of sales and marketing. Fraternal relations began to unravel when Robert began pushing Peter to experiment with higher quality wines to be marketed in expensive restaurants. Peter took Robert's advice as criticism and began objecting to Robert's fast-paced promotional schemes and lavish expense accounts. According to press accounts of the time, the brothers' philosophical disagreements went so far that they even began to pronounce their last name differently. Peter called himself a Mon-DAVE-i while Robert called himself a Mon-DAH-vi. Fist fights between the brothers led to lawsuits, and in 1965, Robert, who owned a 27 percent interest in the Krug winery, was voted out of an active role in the family business.

By 1966, with lawsuits still pending, Robert borrowed $100,000 from friends and began the Robert Mondavi Winery with his son Michael. Several months later, the lawsuits were settled, and Robert walked away with $11 million in land, vineyards, and bulk wine. Part of the prize was the To Kalon vineyard, the main grape source for Mondavi's Reserve Cabernet Sauvignon, a long-aging premium wine. In 1969, when gourmet cuisine and the fine wines to accompany it were becoming a trend in Southern California, the Cabernet Sauvignon won a highly publicized tasting, and the Mondavis were able to ride the crest of the craze for "nouvelle cuisine." Within three years, they tripled their production and earned their first profit.

Robert and Michael built the graceful, arching stucco winery that still stands in Oakville today, and in 1975 Robert's second son, Tim, graduated from the wine-making program at the University of California at Davis and joined the company. Like his father, Tim has worked hard to match grapes with the appropriate soils and climates to create new varieties of wine. In fact, though the Mondavis didn't invent Chardonnay, they were responsible for calling attention to it as a great California wine. They are, in fact, the only California wine makers of Italian descent to experiment with America's penchant for white wine.

In the years that followed, the Mondavis added four other wineries to the original vineyards, increasing the style, price, and variety of wines available to the public. The diversity of wines particularly appealed to restaurants, which soon made up 70 percent of the company's sales. Today, restaurant sales are only about 30 percent.

In 1979, the Mondavi family opened Robert Mondavi Woodbridge, a 100-acre vineyard that annually produces over 3 million cases of varietal table wines, such as Chardonnay and Zinfandel. These wines average $7 per bottle and bring the Mondavi name within reach of lower-end consumers.

They also added Opus One, a joint venture with the Rothschilds of Chateau Mouton-Rothschild, a one-wine operation. Though it carries no varietal description on the label, Opus One is a Cabernet Sauvignon-based red that includes smaller portions of Cabernet Franc, Merlot, Malbec and Petit Verdot grapes and is currently one of the most expensive California wines on the market. After a slow start caused by the loss of nearly half the vineyard to phylloxera, a disease that damages vines right down through the roots, the vineyard recently enjoyed its first successful vintage year.

In 1980, they acquired the Vichon vineyard, a five-acre vineyard that produces grapes for a number of premium Chardonnays, Cabernet Sauvignons, Merlots, Chevrignons, and Sauvignon Blancs. Without the Mondavi label, the wine has been slow to take off and must compete with dozens of similar quality brands. Recently, however, Vichon began producing California "Coastal Selection" wines from non-Napa grapes. The Mondavis plan to expand production to 200,000 cases by 1995.

The Byron Vineyard and Winery in Santa Monica was added in 1984. This 640-acre vineyard produces Burgundy-style wines including several higher priced Chardonnays and Pinot Noirs.

"I set out to have a large business, without losing the basic goal of excelling in each category of wine," explains Mondavi. "My goal was to become the Mercedes of the wine business. Mercedes makes everything from cars to trains to trucks that cost anywhere from $20,000 to $250,000. Well, I wanted to do the same for wine. I want to make high-end wines — like Opus One — for wine lovers. With our Woodbridge wines, I wanted to go back to our roots and make wines for people to enjoy on an everyday basis."

With characteristic candor, Mondavi makes no bones about the fact that the road to the company's success has been pitted with both financial and emotional difficulties. The demands of work and travel caused his first marriage to end in divorce. And then there were the problems with his brother at Charles Krug, which have only recently been resolved to the point that the brothers speak cordially at large family gatherings.

Nor has running his own family-operated business been without its share of difficulties. Several years ago Robert tried to have his two sons — Michael, now 51, and Tim, 44 — serve as co-chief executives of the company. Their differences were so strong and so hotly defended that the family finally came to the agreement that Michael would take overall charge of the company and Tim would remain managing director in charge of wine-growing operations until Michael retires. Daughter Marcia Borger, 46, is also a winery partner and oversees business from her home in New York.

"Five years ago, we called in several consultants, all of whom said, 'Your sons don't really believe you want to transfer the business to them,'" Mondavi explains. "I have finally developed inner peace about how to run the company. It took me years to really accept my sons' differences, but I finally have. And now we all adhere to the policy that in this company, Michael makes the final decisions. We can all express our opinions, but his is the one that we go with . . . I just want everyone to speak the truth and the people with authority to take responsibility." With a generous laugh that all but dismisses what must have been some pretty turbulent father-son discussions, he adds, "And now I love everyone."

Mondavi insists that one of the keys to the company's success has been hiring people who adhere to the Mondavi philosophy of making the highest quality wine possible. "I try to convey to all of our employees that they are the ones that make our company," he says. "All of our people — including my children and even my first wife — trust that I will make decisions that are best for them . . . What I hope for is to develop a family heritage that will teach my grandchildren the distinct differences that are possible when different people are interpreting the same thing. Ultimately, the family is the integral unit of human life and I'd like us all to feel that we are all contributing something that is mutually beneficial to all of us." To date, Mondavi has nine grandchildren and hopes that "at least half of them" will be involved in the business either directly or indirectly.

In the meantime, he continues to pursue his mission of teaching the world that wine is "a necessary part of the good life." In fact, several years ago, amidst growing and widespread anti-alcohol sentiment, Mondavi founded "The Mission," a project designed to research wine's medicinal values. To this end, Mondavi has developed countless wine tours, tastings, and lectures, all designed to educate the public on the virtues of wine. He has worked hard to teach the public about the beneficial health properties as well as the aesthetic pleasures of wine.

Now that he has successfully organized the transfer of the company's operations to his sons, Mondavi has time to enjoy his well-deserved success. He and his current wife, Margrit Biever, live in a handsome, 10,000-square foot home on a hill overlooking the Napa Valley. He maintains his youthful sex appeal by a daily regime of aerobic exercises, stationary bicycling, and a twelve-minute swim in the pool he had built into his living room. He tries to play tennis at least two times a week, get a professional massage every day, and, above all, drink a couple of glasses of wine with supper.

For the rest, he lives rather modestly, preferring to put his money back into the business rather than spend it on fancy cars or second homes. His pet project is the creation of a wine museum, and, in conjunction with master chef Julia Child, the formation of the American Institute of Wine and Food. He would like to house both structures in a development that will include a deluxe hotel and spa and an amphitheater for cultural events.

"Now that we have fine food and wine here in America, we need to educate the world about what we can produce and teach them that an appreciation of wine making goes along with an appreciation of food and even art, music, and culture," he adds. "We don't have a master cooking school like the *Cordon Bleu,* and we don't have any ongoing research work in vintnology. I felt we should build a city within the city here in Napa that would be a world-class cultural center. I've already committed myself to buy $2.2 million worth of land for the project. I'm working in conjunction with the city and state to coordinate what will be a $25-million cultural center. We hope to be breaking ground within three years."

But his aspirations are far from finished in the area of wine making itself. "I have a tremendous amount of confidence in myself," he says. "I've traveled the world over to understand my business. Risks are only short-range. I know that if you proceed from a place that is practical, logical, and has common sense, you will succeed. What doesn't work out in the beginning will eventually. My competition is world-wide. We already have wines in 67 countries. There are many more varieties to be discovered and there's plenty of room to enhance the industry. My goal is to keep excelling, to make a wine that is lighter, more harmonious, and gentler. It will have layers of flavor."

What will it taste like? Hazel eyes twinkling, and without missing a beat, Mondavi replies: "It will have the softness and tenderness of a baby's bottom and the depth and power of Pavarotti's voice."

"If you set out just to make money, then you will probably fail. If you concentrate on doing the best job you possibly can, then the money will follow."

STANLEY SELENGUT

Creator of Harmony: A Center for the Study
of Sustainable Resort Development

~

"Life is like fishing," says Stanley Selengut, ever the philosopher. "You put your bait on the end of a hook and cast your line under the water. When you pull up your fish, either it's tasty and you eat it or you throw it back in. Well, your bait is your talent — the things you like to do — and the fish is what you make of your talent."

No one could accuse Selengut, 65, of not making the most of his "bait." For the past forty years, he has carved a continuous series of successful enterprises out of a talent for perceiving what he calls "indigenous assets" and turning them into something marketable in a way in which everyone involved benefits.

His most recent venture — and, in Selengut's case, adventure — is "Harmony: A Center for the Study of Sustainable Resort Development" on the island of St. John in the U.S. Virgin Islands. Harmony is a two-and-a-half acre solar- and wind-powered resort that Selengut designed, financed, and built as a research model for resort developers, environmentalists, and economists in the relatively new field of "ecotourism."

Perched on a hillside overlooking turquoise Maho Bay, Harmony opened in December 1993 to offer adventurous tourists an educational as well as recreational vacation. The resort consists of a scattering of two-story "luxury cabins" built mostly from recycled lumber, glass, and plastic. The eight cabins operate entirely "off the grid" — that is, independently of St. John's electrical system. Visitors cook their own dinners in solar-powered ovens, drink juice cooled by solar-powered ice machines, dry their hair with solar-powered hair blowers, and stay comfortably cool without air conditioning — all thanks to wind scoops and architectural design that makes maximum use of the local trade winds. Even Harmony's carpets and sheets are made of undyed natural fibers and are cleaned without using chemical detergents.

Guests, who must stay for a minimum of a week, participate in the educational and research aspect of the resort by working with individual personal computers that monitor the water consumption and the power used in each cabin. In a kind of symbiotic arrangement usually found only in nature, the visitors get the upfront benefits of the latest in ecological technology, while their experiences are gathered in a data base used by Sandia Laboratories in Albuquerque, New Mexico, to develop more and better energy-efficient products.

"Most people think of ecotourism as a group of vacationers tiptoeing around nature without disturbing it. I really think human beings are capable of much more. We can use our intellect to help restore and enhance the environment. The purpose of studying sustainability is to allow future generations to have at least as good a lifestyle — aesthetically, culturally, naturally — as we do now," says Selengut, whose white beard, Caribbean blue-eyes, and copper eyebrows, arranged like a tangle of daddy long-legs, have the uncanny effect of making this Bronx-born New Yorker resemble a Victorian anthropologist on a jungle expedition. All that's missing is the pith helmet. "Ecotourism has led me to believe that we really must take responsibility for everything around us, [and] if we do, we will all be much better for it."

In the past several years, Harmony has attracted the attention of international teams of architects, landscape designers, and environmentalists and earned Selengut a reputation as the "Green Guru" in the travel industry. An articulate and passionate visionary with a cause, he serves as a consultant to governments and resort planners from as far away as Alaska, Bolivia, and Tasmania, and his resort has earned a tidy profit in the process.

"Entrepreneurship is not just about money; it is an art form," Selengut says, leaning back in his desk chair in the first floor office of the pristine, neo-classical townhouse he owns on 73rd Street just off posh Madison Avenue in Manhattan. "And just like any art form, there are standards to it. I'm the last one to say money isn't important, but there are so many other rewards to get out of a business. If you set out just to make money, then you will probably fail. If you concentrate on doing the best job you possibly can, then the money will follow. My vision of an enterprise is to go after it all. I like to create a plan in which everybody wins. Almost every venture I've gone through has had that quality, and the most amazing thing is that I've never had a failure."

One of the reasons Selengut looks for projects that benefit so many may be the absence of that kind of generosity in the environment in which he grew up. He remembers being difficult and "willful" as a child, getting into the kind of scrapes that once forced his mother to tie him in a chair for an entire afternoon. "My mother never really meant any harm, but I was tenacious," he recalls with a grin. "I sucked my thumb longer that I should have because it was *my* thumb and I had the right to do with it as I pleased. I had a pet skunk which I walked around on a leash because I thought it was cute. I had absolutely no fear of turning a thought into an action."

Cursed with what he calls "a memory problem" in childhood, he was never much of a student, either. He spent many of his elementary school days sitting in a corner, literally forced to wear a dunce cap, and was held back several times. "They didn't understand learning disabilities in those days," he says. "So I was forced to find other ways to learn and other ways to solve problems. The feeling was always, 'Okay, I've hit another wall. Now what do I have to do to get around it?' I'm sure this kind of thinking served me well later on." Indeed, what young Stanley lacked in discipline he more than made up for in curiosity. He read books like *Bomba, the Jungle Boy* and escaped into fantasies of travels to exotic places where he could rule amidst the wildlife and the indigenous people.

When Selengut was kicked out of DeWitt Clinton High School in the Bronx for poor grades and what he describes as "playing hooky once too often," he decided to join the Marines and start doing some of the traveling he had been fantasizing about. "I was probably the world's worst Marine," he says with a gleeful snort. "But I spent two years in Tsing Tao in China. It was fascinating, and I was exposed for the first time to abject poverty. It was there that I first learned to be an understanding person and try to see things from other peoples' perspectives. That, too, would serve me later on."

Barely twenty and just back from China, Selengut came to the conclusion that it was time to go back to school. He earned a high school equivalency diploma, then begged his way into Bergen County Junior College in New Jersey, later finishing a degree in civil engineering at New York University night school. This was mostly to please his stern father, who was a general construction contractor in the New York area and wanted his boy to make something of himself in the business. "Civil engineering was wrong for me," says Selengut. "I was attracted to more creative and exotic work. But it was also a wonderful choice because it forced me to be practical and worked as a real counterforce to bring me back to reality."

Working in construction didn't last long for the "willful" Stanley. He was fired from his first job as a construction supervisor for asking for a promotion after only a week on the job, and, he says, "never worked for anyone again." Overseeing the planning and construction of buildings would remain Selengut's bread and butter for the next forty years. He built a housing development in Lake Hopatcong, New Jersey, as well as ten houses on Fire Island, some of which he still owns and rents out. He specialized in "taking small, elegant Manhattan buildings that had fallen into disrepair and turning them into elegant cooperative apartments," including his own home off Madison Avenue. His construction work allowed him to seek other opportunities to use his creative talents in projects that benefit a broader community.

The ventures that resulted from Selengut's decision to follow his own path are all carefully documented in a set of portfolio-sized scrapbooks kept stacked in a closet in Selengut's office. Originally assembled as a marketing tool to promote his early businesses, the meticulously maintained books brim with artfully captioned pictures and literally hundreds of newspaper clippings that bear eloquent testimony to Selengut's busy and varied life.

In 1958, Selengut read an article about the newly built section of the Pan-American highway that stretched from Mexico to Guatemala and convinced the first of his three wives to make an expedition south through much of Latin America. Smitten by the exquisite and exotic handicrafts of Bolivia, Ecuador, and Peru, the couple loaded up their '57 Chevy with a glorious collection of colorful, hand-woven sweaters, hats, and masks, sheepskin-lined mittens and slippers, and an assortment of jewelry, pottery, mirrors, and rugs. It wasn't long before they were in partnership with another couple and running Piñata Party, a handicrafts store on MacDougal Street in New York's Greenwich Village.

In the early sixties, Selengut turned the handicrafts of the Altiplano area in Peru into a multi-million dollar industry, using award-winning marketing promotions that included flying families of Peruvians to New York for weaving demonstrations, musical concerts, and food festivals. A second Piñata Party store was opened on Park Avenue and most of the country's major department stores began carrying the hand-woven woolen items as chic ski apparel. Fashion models clad in Peruvian sweaters and hats graced the covers of *Vogue* and *Mademoiselle*, *Life* and *Look*. Before long, the Selenguts and their partners, George and Rita Grossblatt, had the inhabitants of whole Peruvian villages employed to weave their updated designs of local hats and sweaters for distribution to more than 1,100 retail outfits throughout the United States.

All went well — until the pendulum of fashion began to

swing back and the fad for South American handicrafts faded almost as quickly as it had bloomed. "Suddenly, we had no market. Here were 2,000 people who had learned for the first time what it felt like to make some money, [and were] about to lose their jobs. I had brought them to this point and I couldn't just abandon them." Selengut then caught wind of the Alliance for Progress, a new program started by the Kennedy administration to help foster job growth in Latin America. "I flew to Washington and just began knocking on doors until I convinced Robert Bonham, the Chief of Cooperative Development for Latin America, to help me. Before long we made a deal with Sears Roebuck. I got some marketing help and design people and Sears financed a number of Andean craft cooperatives, which produced about 3,000 home furnishings products for the Sears chain.

"I would go to Peru and Ecuador and try to figure out what new things we could do with all that indigenous talent. We created a revival of Panama hats to help the weavers of Ecuador; then we moved into shoes and pocketbooks and even Christmas tree ornaments."

His success was so great that in 1962, Selengut was asked to work as a consultant on the development of crafts in the United States with President Kennedy's Office of Economic Opportunity. The job brought Selengut to poverty-stricken areas around the country, where he was soon consulting with Native Americans, Kentucky mountain people, black quilt-makers in Alabama, and a wide variety of elderly folk artists on how to develop craft products.

"You had to be quite ingenious," Selengut recalls. "I remember going into a dismal coal-mining town in Kentucky. All the young people had left, the town was completely run-down and depressed, and I thought there was nothing I could do for them. Then they invited me to lunch at a small local church. The meal was meager, but the bread they served was spread with a delicious honey with a very tangy taste. I asked them what the taste was and they replied, with a grin, 'Why that's moonshine!' Bam. I knew we had it. We developed a line of 'Moonshine Products,' — honey, jams, and jellies packaged in a jug with a triple X on the front . . .

"It was the most exciting time in my career. I got to do the things I do best. I knew how to take an indigenous product and turn it into a profit-making market, and I was good at bringing the talents out of the local people and marketing them so that they would sell. I knew how to show respect for the locals and how to allow them to feel that [the] product was their own. We helped create the demand for Native American jewelry, as well as folk quilts and an assortment of local handicrafts. It was all very exciting because I felt I was actually helping these people and that what I was doing could make a difference."

When the OEO's funding was cut back after President Kennedy's assassination, Selengut continued his work with his own design consulting outfit, funded by his ongoing construction work in New York. "The rewards were very complex," he recalls. "I married my second wife, a quilt buyer for Bloomingdale's, in a quilt factory we had built in Alabama. Just imagine it. A Jewish guy marrying a white woman [in a service conducted] by a black minister. The community made us a beautiful double wedding-ring quilt that they hung on the wall as a decoration. We ate cows and pigs and 'possum and walked down the aisle while someone played 'Here Comes the Bride' and then 'We Shall Overcome' on an old rickety piano. The sense of community was overwhelming."

Selengut's next venture, Children's Motivational Environments, sprang from his work with children in Alabama and Kentucky. "You see the children in these areas imitating their parents and becoming victims of poverty just like their parents," he explains. "I wanted to come up with something that would really help children to learn. I began thinking about the way childrens' rooms are designed and how little the design had to do with the way children think. I began to key into the sequential thinking patterns of kids and started a line of furniture that kids could put together and take apart like giant Tinker Toys. They could shape part of their world and teach themselves about building and organization in the process." The product began to sell like hot cakes, and the company soon branched out to include soft furniture shaped like fruits and vegetables, life-sized toys that the children could construct themselves, and hand puppets. Several pieces were even purchased by the Smithsonian Institute for its permanent collection.

"The whole venture was enormously complicated and something I wasn't really equipped to deal with," recalls Selengut. "The orders rolled in, and each client presented new problems in packaging, shipping, and promoting. The stress was unbearable. I developed acute high blood pressure, and my doctors told me that if I didn't take it easy, I would die. Plain and simple."

So at the ripe age of 44, Stanley Selengut, world-traveler and builder, organizer and promoter extraordinaire, retired. Well, almost. After a year spent learning to play tennis (still self-conscious about his lack of athletic abilities, he huffed and puffed his way through a summer course, the only middle-aged tennis player in a class of eight-year-olds), he began to fantasize about owning and running a lodge or an inn, a place where he could further tune into the needs of others.

In 1974, when his old Washington friend Robert Bonham asked him to consult on the design of a low-income housing project that was being sponsored by the Rockefeller family, he learned of the presence of a Rockefeller family resort on St. John in the Virgin Islands. That got him thinking. After visiting the island, replete with exquisite panoramic views, lush vegetation, and a diversity of wildlife, "Bomba, the Jungle Boy" once again heard the beat of the drums. Within a year, Selengut had leased fourteen acres on Maho Bay in the U.S. Virgin Islands National Park and began construction on the Maho Bay Campground, an environmentally sensitive resort that now boasts 116 tent cabins lodged amidst its trees.

"The local people were very resistant to the idea of a New York developer coming in and building a resort," Selengut recalls. "They were worried about my building on a hillside and destroying the land; they were worried about pollution and the ecology of the island. I saw things from their perspective, and it became very important for me to be a good neighbor. I found that if you don't get hostile and arrogant and are sensitive to people's needs, [they] will do right by you. I managed to turn the adversity of their opposition into an asset. The course of our development depended a lot on the feedback from the local people and from our customers . . . We learned that good design doesn't come from the inside out, but rather inward, from the outside indigenous life. Natural law dictated a lot."

The Maho Bay tents were constructed of light, inexpensive materials and erected on stilts and without heavy construction equipment so that the ground cover was left intact. Solid and liquid wastes were processed on-site and used to fertilize local vegetation. The resulting increased vegetation attracted native frogs, lizards, and birds, which, in turn, helped control the insect population.

"We developed a good relationship with the National Park Service and they began advising us on environmental issues and showing us off as a model facility. I learned that a lot of people were attracted to our campground because we were sensitive to the ecology," Selengut adds. "We were successful from the day we opened. We kept it simple and spent no more than $7,000 to construct each tent. We made our money back in the first 100 days we were in operation. With 7,000 visitors a year, we could gross at least $200,000 annually." Not only has the campground been a financial success: it has also won numerous environmental and architectural awards. In 1991, it was the site for a workshop in sustainable design that attracted over 60 experts in the field.

"As our success grew, I became enamored with the idea of sustainability and decided to build a smaller campground using all of the principles that were being discussed. Basically, sustainable development is the practice of using natural resources no faster than they can be regenerated. My idea was to create a kind of Disneyland that was based not on fantasy but on sustainable realities. And that's how Harmony came about."

Harmony opened in December of 1993, financed solely by Selengut. "Can you imagine the profitability of a resort that operates independently of the island's electrical system?" he asks. "There are no electric bills, no water bills. The land-scaping is all indigenous and requires little maintenance ... The community was built entirely from recycled materials — wood scraps, plastic bottles, crushed glass, and ground tires. My gut instinct was towards a spiritual design that would foster human creativity. I wanted to keep it as simple as possible, so that guests would like it and take it back with them as a model for their own homes.

"We charge $150 a day for two people, and the universal reaction we get is, 'Why isn't everybody doing this?' It's totally comfortable. The refrigerator keeps everything cold, the microwave oven works, and yet you don't burn any fossil fuels at all ... In fact, the luxury cabins cost almost $60,000 to build, a lot more expensive to build than those at Maho Bay, but we'll get our money back in three years. Most developers would jump through a hoop for an opportunity like that."

These days, Selengut is fielding more requests for getting involved in ecological resort projects than he has the time or the energy for. He and his third wife, Irma, prefer to divide their time between their Manhattan home and office and their country home on Bridgehampton, Long Island. Never one to neglect any indigenous assets, however, he is hopeful that one of Irma's three children will ultimately join Stanley Selengut Consultants, Inc. and pick up the torch from him. He insists that he is by no means finished marketing his vision of the future of resort ecology. If he has his way, 51 acres of Estate Concordia, a property he purchased on the side of St. John opposite from Maho Bay, will be devoted to establishing a model project for the Clinton administration's Council on Sustainable Development. "Ideally, I will be able to promote an advanced educational system that will train students in sus-tainability," he says. "Like Harmony, it will be a collaborative effort, where companies like Sandia will supply the newest technology and our guests will test the products and give their feedback.

"We've gotten the world into such a mess that just leaving things alone doesn't cut it anymore," Selengut insists. "Sustainability doesn't just mean stopping the destruction of nature — it means managing nature. This past month, we entertained our one millionth customer at Maho Bay, and our land is in better shape than it was on the day we found it. There's an incredible reward in knowing that. The way I see it, you can't be successful if you don't enjoy yourself . . . There is something almost spiritual about being in a place that is as it should be . . . What drives me is the joy of using my capacities and seeing to it that everybody wins — not just me, but my guests, the island, and every aspect of the environment."

"The biggest obstacle for black kids today is still their blackness. I believe in pushing the black agenda and putting people in the right place to create a framework for real change. I believe in that with all my heart and soul. The people who really succeed in this world are the ones that have that extra special degree of passion."

JACK TRAVIS

Acclaimed architect and educator

W hen Jack Travis was ten, he used to accompany his mother on shopping trips to the butcher. He would ask the man wrapping meat for their supper to tear off sheets of butcher paper so that he could bring them home and draw housing plans on the long white curls. In junior high school, he moved on to three-dimensional models, building Bauhaus igloos out of stolen sugar cubes. For inspiration, he would spend his play time at the housing projects springing up around his Las Vegas, Nevada, neighborhood, watching the construction workers dig foundations, frame walls, and lay beams and joists.

"But it wasn't until the ninth grade that I actually heard the word *architect*," says Travis, a broad grin lighting up his usually sober expression, made all the more serious by round, wire-rimmed spectacles. "My English teacher, Sister Juanita Marie, read one of the essays I had written in which I pointed out the dangers of our school's rustic, rough brick-and-mortar exterior. I said something about its being no place for playing children. Sister Juanita Marie said, 'Well, Jack, it sounds like you want to be an architect.' When I heard the word, I ran to the library and took out a book entitled, *So You Want To Be An Architect* and read it several times over." What followed would make a terrific sequel.

Today, Travis, 42, is one of a small but growing number of successful African-American architects and the founder of

Jack Travis Architect (JTA), his own architectural firm. He has received numerous awards for his work as a high-end architect for such well-known motion picture stars as Spike Lee and Wesley Snipes, as well as for corporate clients like Gulf & Western, Macy's, Giorgio Armani, and Revlon International. He has been hailed by the media for his innovative, modernist style as well as for his efforts to bring African-American cultural perspectives to architectural design.

Travis says he relies frequently on African and African-American history to suggest the forms, motifs, building materials, and colors with which he works. This preferred aesthetic is reflected in JTA's offices, a 1,500-square foot loft on West 29th Street in Manhattan. West and Central African sculptures and East African medicine jars, fetishes, and musical instruments stand in stark contrast to the concrete space divided by curving cinder-block walls and perforated steel screens and entryways. The merging of elements from such distinct cultures has the powerful effect of celebrating their differences even as it establishes the ways in which they complement one another.

"I like to create designs that make statements that go beyond the architectural quality of the space. More important, I want to establish an African-American aesthetic," explains Travis, whose bold, black-and-white African print shirt and leather and silver African bracelets further illustrate his ethnic sensibility. "That aesthetic should be informed by an Afrocentric understanding of history and of the African Diaspora in particular. [The] styles [that] evolve will never be purely African, but we can draw from many cultures and still call the style that emerges our own.

"In fact, any place that black people have settled, whether it is the Caribbean or Brazil or the United States, will [develop] a style that is not purely African. As a people, we don't have a problem with other people's cultures. The African cultural perspective is so deeply rooted and so spiritual that it is easy to combine with other influences. It is our good fortune that we can go beyond our African origins and choose from whatever influences around us and then combine them with our own. An Afrocentric focus should, in fact, merely create a foundation so that we can go beyond it with other cultural influences."

Although Travis acknowledges that becoming an architect has always been his dream, inspiring more black Americans to practice in his field is his true passion. In his 1992 book, *African-American Architects: In Current Practice*, published by Princeton University Press, as well as through articles, speeches, and a variety of teaching commitments, Travis laments the limited opportunities for African-American architects, including the fact that although blacks make up 12.5 percent of the U.S. population they account for only one percent of the country's registered architects. What's worse, he adds, not one African-American is a founding or a design partner in any of the country's largest architectural firms, has a high editorial staff position in any architectural magazine or book publisher, or has an upper managerial and policy-making position at any of the country's predominantly white architectural schools.

"It isn't easy to succeed as an architect," says Travis. "What keeps me going is a passion for what I do. My goal is to get as many black faces as possible into the profession and then to enhance the landscape with our vision. Black Americans have the potential to be as successful in this field as we already are in sports and entertainment. We must quit waiting for the government to solve our problems and begin doing it ourselves. We are going to have to make people respect us through a body of solid work. One of the things we do have is the power to control the visual context of our communities, and there is a certain amount of dignity and respect in at least controlling our own environment."

He says that African-Americans can contribute to a new architectural style of and for African-Americans and cites the African-American architect Harry Simmons, whose practice is in Brooklyn, New York, as an example. If Simmons designs a public building in a black or Hispanic neighborhood, its appearance is somewhat different from one that was designed by a white architect. There is more "meaningful" outdoor space, for example, because minority males tend to gather outside to socialize and pass along information.

Although Travis's firm does very little of this kind of public housing work, his vision of a culture-based architecture is apparent in such projects as his recent installation at New York's American Craft Museum. The show, entitled "Uncommon Beauty in Common Objects," was a tribute to African crafts and was housed in a series of contemporary wood, metal, and canvas structures reminiscent of an African tribal village. "The architecture of the space," explained Travis, "was designed so as not to overpower the art but to give it a cultural context."

Travis cites his father's work ethic, his mother's dedication to exposing her son to as many opportunities as possible, and his experiences at a culturally diverse Catholic school in Las Vegas as comprising the environment that nourished the political vision he has today. Perhaps it was these factors, in combination with what he calls his "tenacity, fortitude, organizational skills, and ability to communicate," that helped him to escape the same future shared by his two younger brothers, Skip and Grant, both of whom have been crack addicts for the last fifteen years and are still living in Las Vegas.

"I was a good kid who believed in authority. I guess my mother put the fear of God in me. I cleaned her house every day and did what I was told," he reminisces. "My father was a different kind of inspiration. He was born in Mississippi and never went to school beyond the fourth grade. He grew up picking cotton in Louisiana and eventually moved to Nevada because there were more work opportunities available. He got a job as a construction laborer for the Atomic Energy Commission at the Nevada Nuclear Test Site and drove 65 miles into the desert every day. He never missed a day. My mom worked cleaning houses until she got a job working at the new hotels they began building in Las Vegas in the 1950s.

"We knew a lot of different kinds of people from the hotel where Mom worked—Mexicans, Cubans, Blacks, Jews, and Mormons. My parents were never involved in any of the civil rights issues going on in the fifties and sixties. They basically never even heard of Martin Luther King, Jr. They simply wanted to get along and not make any trouble. There was plenty of racism in Las Vegas in my childhood. I remember white people driving by as I walked down the street and silently mouthing 'Nigger' at me through the window as they passed me by. I remember my father being stopped as we drove to Louisiana for his mother's funeral and a police officer stopping us in Texas and telling us we'd better not stop until we'd left the state . . ."

Though Travis met almost no black professionals in his childhood, he never once doubted his decision to become an architect.

"I remember my mother bringing me to see a local black man who was working as a draftsman. He lived in a small house with his wife and eight or nine children, and he had a small, cluttered drafting table in a corner of his living room. It was dirty and somewhat depressing, but I didn't mind. I knew that was what I wanted to be doing.

"So I studied *So You Want To Be An Architect*. The first thing it said was that you had to be competitive and a leader. Well, I was *that;* I played football and basketball and tennis, and I was a very good athlete. It also said you had to be good in math. Well, I was *that* too. I always loved numbers. But it also said you had to be able to draw. That was a problem. I couldn't draw to save my life." So he enrolled in a drafting class at Las Vegas High School night school and went to work on his drawing skills.

Always willing to do whatever was necessary to find his way to a career in architecture, Travis then met architect Bob Fielden and got his first break. "When I was fourteen or so, I passed a sign on one of the main thoroughfares in Las Vegas that said 'Architect Jack Miller,'" he recalls. "Well, I saw the word 'Architect' and I saw the word 'Jack' and I told my mother I had to go over there. The next day, my mother drove me there. I knocked on the door and told the secretary I wanted to be an architect. I guess she thought I was cute, and she took me in to see Bob Fielden. I showed him my drawings and he said, 'Let me give you some advice. Don't draw. You will develop a lot of bad habits once you start your formal training.' I couldn't believe he just assumed I would have formal training. Then he said, 'You need to look around you. You need to *see*. Don't draw. Look and sketch.' I knew I wanted to sound just like him one day."

Travis's studies improved dramatically in high school, and Fielden gave him his first architectural job the summer after he graduated. "This was a small branch office for Jack Miller, a firm that was doing a lot of work in Los Angeles. There were eight people in the office and only one black besides myself. I remember that job because I learned how to build models and because I met Carl Hauser, an architect who, like Bob Fielden, would remain my friend to this day. Carl was a real sixties radical, and he used to [say to] me, 'Jack, you're a black man. Who are you going to build buildings for? When you go to college, don't listen to anything they teach you. They won't be on your side.' He would sort of test me each week — ask me about how I perceived the role of a black architect — to see if my consciousness was getting raised."

Travis ultimately chose to attend Arizona State University to participate in their five-year undergraduate program in architecture. He liked Arizona State for its proximity to home, but, also, and even more importantly, for its hot, arid climate, which was similar to the climate in South and West Africa. In addition, the school had a solar energy program lead by John I. Yellott, a leading expert in the field. "I was the only black student in architecture," adds Travis. "Donald Hinshaw, the Assistant Dean, became a sort of father figure to me, and my advisor, Calvin Straub, was a terrific help. It was at ASU that I also met a black architect for the first time. His name was Rushia Glenn Fellows. It was at ASU that I began to understand the language of architecture. Most of all, I learned that I could do it if I tried."

After ASU, Travis knew that he wanted to teach architecture and inspire other black Americans to pursue a career in the profession. Knowing he needed a graduate degree to teach, he chose the University of Illinois on the advice of Carl Hauser. The program was small and was reputed to have a number of excellent programs, both in public housing and in prison architecture. "The program was much more rigorous there," says Travis. "I guess I felt that when I got to the University of Illinois, I had to grow up. The level of expectation was much greater. I also met a white architect named Jack Baker, who was a tremendous inspiration to me. He was doing a lot of [real] quality work out in Champagne, Illinois. I felt that if he could do that kind of work in such a provincial environment, then I would have to work to be the best that I could be — whatever the obstacles."

After graduate school, he spent a few years in San Francisco, but it was a visit to New York that ultimately became the next turning point in his career. "Something happened to me when I headed over the George Washington Bridge," he explains. "I instantly realized that New York was the basis of everything that happens in my profession and I knew that was the place I had to be."

It wasn't long before Travis networked his way into a job at the New York office of Skidmore, Owings & Merrill, one of the most prestigious architectural firms in the country, and one, in fact, that employed very few black architects at the time. In fact, when Travis applied for a job, there were no black architects at all in either the design or production departments. "I had tried four times to get a job there on my own," he recalls. "Each time I met with someone different and each time I didn't get a job. Finally, on the fifth time, I went in on the recommendation of a friend and I was hired on the spot."

Travis's experience at Skidmore, Owings & Merrill was seminal to his future in architecture. "One thing I was struck by was just how many truly talented people there were," he says candidly. "There were 240 architects in the office at the time, and everybody there was incredibly artistic and creative. When I saw the level of people like these, it was easier for me to understand exactly what I could accomplish. I realized I didn't really have an artistic or spiritual sensibility. I have excellent management and organizational skills and excellent communication skills. I knew that I could design, but my design talents were not on the level of the architects that were around me. I was immediately put in interior space planning, and I realized that I would be pigeonholed there for as long as I remained at SOM."

In 1982, Skidmore began to downsize and Travis knew that he wouldn't make the cut. "I knew it was time to leave," he recalls. "I had to move to a smaller office, where I could get more experience. I knew it wouldn't be too difficult because once you've worked at SOM, you can get a job just about anywhere."

From 1982 to 1984, Travis moved through a series of jobs at smaller firms, including a job in the design department of the Switzer Group in New York, a prominent black-owned architectural firm. Artistic differences, based mostly on the fact that Travis's experiences with SOM's wealthy clients had "spoiled" him by allowing him to work with the kind of limitless budgets unavailable at other firms, kept him on the move.

"I guess I was a bit of a jerk," he says in retrospect. "I played the artist and didn't want to stint on the budget. I felt I was about another level of quality, where art and aesthetics should rule over money... The clients at SOM were Saudi Arabians and Iranians, people who were willing to spend $25,000 on an inlaid end table for a reception area. Suddenly we were dealing with people who had budgets and it took me a while to come to terms with that." Not, unfortunately, before Travis was fired from Sidney Philip Gilbert Associates, the last architectural firm that employed him.

By November of 1984, Travis realized it was time to go out on his own. "It was Christmas time," he recalls, "and lots of my old friends and co-workers were having Christmas parties ... I left a party one night and began to feel really sorry for myself. I simply decided that I had to get my own office ... Of course, the idea made me nervous but not to the point that it would stop me. I said to myself, 'Everyone else can do it. Why not me?'"

So without an office, a game plan or, for that matter, a single client, in January of 1985, Jack Travis started JTA in the loft he was sharing with a girlfriend on West 20th Street. Fortunately, his courage was matched by a considerable amount of the kind of luck usually found only in fairy tales.

For six months, Travis went into partnership with Julio George and Walter Maffei, two friends he had met while working at the Switzer Group. Maffei tried to drum up some work while Travis worked at NBC in facilities management and space planning. "We weren't getting anywhere until Walter got a call from Gabriella Forte, an executive at Giorgio Armani Worldwide," Travis explains. "Gabriella walked into my office and basically said, 'I like him. You're hired.' She never even asked to see my work. 'My only requirement,' she said, 'is that I'm your only client.' Then she asked me how much it would cost to start up my own firm. I said, '$20,000.' She said to her colleague, 'Write him a check.'"

Over the next five years, JTA grew to a six-person firm and did a series of projects for Giorgio Armani, including the design implementation of the Emporio Armani store on lower Fifth Avenue, some renovation work in the Giorgio Armani boutique on Madison Avenue, and a series of smaller Armani boutiques in some of Manhattan's poshest department stores. Travis's work, touted for its clean lines and its powerful blend of warmth and minimalism, put JTA on the map. Soon he had a number of jobs designing residences and other upscale boutiques like Madison Avenue's Cashmere Cashmere store.

At the same time, film director Spike Lee contacted Travis to be the architectural consultant for his film *Jungle Fever*. His job was to help the film's star, Wesley Snipes, better understand the role of a black man in what had long seemed to be a white man's profession. Work on Lee's five-story Victorian home in Fort Greene, Brooklyn, as well as for the new offices of Lee's production company, 40 Acres and A Mule Filmworks, Inc. followed, along with three residential projects around the country for actor Snipes. "Up until my work for Spike, most of my clients were white. Now, we are becoming a premier, high-end black firm," affirms Travis. "The number of projects we do is still small, but the costs of each project are high. We're now doing several million dollars worth of work."

As his success continues to grow, Travis works even harder at his real passion — bringing more black students to the profession of architecture.

He speaks in prisons and juvenile detention centers and teaches a course in architecture at the Fashion Institute of Technology in Manhattan. For the past three years, JTA has sponsored an annual Student Summer Workshop. "The focus of the program," says Travis, "is to bring together students, particularly African-American, from all points of the U.S., the Caribbean, Africa, and other countries to study Afrocentricity as it might relate to architecture, design and planning." The six-week seminar brings together between 25 and 40 students and exposes them to a variety of African-American professionals to help them learn Afrocentric design and presentation techniques. The $50 tuition fee is waived for any student who can't afford it. Although it costs Travis several thousand dollars a year to organize, the low tuition makes the program available to a wider range of African-American students.

"The primary message of the program," notes Travis, "is about doing, about teaching African-American students how to make their way through the gauntlet of racism. The biggest obstacle for black kids today is still their blackness.

"I want everyone in my firm to be black, if for no other reason than it's never been done before. I believe in pushing the black agenda and putting people in the right place to create a framework for real change. I believe in that with all my heart and soul. The people who really succeed in this world are the ones that have that extra special degree of passion."

"I was given the opportunity to live in the best country in the world with a strong, healthy body, good mental abilities and the best education available. For me to be proud of how I've lived, I feel that I have had to take these opportunities as far as I can go."

SCOTT McNEALY

Co-Founder, Chairman and CEO
of Sun Microsystems Inc.

ven though his business is computers, Scott McNealy likes to talk in transportation analogies, especially when he is explaining what he calls his "vision."

"The history of computing is a lot like the history of transportation," says the 39-year-old co-founder and CEO of Sun Microsystems, Inc. "In the old days, all we had were trains and buses. Nobody personally owned a train or bus because they were big, expensive, hard to maintain, and, though they usually left on time, almost always arrived late. Worst of all, a bus or a train accident usually meant headline news, a major disaster involving hundreds of people.

"Well, that was mainframe computing in the sixties and seventies. Those big machines, made by companies like IBM, DEC, or Hewlett Packard, were capable of hauling huge amounts of data, but the machines were impersonal, inflexible, and expensive to maintain. It was master-slave computing. If the mainframe — the master — broke down, it was a major disaster. All the slaves stopped working.

"Now we've entered a new world, where trains and buses are still around, but there are bicycles and cars, too. PC's are the bicycles. They're easy to use, easy to maintain, and they get you to most places in the bike lane of the information super-highway. What Sun makes — workstations — are the automobiles. By adding the right microchip and joining a sophisticated network of file servers, system software, printers, and network services, we can virtually re-engineer how we work.

"At my desk right now, I can send an e-mail letter in eight seconds to a colleague in Europe or transmit a message to my fianceé a few blocks away. I can call up any video I want, check my appointment calendar for the next six months, balance my checkbook, or order a bouquet of flowers for my mom. We are hooked up to a wide range of services, and the computers we manufacture are the cars that can travel on the autobahn instead of the bike lane of the information super-highway."

Since Sun Microsystems, Inc. entered the computer market twelve years ago, the firm has changed the face of computing as we know it by introducing McNealy's "automobiles" — that is, fast, inexpensive "workstations" for engineers, publishers, financial brokers, and anyone else whose job requires more power than ordinary desktop computing can provide. Relying on what the press calls his "traditional us-against-the-world attitude," McNealy and his partners found a niche for themselves by coming up with innovative and economical ways of satisfying the mainframe computer market that formerly belonged to such hi-tech giants as Intel, Microsoft, Novell, DEC, and IBM. Today, the company is the world's leading provider of UNIX workstations, servers, and related software and hardware technologies based on open, distributed network computing.

"Sun created two waves of change in computing," McNealy explains, visibly warming to his subject. "The idea of network computing was one of them. The other was to move from proprietary interfaces to open operating systems." McNealy prides himself on "bringing an understanding of what we do to Joe Six-Pack," and his pride is well-founded. Picking up steam, he relies on a different analogy to illustrate the second wave of change. "Just as nations do, computers have different written and spoken languages, different alphabets, and different dialects. Until now, the major computer companies have created different operating systems — or languages — and different user systems that make it virtually impossible for one computer to interact with another.

"At Sun, we believe that we should be able to create a barrier-free computer system and put all proprietary language into the public domain. All of our interfaces are publicly available. Only our implementation — the particular design for how that 'language' is used — is proprietary. Either network computing or open systems alone would have made us a *Fortune* 500 company. The two together will make us a *Fortune* 120 company ... I'm a believer. I go out and tell everyone to get off the buses and trains."

Indeed, McNealy spends much of his time on the soapbox, preaching his belief in open operating systems. He lectures to industry leaders, lobbies for his cause on Capitol Hill, and sits on various educational and manufacturing boards. The goal of open systems, he asserts, is to provide customers with choices: the ability to select among multiple products from multiple vendors and integrate them on powerful networks. His audience is not only the U.S. government, which, he claims, purchases one out of every four computers sold in this country, but the world.

In fact, in the last twelve years, his ideas for network computing have virtually revolutionized the computer establishment and have turned Sun Microsystems, Inc. into the world's number-one workstation and server vendor for the UNIX system, an open software environment. In its last fiscal year, the company took in $4.3 billion in revenues and commanded close to 40 percent of the worldwide workstation/server market, giving the company a ranking of 139 on the *Fortune* 500 list. In short, Sun is the most successful 12-year-old computer company *ever*.

"I've made more money that I ever wanted to make," insists McNealy, his blue eyes flashing, "and I've accomplished more than I ever imagined. But I still have two goals: I'd like to see everyone hooked up to the same data highway, and I'd like to see every man, woman, and child working in the same computer language."

Dressed in a sweatshirt and chinos, McNealy's boyish grin, prep-school haircut, and obvious enthusiasm make him seem impossibly young to be heading up a company worth $4.3 billion. Yet he is clearly at home with his success.

His glass-walled office is a clutter of hockey sticks and souvenirs from his frequent business trips to Europe and Asia. Corporate art includes a cartoon poster of Bill and Hillary Clinton, a host of wall plaques testifying to his industry achievements, a kimono-clad porcelain doll encased in a glass display box, and a whiteboard scrawled with enigmatic diagrams of what are possibly sales and marketing strategies. He appears to inhabit an island of casual accessibility amidst the considerably more formal corporate headquarters of the company he founded in an "oversized garage" in Santa Clara, California only twelve years ago.

Sun Microsystems now inhabits a huge, futuristic concrete-and-glass structure and several satellite buildings straddling Highway 101 in Palo Alto, California, on the northernmost tip of California's ever-extending Silicon Valley. Yet, despite the stark, modern architecture, the security system that requires all visitors to display plastic I.D. badges, and the gray-suited Japanese businessmen arriving in bunches to attend corporate meetings, McNealy insists that he prefers to keep the atmosphere as "non-corporate" as possible.

"The tie is one of the most dysfunctional articles of clothing ever invented," he once told a reporter. "The only dress code we have is that you must." A similar informality governs his management style. "You don't see a big walnut desk or any wall-paneling here, like you do in the offices of most CEOs. We have no corporate parking lots, no unions, no corporate benefits packages. In fact, I don't really know where labor stops and management begins. I have friends all over the company. My chief information officer, for example, was my thesis advisor at Harvard, and he's about to be the best man at my wedding."

Indeed, Sun Microsystems began as a collaboration amongst friends. At 27, McNealy was working as a director of operations at a small high-tech firm called Onyx when he was contacted by Vinod Khosla, a fellow MBA graduate from Stanford University, to help start Sun.

Khosla, a native of India, had a dream to found a company in Silicon Valley and to retire before the age of 30. Intent on his belief that the industry needed a general-purpose workstation that could do most of the same tasks as a mainframe computer at a much lower cost, he had contacted Andreas Bechtolsheim. Bechtolsheim, another Stanford graduate, was licensing the rights to an inexpensive workstation called "Sun" (for *Stanford University Network*), that he had designed from off-the-shelf parts. Recognizing the need for someone to take charge of manufacturing for the company, Khosla then invited McNealy to dinner at McDonald's and made him an offer.

"I came out of the automobile industry," explains McNealy, whose father was vice-chairman of the American Motors Corporation. In fact, he spent much of his childhood listening to his father chat about business with family friend Lee Iacocca on the golf course. "Most of my early jobs involved working in garages and around cars. My first job was washing cars in an auto dealership for $1.75 an hour. Then I got a job as a foreman in a United Auto Workers supply plant. Frankly, my early dream was to own my own tool and die shop. After I graduated from Harvard, I gravitated towards manufacturing and worked at Rockwell for a while." Following the completion of his MBA at Stanford, he further developed his skills as a manufacturing manager by building military tanks for FMC Corporation.

"I never really considered going into computers. Onyx was simply next door to FMC, and I had the kind of manufacturing experience they were looking for . . . When I was contacted to help establish Sun, I figured, 'Why not?' I had three years of business experience, so I wasn't yet steeped in bad management practices. I figured I had nothing much to lose."

To start Sun, he borrowed $25,000 from his father to buy founders' stock. "My dad and I had a deal," he explains. "He agreed to pay for my undergraduate studies in economics at

Harvard and for my MBA at Stanford. He covered my room, board, and tuition and nothing else. Not a penny for entertainment expenses. But the minute I was out of school, the money stopped — not a penny more. It was the best deal in the world. If parents can't cut that deal with their children, then they shouldn't have them." Indeed, it wasn't a bad deal for McNealy's father, either. Today, a single Sun share sells for $20.

McNealy clearly had a knack for leadership. In 1972, he captained his suburban Detroit high school tennis team to a state championship and narrowly missed doing the same for the hockey team. As a manufacturing foreman at Rockwell, he was temporarily hospitalized for exhaustion after working fifteen-hour days, seven days a week. At Onyx he was credited with turning the company around after solving a number of quality problems.

"I guess what drives me is a basic, innate insecurity," says McNealy about his work ethic. "I know you have to be honest — that's easy. I always wanted to be the good guy who succeeds, and I've certainly been handed more than enough. I guess I felt I was given the opportunity to live in the best country in the world with a strong, healthy body, good mental abilities, and the best education available. For me to be proud of how I've lived, I feel that I have had to take these opportunities as far as I can go. Someone once said, 'Only the most secure can do nothing. Insecurity is the root of all motivation.' But you can be insecure and channel it in a positive way.

"I brought a sense of fairness and some real basic business knowledge to Sun," he adds. "I'm not very technically minded, and I've never really had any mentors, either. In some ways, everyone is a mentor. Some teach you what to do; some teach you what *not* to do . . . I entrusted the technical founders to create the best product. I came here to run the manufacturing and to serve, in a way, as the company spokesman. Basically, I'm a hard-wired capitalist. I don't like to spend money unnecessarily. Many people in charge of companies overspend. I think about business in terms of lifeboats. I ask 'How many people can we put in a lifeboat?' and then 'How can we build more lifeboats?'"

Within a few weeks of acquiring the initial venture capital funding, Sun Microsystems incorporated in 1982. And the rest is a high-speed success story. The company hired Bill Joy, a Berkeley graduate student who was known as a UNIX guru for having designed a cheap, popular microprocessor version of the operating system then used only by scientific nerds. Joy was also a believer in low-cost, open systems, and his software expertise blended perfectly with Bechtolsheim's creativity in hardware.

When Sun workstations first rolled off the assembly line in 1982, they were eagerly grabbed by technical personnel in academic and industry labs. Within seventeen months, the company had begun providing workstations to ComputerVision, a major CAD (Computer Aided Design) supplier, which put Sun on the map in the mainstream technical market. Revenues quickly went up to $9 million. By 1984, the firm had opened a European office to begin international sales and had launched Sun Federal, a subsidiary to serve the government market. In the years that followed, the company began distributing in 27 countries around the world and spread to the commercial market, signing on customers like McDonald's, Federal Express, American Airlines, and the London Underground.

Sun designed its own powerful Reduced Instruction Set Computer (RISC) processor, called Scalable Processor Architecture (SPARC), in 1987. The chip was aimed at giving Sun's hardware expanded yet inexpensive capabilities. Installed in a new desktop machine, the system — called SPARCstation — was installed in a "pizzabox" style desktop machine and launched two years later. It wasn't long before it became the most powerful RISC workstation on the market, and it was imitated by many competitors in the years to come.

By 1992, Sun replaced Wang on the prestigious Standard & Poor's 500; *Fortune* magazine named the firm the second largest exporter as a percentage of sales, right behind Boeing; and the company made the *Fortune* International 500. Sun's subsidiaries grew to ten, including its two largest — Sun Microsystems Computer Corp., the workstation and server manufacturer, and SunSoft, Inc., which develops and sells system software.

All the while, the company continued to champion open systems, which were avoided by most large computer companies, and began designing and licensing to all Network File System (NFS) newcomers, the file sharing software that soon became the industry standard. It was Sun's belief in open systems that drove sales way past any of their competitors.

"I believed then and I still do now that open systems were the only way to protect capitalism," says McNealy, whose innovative theories, casual clothing, and articulate, if irreverent, speeches about a brave new world of computing set him apart from his more conservative competitors.

The way McNealy explains it, Sun's customers are able to make every resource on the network available to any user who needs it, from any physical location on the network. The open systems approach also lets customers protect their previous investments in equipment and training while allowing them to take advantage of new technologies as they emerge, because it allows existing systems to be integrated with newer technology.

And with open technologies, computer vendors can choose among multiple suppliers for the hardware and software components they need, without fear of incompatibility or the requirement of paying huge royalty fees. In addition, openness fosters market growth — as more and more vendors embrace the technology, volume goes up and prices for machine components go down. In short, Sun encourages the creation of industry-wide hardware, software, and networking standards. Open standards make life easier for customers and vendors alike because they reduce confusion and unnecessary product development time while still allowing for innovation. Where a volume standard already exists, Sun supports it. Where none exists, Sun attempts to build industry consensus so that a standard can be established.

Although Sun now employs over 13,000 people, there has been great effort to keep intact the energy, ideas, and unconventional attitudes that helped the company grow. Andy Bechtolsheim and Bill Joy, as well as other technical innovators, still do what they always did. These days, Joy is working on a computer that will disappear right into a desk and have a screen as its surface. Bechtolsheim is working on the next generation of desktop computers and talks of a day when computers will be the size of credit cards and simply plug into a keyboard.

Despite the commitment to his vision and the astronomical growth of Sun, McNealy still attributes much of his success to chance. "I believe in accidental empires," says McNealy. "I wouldn't bet on my starting Sun a second time. When we started the company, I was the manufacturing manager. Two years into it, we got rid of our president and my colleagues asked me to take over temporarily until they found someone. Well, they never did, and now I'm CEO.

"A lot of it was good timing, luck and fate. I believe in fate . . . People ask me all the time if I am a risk-taker; I'm not. Nobody ever missed a meal starting his or her own business. When you start, there is no risk because there's nothing to lose. If you're successful, then you have risk. Now, I employ 13,000 people and have to keep a $4.3 billion business running. *Now*, the risk is huge. If you ask me, people should fear success more than failure."

Although he admits that the rewards have been great, he is careful to add that the costs have been great as well. "There is a high level of satisfaction for having made a difference in the industry and for granting enough stock to all of the members of my family to enable them each to buy new houses. And, hopefully, there will continue to be enough money to establish a trust fund that will help many more people outside of my family.

"But the cost is not small. All of this success happened for me at such a young age. Being responsible for so many people became very consuming and didn't leave time for much else. I should have had five kids by now."

When he's not overseeing Sun's subsidiary companies, making speeches to the computer industry, or arguing on Capitol Hill on behalf of network computing, McNealy is serving as vice chairman for trade of the Computer Systems Policy Project, a consortium of thirteen of the largest U.S. computer companies that addresses public policy issues affecting the industry and the country.

In what little spare time remains, he plays hockey, takes advantage of his season tickets to the San Jose Sharks, and spends time with his mother, an artist and interior designer. "I may not have her artistic temperament, but I'm a momma's boy," he quips. Now, he tries hard to spend more time with his friends and — most recently — his fiancée, Susan Ingemanson, a 24-year-old researcher at Stanford University.

In the spring of 1994, McNealy gave Ingemanson a rather substantial diamond engagement ring — packaged, incidentally, in a box that contained a tiny, battery-powered spotlight to illuminate its contents — and the two are now planning a wedding. For the time being, they will live in McNealy's modest, four-bedroom home in the Bay area.

"People blessed with abilities should use them to help the planet in any way they can. I have got to prove every day that I'm right about network computing and that I'm right about open interfaces. And that's got to stand the test of time.

"If anything," he insists intently, "I am a raging capitalist. I believe the solution to our social problems and our standard-of-living problems is a capitalist solution. If we ultimately convert the world to a network computing system, we will be able to do almost anything by computer. We could get rid of hundreds of thousands of unneeded government jobs and put those same people into jobs that would add to our quality of life. We could fundamentally make the world a stunning place to live."

Post Script: In April of 1995, Sun Microsystems posted an 87 percent increase in earnings, far exceeding even the most optimistic of Wall Street analysts' expectations. Scott McNealy announced that much of the growth was spurred by enterprise network computing, which is the replacement of mainframes and minicomputers with groups of smaller machines and by the increased popularity of the Internet since 56 percent of the Internet access servers now operating have been made by Sun.

"Things happen in life that you can't control
so it's best to do what your heart tells you to do
and not worry so much about the end result."

EMILIO ESTEFAN, JR.

**Creator of the Miami Sound Machine, President
and Founder of Crescent Moon Records**

midst the sponge-painted walls, potted palms, and art
deco mirrors in the restaurant of Miami's Cardoza Hotel,
Emilio Estefan, Jr. looks happy as a clam at high tide.
Outside, under lavender sidewalk umbrellas, Cuban
businessmen in summer suits and melon-breasted girls in low-
cut bikini tops are sipping cappucino. A few tanned young
parents are spooning Catalonian vanilla custard and tropical
flavored sorbets into their toddlers' mouths on the hotel's ve-
randa. Obviating the hypnotically turning fans suspended
from the restaurant's high ceilings, a gentle breeze blows in off
the Atlantic and stirs the palm trees along Ocean Drive. The
voice of Emilio's wife, singer Gloria Estefan, is piped through
the restaurant's sound system, and the sultry Latin sound
seems the perfect accompaniment to the view of powder-blue
sky, aqua water, and the neon-lit strip of birthday cake-colored
restaurants, hotels, and bars that parallel the beach.

Emilio has every reason to look happy. The restaurant,
Allioli, is running smoothly, and he and Gloria own it, along
with the Cardoza Hotel and Lario's on the Beach, a trendy
Cuban-American cafe a few blocks down the Drive. His recent
real estate ventures in the newly gentrified South Beach art deco
district are proving as successful as his career as a percus-
sionist, songwriter, and record producer. He recently concluded
a multi-million-dollar distribution deal with Sony Music Entertainment for his own recording company, Crescent Moon

Records, and his lifelong dream of reinventing the way Latin music is heard in the United States is being fulfilled.

Add the fact that Gloria, his wife of fifteen years, will give birth to the Estefans' long-awaited second child any day now, and you've got one happy camper. As if suggesting a comparably good reason for his contentment, he tells a pair of journalists who are lunching with him that this same morning, while he was driving his wife to the doctor for a routine prenatal check-up, the couple saw an injured pelican along the side of the highway. They pulled the car onto the shoulder of the road, wrapped the limp bird in a towel, and brought it to the local animal hospital to mend. "I think we saved it," he says, his concern evident.

Talking to Emilio Estefan makes you smile. Maybe it's the Cuban accent that still causes him to roll his r's and confuse his prepositions after 25 years in the United States. "I always tell people my favorite show is CNN," he jokes, offering no explanation why such a smart guy can't perfect his English. "I can understand it because I get to see and hear everything at least twice." Or maybe it's the incongruous mix of hip sophistication — the close-clipped, graying goatee, the expensive linen shirt and alligator shoes, the silver hoops piercing both ears — and boyish enthusiasm. In part, the pleasure comes from discovering that a 41-year-old entrepreneur whose net worth has been estimated by *Hispanic Business* magazine at about $40 million, who is a world-famous producer of two Grammy Award-winning records, the husband and manager of megastar Gloria Estefan, and pal to the likes of Sylvester Stallone and Madonna, is such a nice and regular guy. Notwithstanding his celebrity status and distinctly Cuban roots, Emilio Estefan, Jr. is very much the boy next door.

"It's the immigrant mentality," he offers as explanation. "We lost everything when we came to this country from Cuba, and you're always afraid you're going to lose everything again. It gives you a very different view of life. I don't take things seriously. I believe that no matter how much you have, something can always happen to take it all away."

In fact, Estefan has had his share of disasters. In 1990, while he, Gloria and their nine-year-old son were touring the country with their band, their tour bus collided with a tractor-trailer on a snowy mountain road just outside of Scranton, Pennsylvania. The accident left Gloria with a fractured spine, and surgery to implant two permanent steel rods eight inches long beside her spinal column proved necessary. Doctors warned that the 32-year-old singer would require months of exercise and physical therapy to return to the stage.

"The first six months were unbelievably hard," he recalls, his face mirroring the pain of that experience. "We were doing so well. The day before, we had performed in the White House; our records were successful all over the world; our tour was sold out. Gloria kept saying that she felt something was going to go wrong, and I said, 'Don't be ridiculous.' It took us both a long time to recover. I didn't leave the house for almost a year. My hair and beard turned completely gray in a few weeks . . . I still remember the day Gloria came home from the hospital. We have a staircase in our house that we used to love to race up together. When I first brought her into the house in the wheelchair and we reached the stairs, I thought we would both fall apart."

Battling unbelievable odds, Gloria maintained a rigorous exercise schedule and fully recovered within the year. "We received thousands of letters and became a kind of inspiration for people," Estefan continued. "But my attitude completely changed after that. Things happen in life that you can't control, so it's best to do what your heart tells you to do and not worry so much about the end result."

This was not Estefan's first encounter with loss. Growing up in Santiago de Cuba in the early 1950's, he and his family enjoyed considerable wealth, thanks to his father's success in the men's underwear business. "In his early days, my father was a famous poker player and made a lot of money," Estefan recounts, recalling his father's high-rolling spirit and adding that Estefan, Sr., now in his eighties, still indulges in his favorite card game in Miami and likes to come around the office to flirt with his son's female employees and bring gifts of perfume. "He used to play the lottery and won it 27 times! But he always gave the money away. He always used to say that all that really mattered was good health. He taught me that if you don't have a penny but you are happy, then you are the richest man in the world . . . He finally went into business in Cuba by inventing a new style of men's boxer shorts with a little pocket in the waistband. He started a company and was very successful. We weren't millionaires, but we had a house with four servants, and we lived very well."

In 1966, under Castro's regime, the government took it all away. The family was left virtually penniless. "When I was eleven or twelve, I told my parents that I must leave Cuba," he continued. "According to the laws at the time, when I turned fourteen, I would be drafted into the Cuban army and would be forced to stay in Cuba until I was 35 . . . I was very mature for my age. I had seen so many things happen under the Communists. My father's sister was put in jail for speaking against the government, and I didn't want to be trapped in Cuba for the rest of my life. I told my parents I could take care of myself. I had to leave."

Emilio's older brother, Jose, was already of draft age and was forced to stay in Cuba with his mother while young Emilio and his father moved to Madrid, Spain. "We spent a year and a half on the streets," he says. "We couldn't get work because we weren't residents, and we were virtually penniless. We had little food and got all of our clothes from Freedom House, a local shelter that distributed used clothing. Fortunately, my parents had bought me an accordion a few years before, and I brought it with me when I left home. I used to play accordion in the local restaurants for tips, and that money paid for our stay in a small pensione."

When Emilio turned fifteen, relatives in Miami arranged a student visa for him and purchased airline tickets for him and his father to fly to Miami. They moved in with his father's other sister, Javivi, who had come to Miami to escape Castro's rule and rented an apartment for herself and six of her nieces and nephews. Not knowing a word of English, Emilio moved in with his cousins and enrolled in Kinlock Park Junior High School in Miami.

"I learned English quickly enough, but I wasn't really interested in school," Estefan continues. "I was always thinking about business, about how to make enough money to bring the rest of my family over to the States." Once again, he supported himself by playing the accordion in local restaurants for tips. When he turned seventeen and became a student at Miami High School, he lied about his age and took a job as a mail boy for the Bacardi Rum Company. "I used to go to Bacardi at seven in the morning," he recalls. "I'd work all day, and then I used to go to school, to finish my night school. Then I used to go to an Italian restaurant every night till twelve or one in the morning to play for tips."

His first big break came soon after that. "One of the Bacardis asked me to play the accordion at a party for a member of the family's 50th wedding anniversary. I brought a conga player along, and we were a big success." He earned $300 for the night's work and made enough contacts with the Bacardis' family and friends to start his own band to play at local Cuban weddings and bar mitzvahs. "These people really liked to throw a party," he adds. "I would usually get paid $120 or so per night for the band. I would get $30 or $40 to play percussion and the accordion and lead the band, but whenever I got paid a little more, I hired another musician instead of pocketing the money. I always believed in quality."

By 1972, Estefan was earning enough money to bring his mother to Miami. (His brother remained in Cuba until Emilio returned there in 1980, during the Mariel boat lift. He worked as an engineer for Emilio for a time before going out on his own.) Estefan and his parents moved into their own apartment. The family used what little savings they had to buy a clothing factory in Little Havana and began subcontracting any piecework they could find. "That's when my second break came," he continues. "One of the Bacardis was doing a Bacardi rum cake promotion and they needed an order of satin banners for their hostesses to wear. I went over to the local funeral parlor and bought up all the sashes that came off the funeral bouquets for very cheap. Then I glittered the Bacardi name on them and sold them to the company for less than half the price they were willing to pay another company.

"After that, I got a job making Bacardi T-shirts. Few people knew about iron-on labels at the time; all of my competitors were charging a fortune to hand-block the colors. Our factory was able to make the shirts very inexpensively, and we sold thousands of them for about 70 cents per shirt. My mom managed the factory, my dad worked there, and we began doing very well."

By 1975, Estefan enrolled in Miami Dade Community College, and his band, the Miami Latin Boys, was bringing the Latin beat to the most stylish Cuban parties in town. "I wanted to study music in college," Estefan says, "but I couldn't really afford it, so I got my degree in business and communications. As far as music goes, I've never really gotten the chance to study it. I've been nominated six times for Grammys, won two, and I play by ear! I don't even know how to read music! As for my business education, well, I think you learn more about how to run a business from instinct and experience anyway. I can't say I ever really had a mentor or someone who taught me how to make a living. I never go by the book, but school did give me the basics and helped me to get organized."

After school, Estefan continued to work at Bacardi as well as in the family's factory and on the wedding and bar mitzvah circuit with the Miami Latin Boys. One evening, while playing percussion with his band at a local wedding, he bumped into Gloria Fajardo, a high school student he had heard singing with a church band several months before. "I asked her to come up and sing a song. The rest of the band didn't want to accompany her because they hadn't rehearsed so I played the piano, and she sang "Tu Me Acostumbraste", a really beautiful ballad. I loved her voice right away, and I had been wanting to add girls to the band. I told her to come join us."

It took several weeks before Gloria agreed to come to rehearsals and even then, Estefan recalls, she always came accompanied by a chaperone. "She emigrated from Cuba when she was very young. Her family was very poor when they settled in America and she had a lot of problems. Her father was captured in the Bay of Pigs [invasion]; then he went to Vietnam as an American soldier. When her dad came back from Vietnam, he developed multiple sclerosis so her mother had it real hard. Gloria spent years nursing her father while her mother was out working to support the family. She was very naive, and I worried about her. I told her that we were serious people — no drugs, no alcohol."

By 1976, the Miami Latin Boys weren't just boys anymore. Emilio's band became the Miami Sound Machine, featuring two female singers — Gloria and her cousin, Merci. In addition to singing with the band, Gloria worked as an interpreter at Miami International Airport and finished a degree in psychology at the University of Miami. For years, the two had a relationship that was strictly business. "I have to really know someone before I fall in love," Emilio says with credible earnestness. "It was her eyes that attracted me, but her sweetness that really won me over." Three years later, in his parent's apartment, Emilio proposed, and Gloria Fajardo became Gloria Estefan. To this day, their marriage is the stuff of romantic legend, particularly in a business well-publicized for its ephemeral relationships and high divorce rate.

From the time the Miami Sound Machine was created, the Estefans worked to bring their Latin sound — which Emilio is fond of describing as "*arroz con frijoles y hamburgesa*," or "rice and beans and hamburger" — into the mainstream. Both he and Gloria had spent their teen years listening to bands like the Bee Gees and KC and the Sunshine Band, and the Miami Sound Machine's performances always offered an amalgam of Cuban standards and American pop favorites.

"From the time I first introduced the band to the American market, I didn't want us to be introduced as Americans," Emilio explains. "I wanted to introduce us with the conga and the timbales and the bongos. That's how we were born in Cuba, that's part of our culture. Some people called me crazy. But my idea was that if we succeeded, I wanted people to know where I came from."

Estefan approached record companies all over the country but found no one who was interested in producing their sound. Instead, he and Gloria produced their first record *Renacer* themselves for $2,000 on the now-defunct Electric Cat label in Hialeah, Florida. "We never saw a penny from that record," he recalls. A year later, they produced a second album, which was very well-received in the Latin American market.

Gloria and Emilio's first child, Najib, was born in 1980. Although Emilio had worked his way up to a $100,000-a-year salary as Hispanic marketing director for Bacardi by that time, he decided to quit and devote himself full-time to the Miami Sound Machine. "Bacardi told me I could come back if the music didn't work out," he says with a laugh, adding that his relationship with the Bacardi family is still strong. In fact, the company was an $18-million sponsor of Gloria's last tour.

The relative success of their second album led the Miami-based Discos CBS International (which ultimately became Sony Disco) to offer the band a contract. "We told them we wanted to do everything bilingual," Estefan says. But the music company was not as optimistic about the success of the Latin sound, and the group's first four albums were all Spanish-language releases. "We were an instant success all over Latin America, but I was determined to bring the sound here to the United States."

In 1984, Sony finally agreed to release their English-language single "Dr. Beat" as the B-side of a Spanish song. Emilio himself visited every disco in South Florida with a free copy of the single in hand, and the song became a hit, soon traveling to Europe, where it was number one on the pop charts. Sony sold the rights to Epic Records, which picked up their next two albums for American distribution, and the new Miami sound was born.

"We were big all over Europe," recalls Estefan. "Gloria suggested we add some congas and go even more Latin. We wrote more songs and before long, we were playing to sold-out crowds — first in England and the Netherlands, and then as far away as China and Japan. The interest in Latin music began growing in the United States, too, largely because of our cross-over sound, and before long, our records were selling gold and platinum."

In 1991, the Miami Sound Machine disbanded and Gloria Estefan began earning new accolades as a solo artist. Her album *Mi tierra*, a collection of traditional Cuban songs, won a Grammy award in 1993, and husband Emilio was nominated for a grammy for producing it. *Mi tierra* became the biggest-selling Latin album ever in the United States and has sold more than 5 million copies worldwide. The success of this album was followed in 1994 by *Hold Me, Thrill Me, Kiss Me*, a collection of American pop classics. The album went gold, selling 500,000 copies before it was even released, and Gloria's $38.5 million gross from these recent recordings has made her the highest paid female Latin singer in the world.

In January of 1994, Thomas Mottola, the president and COO of Sony Music Entertainment, offered Estefan a deal he couldn't refuse. Estefan would earn a seven-figure salary as president of artist and talent development for Sony and be free to produce and publish the artists of his own choosing on his own Crescent Moon Records. The music would then be distributed by Epic Records.

"Tommy had been trying to offer me a position at Sony for a long time," Estefan reflects. "I kept telling him I didn't want to do it because I wanted to be free to do the kind of music I wanted to do. Then he called and offered me total control."

Estefan arranged for Crescent Moon to handle production and publishing in his own office on Bird Road, just west of Coral Gables, Florida. This meant that he would be able to pick all of the talent that goes into making a record. As a result, singers could occasionally double as songwriters for other performers and background vocalists could be featured on their own records. Most of the time, Estefan has complete ownership of song rights. This is important, because each time a song is played on the radio, a royalty fee is split equally between the songwriter and the owner of the song's publishing rights. If Estefan owns the rights to each song recorded on his label, the royalties go back into his own company. And if he also happens to have written the song, he gets 100 percent of the royalty fees.

"I would not make a deal with someone who is going to sell 500,000 units worldwide if I do not own the publishing rights," he has told the press. "We don't make money on the live performance . . . That's why we're so lucky — because we write every song we publish."

Plans are now on track to move Crescent Moon Records to a larger warehouse space in the South Beach area, near Estefan's other real estate holdings. Estefan Enterprises comprises a 300-employee company that includes the Estefans' real estate holdings, Crescent Moon Records, and Foreign Imported Productions and Publishing, which owns the rights to most songs sung by Gloria, recording star Jon Secada, and some 29 other singers and songwriters. The studio, widely considered a world-class facility, has attracted the likes of Whitney Houston, Bette Midler, Pink Floyd, and even Frank Sinatra to take advantage of its technology.

"What we want to do is take Latin music to the next level," Estefan recently said in an interview with *New Times,* a local Miami publication. "For years, [albums by] Latin people have been given small budgets because sales have never been what they should be with such a great flavor of musicians in our culture. But they've never been able to record the way we're recording now, with 80 channels digital. When you listen to a Latin album, I want it to have the same sound as when you listen to Michael Jackson."

Although he has been likened to music producer Berry Gordy — for doing for Latin music what Gordy did for the Motown sound — Estefan does not want to limit Crescent

Moon artists to Latin musicians only. This past year, he produced the sound track for *The Specialist,* an action film set in
Miami and starring Sylvester Stallone and Sharon Stone. The
company has also signed on a number of rhythm and blues
artists and an eclectic group of singers that includes La Gaylia,
an African-American singer of pop ballads, Albita Rodriguez,
a Cuban-born torch singer, Roberto Blades, who performs
Spanish rock, and Donna Allen, a funk rock/rhythm and blues
singer.

"We literally get thousands of tapes every day, but I don't
generally listen to them," Estefan says, adding that because he
and Gloria write songs themselves, if any of their songs were
to sound like the tapes they have been sent, they would be
opening themselves up to lawsuits from the prospective artists.
"I prefer to go and see people live and sign them on if I like
them. When I decide to do an album, I don't do it just because
I think it will sell. I have to do what comes from my heart. I
am determined to do something for the Cuban community in
Miami . . . I also want to keep the operation relatively small.
I'm a perfectionist and this way I can stay close to what's
happening in the company . . . And if I put out a record that I
believe in and it fails, I don't really care. I would just go back
to playing the accordion and that would be all right with me."

Despite her extraordinary success in recent years, most
major newspaper and magazine interviews describe Gloria as
"a regular gal" who disdains expensive jewelry and prefers to
wear T-shirts and jogging pants rather than the tight satin
evening gowns that give her a femme fatale look on her album
covers. And although Emilio likes expensive clothing and cars
(he drives a Range Rover and the couple own a Rolls Royce and
a Lexus) he seems perfectly at home jogging or riding his bike
along Ocean Drive at six a.m. every morning.

He says he thinks of Estefan Enterprises as a "very family-
oriented thing," although "Gloria never gets involved in the
business. She hates business. This is my company, but she and
I talk about it all the time . . . Most of the people working here
have been here for ten years or more. The woman who heads

our publishing company started out selling T-shirts for us; Gloria's best friend from ninth grade, Patty Escoto, is my assistant; and my cousin runs the production facilities on Bird Road... When I hire somebody, I don't look at whether they went to a great school or whether they worked for a lot of big companies. I look for good will. I believe if you have good will and you have initiative, you can learn anything. I give my people a lot of responsibility and they can go pretty far.

"As for myself... well, I always try to do things better. I get bored, but the problem is that my mind is faster than what I can actually do. Like this hotel. Ten years ago, Gloria was bugging me to buy some land down on the beach. I thought she was crazy. Then I came down here and took a look and began buying and buying. We own a lot of property along the beach, which we haven't even developed yet. First we opened Lario's, then the Cardoza Hotel. But it's two years since we opened the hotel and the last room is just getting finished. Things take time. I wake up every morning around six o'clock, and while I'm riding my bike I think about what I can do that day that will make me feel good. It doesn't have to be a big thing, but I try to accomplish something every day."

With an innocence that seems almost incredible considering how far he's come and how much he's seen, Estefan sees himself as the living embodiment of the American dream. He and Gloria are very active in the Miami business community and are known for their local charity work. "I will never leave Miami," he insists. "Miami has been great to us. You feel the energy when you come here. I've been all over the world many times, and when I come back to Miami I feel the energy."

After Hurricane Andrew devastated the city in 1993, the couple organized a superstars' hurricane relief concert that raised $3.5 million for programs to rebuild the city. This past year, the two masterminded a gathering of over 20,000 Cuban-Americans at Miami's Orange Bowl Stadium to pray for a free Cuba. The couple have also donated millions to the United Way over the years. "We do a lot of charity work that most people will never hear about," adds Estefan. "The other day, for instance, I found $16,000 worth of American Express bills for a New York hotel. When I asked Gloria about it, she told me that she brought some people to New York who needed a kind of back surgery that they couldn't get anywhere else."

Estefan says that although he was raised a Catholic, he has no particular religious affiliation anymore. He firmly believes, however, that there is a God that takes care of everyone. "Everything happens for a reason. We've been through some very hard times, but we've managed to stay on top. That's something I want to teach other people. If there's one piece of advice I can offer, it's 'Be persistent and don't let anybody tell you that you can't do something. If you believe in something, do it with all your heart and things will work out.'

"When God has been good to you, you've got to give back. There's nothing better in life than being able to help people. If you are able to minimize someone else's pain, then you must do it. I believe we're on this earth for two reasons," he says, leaning back in his chair and surveying the busy restaurant scene he has created. "One reason is to improve ourselves. The other is do something for other people."

Estefan is quite clearly doing both. The couple share a beautiful home with their son and five Dalmatians on exclusive Star Island in the Bay of Biscayne, just off Miami Beach, and Estefan Enterprises continues to grow. After the newest Estefan settles into the family (they are expecting a girl, whom they plan to call Emily), Emilio will be producing the half-time show for the 1995 Super bowl and is planning a world tour for Gloria for the following year. His dream now, he says, is to enjoy his family — all three generations of them. In recent months, he has begun construction on Star Island. He has just bought a home to the north of his house which he is making into what he calls "a kind of country club" for his family, complete with theatre, gym, and thatched roof *bohio* shack by the pool. "I want to build a new house for my mother on Star Island so that she and my dad can be near their grandchildren," he adds. "My mother lived her whole life for me and my brother, and I love to make her happy now. Besides, I've already built her one home, so she's getting very good at talking about construction. She knows exactly what she wants."

Like mother, like son.

"In order to make it, you have to be extremely naive and have a lot of self-confidence and not worry about the competition. You've got to just do it. So long as you have more winners than losers, you'll be okay in the long run."

EDWARD GARDNER

**Founder and Chairman of Soft Sheen Products Inc.,
makers of hair-care products for African-Americans**

W hen Edward Gardner told his friends that he was giving up the steady job he had held for thirteen years to support his wife and kids by pursuing an uncertain future in a new business, they all thought he had lost his mind.

That was 30 years ago. Today Gardner, his wife Bettiann and their four children own and operate Soft Sheen Products, the ninth-largest black-owned business in America.

"Taking risks is part of what it means to be an entrepreneur," says Gardner. "In order to make it, you have to be extremely naive and have a lot of self-confidence and not worry about the competition. You've got to just do it. So long as you have more winners than losers, you'll be okay in the long run."

As he speaks, Gardner's warm brown eyes are glistening almost as brightly as the large diamond ring that he sports on his left hand. Dressed in a conservatively cut dark blue suit, white shirt, and muted tie, the 69-year-old chairman of the board has the warm smile of a favorite uncle and the soft-spoken diction of a born politician. His modest demeanor and his gentle manners notwithstanding, Gardner maintains that he owes his success to his willingness to be a high-rolling, assertive risk-taker.

In fact, risk-taking has been very good to Mr. Gardner. In 1994, Soft Sheen's sales topped $96 million, making it the largest ethnic hair products company in the world. Care Free Curl, a perm designed specifically to wave African-American hair, and Optimum Care, a shampoo, conditioner, and hair spray line specifically formulated for black women, are only a few of the more popular products distributed throughout the United States, Canada, the United Kingdom, the Caribbean, Europe, and, most recently, South Africa. What's more, Gardner has parlayed his success into a number of other ventures, including his own entertainment company, called Lady Roll productions, the renovation and management of a landmark 2,500-seat Gothic Revival style theatre on his native Chicago's south side, ownership of the several blocks of prime local real estate that contain Soft Sheen's manufacturing and distribution facilities, and a share of the Chicago Bulls basketball team.

"Let's face it," says Gardner, clearly at home in his office, amidst such treasured objects as a group of African ebony sculptures, autographed photographs of himself shaking hands with President Bill Clinton and First Lady Hillary, several outsized examples of his work as an amateur photographer, and a photograph of his hero, Martin Luther King, Jr. purchased at auction. "How many people with two degrees, including a master's in education, would give up an assistant principal's job to walk the most dangerous streets of Chicago in dirty clothes, just to carry around a cardboard box full of hair supplies to local black beauty parlors?"

That was back in 1963, when Gardner worked as an assistant principal at an elementary school in the Robert Taylor housing project on Chicago's south side. "Working with these youngsters was very rewarding," recalls Gardner. "The projects were not so dangerous back then. Many of the mothers, most of them single parents, were very poor, but they would get very involved with their kids' educations . . . I had gotten my undergraduate degree from Chicago Teachers College and had gone on to the University of Chicago at night and in the summers to complete my master's degree in education. I began working as an eighth grade teacher at a different project on the south side in 1951 and realized I could be more effective as an assistant principal. When my principal moved to Robert Taylor, I followed him there. I enjoyed working with the teachers. We created a lot of good programs to help these kids get ahead, and many of them grew up to be professionals."

But the work was hard, and the salary — $10,000 a year — was barely enough to support a family of six. "I knew we needed more money, so I took a job after school," continues Gardner. "It really could have been anything, but I had gotten a job working for a beauty products company one summer and it seemed as good a business as any. So I contacted various beauty supply companies and purchased all kinds of products — combs, brushes, pomades, dyes, and so on.

"I would go home after school, have an early supper and then, every night, in the heat of summer and during the freezing winters, I would carry a cardboard box filled with these supplies and sell them to all the beauty shops along the major thoroughfares of Chicago's black communities." By eight or nine o'clock at night, the streets were dangerous, and Gardner chose his tattered clothing carefully so as not to look like an easy mark for muggers or youth gangs. Fortunately, the beauticians liked his articulate conversation, his prompt filling of their orders, and, most of all, his willingness to accept delayed payments from time to time.

"I really got my first education in business walking those streets," explains Gardner, who grew up on 91st Street and Michigan Avenue, the rural outskirts of Chicago in the 1940s. "My parents were a real inspiration to me. My father made $19 a week as a laborer for a carpet company. He had only a grammar school education, but he managed to save enough to buy his family a nice home with a front lawn. Both he and my mother were very devoted to my brother Frank and me. They gave us a whippin' when we were bad and tried hard to raise us with discipline. In fact, both my brother and I ultimately became teachers. Frank still is.

"We were enrolled in Finger High School — two of only a handful of black kids in an otherwise all-white school —

because they wanted us to get a good education. I was a small, skinny kid with a stutter, but it never got in my way. I was a decent enough student, and I got along with most of the white kids I went to school with. There was very little racial tension. It was important to my parents that we get along in the community."

After high school, he was drafted into the armed forces, serving in Asia and New Guinea during World War II. It was in the army that Gardner had his first experiences with racism. He recalls many instances of white soldiers taunting the members of his all-black division with racial epithets. From that time on, he became committed to finding a way to help members of the black community. When he returned home, he enrolled in Chicago Teachers College on the G.I. Bill.

"I liked the idea of working with young black kids, and I was a good teacher," he reflects. "But I had business blood in me, and I wanted to see where it would take me. I had absolutely no business training. No courses. No advice. No nothing. I did everything myself."

By 1964, just a year after he had begun working nights to sell hair products, he was making as much money in the beauty business as he was as an assistant principal.

"I began to think of ways to develop the business," he said. "I started buying products directly from the manufacturers to save costs. Then I decided to quit working in the school system and took the $10,000 I had earned in pension money and started making the products myself. In fact, it wasn't that difficult a decision. The future was uncertain, but I already knew I could make money."

In 1965, he and Bettiann rented a small room in a building in suburban South Chicago and began experimenting with a product Gardner invented and called "Soft Sheen Hair and Scalp Conditioner."

"The working conditions were incredible," recalls Gardner. "Our room had no lights, no water, not even a bathroom. I bought some petroleum, some wax, and some color and began mixing. I bought some jars, designed a label, offset it and glued it on, and started carting it around . . . I still remember the first time I brought it to Mrs. P. D. Morse's beauty shop. I told Mrs. Morse: 'I got a new product from one of my distributors. Let me know how you like it.' The next day, I came back and Mrs. Morse told me, 'Mr. Gardner. I don't know where you found that product, but never buy it again.' " Undaunted, Gardner began remixing his chemical combinations until Mrs. Morse said, "You've got it just right." And the rest is Soft Sheen history.

Every weekend, the Gardners and their four children, Gary, Terri, Guy, and Tracy, who ranged in age from seven to two, began working at the room the kids called "the place," manufacturing, bottling, and labeling Soft Sheen Hair and Scalp Conditioner all by themselves. It would be several years before the family could afford to hire help.

"By the end of 1965, I decided we had to hit the drug store market," continues Gardner. "So I took a couple of jars to Walgreen's. I think they realized there was a growing market in ethnic hair care products so they put in an order for 24 dozen jars. Boy, that was exciting. Of course, we didn't even *have* 24 dozen jars, but you can believe we made them up real quick.

"In the meantime, we began developing new products based on advice from our chemical suppliers and the beauticians [we sold to]. Our beauticians told us they didn't like our tall bottles because they couldn't reach the bottom of the jars with their fingers, so we changed to a jar that was more squat. Then we decided to get rid of our paper labels and bake them right onto the jar.

"We did some market studies and learned that black women traditionally spend as much as five times the amount of money on hair care products that white women do, and we began creating more variety in our shampoos and conditioners."

By the late 1960s, the Gardners had hired a few people to help manufacture their formulations and moved to a new storefront factory on 71st Street in South Chicago. The death of Martin Luther King, Jr. in 1968 played a strong role in the direction the company was to take in the years that followed. "Reverend King used to make speeches about the need to open more doors for black people, and we felt we should build a business that would help support his beliefs," explains Gardner. "He really inspired me to help other blacks succeed in business, and we actually went into business with the goal of supplying more jobs to the black community. My wife was totally behind me . . . er, she wouldn't like that I said *behind* me. That is, she worked very closely with me to try and fulfill this goal."

Throughout the 1970s, the couple managed to obtain a series of loans, many of them from government-sponsored programs for minority businesses, which supported the growth of Soft Sheen into a company of over 600 employees. They also moved into the buildings they currently own on both sides of East 87th Street, a heavily trafficked Chicago where the prominence of their location, says Gardner, "reminds everyone who drives by how successful a black-owned company can be."

"By the mid-eighties we were a one- to two-million dollar company, but we were ready to take on the giants," adds Gardner. Anticipating the popularity of the soft curl look among African American women, Gardner directed his newly hired researchers and chemists to come up with a product that could condition frizzy African-American hair into the silky curls traditionally worn by white women.

"There was a man out in California selling a similar product, and I just knew we could do it better," recounts Gardner. "Most of the other ethnic hair care products companies, like John Johnson's Fashion Fair Cosmetics, a multi-million dollar enterprise, took a pass on the product. They just didn't see it coming. We came up with Care Free Curl, and it sold like crazy. We had a huge boom in business and hired as many as 800 employees to help distribute it around the world."

Success couldn't have struck at a better time. "I was actually getting bored," says Gardner. "I felt I had exhausted my marketing skills, my artistic skills, and my ability to find and select the best people, and I wasn't sure whether we would be able to go any further. And then, just when I thought I had reached a low point, my kids saved the day."

In fact, while Soft Sheen was growing in size and profitability, Gardner's son Gary attended the University of Illinois and then Northwestern to obtain a combined MBA and law degree, Terri went to the University of Illinois and got a degree in photography, Guy attended the Illinois Institute of Technology and got a degree in engineering, and Tracy received an undergraduate degree in chemical engineering from Northwestern and an MBA from the University of Chicago. Through the years, they all fondly remembered their childhood weekends at "the place."

"We never formally asked them to join the company," says Gardner. "But they simply grew up with it. They remember buying the machines with me, making the formulations, designing the labels, and everything else that had to do with the company. It was part of their lives." Gary eventually became president of the company and took charge of the overall running of Soft Sheen, Terri naturally fell into the role of vice president of marketing in charge of Soft Sheen's advertising campaigns, Tracy took over the financial holdings of the company and charts future growth and development, and Guy became executive vice president of manufacturing and president and operations manager of Bottlewerks Inc., a full-service packing operation specializing in the bottling and silk-screening of all Soft Sheen Products.

"I always gave them a lot of responsibility," says Gardner. "I wasn't only teaching them about the company, but raising them to be good people as well. That meant letting them make mistakes so that they would learn and grow . . . My wife always tells me I tell the kids what to do, but I never tell them how to do it. Well, that's intentional."

The same goes for his employees. "I look for people who have the ingredients that make for success in business. They have to be tough [and] competitive and know when to push. More than experience, they need to have the desire to succeed.

"We're a family-run business, and everyone in the company knows that. We have no unions, and we are privately held. It's important to us to retain control and use our money the way we choose, without worrying about whether we are making decisions that our shareholders won't like."

In particular, Gardner is referring to the many programs his company finances to help improve Chicago's black communities, such as the Program to Replace Black on Black Crime with Black on Black Love. The program arranges for speakers to visit local schools and jails and lecture about the ways in which individuals can help within their communities. Soft Sheen also sponsors the "Adopt-a-School" program, which provides financing for improved school feeding programs and guest lecturers who speak to students about positive community action.

"We take money from the black community and we believe in giving some of it back," says Gardner. "So many black Americans simply haven't had a chance to grow and succeed. I like to encourage, motivate, and finance members of the black community to get into jobs they might not ordinarily have the opportunity to pursue. We have a few dollars, and we are glad to contribute to making life better here in Chicago. We are fighting against black crime by lecturing in jails and by taking out full-page editorial advertisements in the city's newspapers, and we are fighting against corporations who refuse to allow their black employees to move ahead by offering better jobs within our own organization. Our goal is to try and create more opportunities for blacks to go further both educationally and professionally."

Although he is well past retirement age, Gardner does not seem to be slowing down. Co-chairman of the board of Soft Sheen, along with Bettiann, he is currently overseeing the production of new products, such as a line of women's hair coloring products and a men's cologne. He is very active in Lady Roll Productions, an entertainment company run entirely by community members and designed to evaluate and book black entertainers for live performances in Chicago's largest

black-owned theatre, the Regal, which Gardner recently renovated at a cost that exceeded $5 million. Though it is currently
the venue for 50 concerts a year and features live performances
by such world-class entertainers as Gladys Knight and the Eisley
Brothers, the Regal is still operating at a loss.

"We will need 100 concerts a year to break even," explains
Gardner, "but that's all part of taking risks. You have to know
when to turn things down and when to take a calculated risk.
We've lost money on this project, but there's plenty of time to
do the research and get it right." On the other hand, others of
Gardner's risks have been much more successful, such as his
choice to become one of the first blacks to be a part-owner of
a national basketball team. Gardner became a limited partner
of the Chicago Bulls in 1983, the same year that superstar
Michael Jordan joined the team.

When he's not doing business, Gardner tries to make time
for tennis, basketball, and taking photographs. Though he
claims he prefers to stay out of the limelight, he is a frequent
lecturer to graduate management students at Northwestern's
Kellogg School of Business and is a member of various local
business boards. In fact, he rarely thinks in terms of "spare
time," since he makes very little distinction between work and
pleasure.

"My wife asks me all the time, 'Why can't you just sit down
and relax?'" he says with a grin. "[But] I relax when I work. I
can't really sit around and do nothing. I like to go from one
challenge to the next. That's enjoyment for me and that's what
life is all about.

"Whenever you go into business, you should want to do
that thing more than anything else in the world. And if you've
got that passion and you can make a positive contribution to
society, then what else is there? I never think of it as work. I
just enjoy myself."

"The way I see it, I never ask God to move a mountain for me; I just ask him for the strength to climb it. All my life, I didn't let nothin' get in my way, and I still don't."

SYLVIA WOODS

**Founder of the world-famous
Sylvia's Restaurant in Manhattan**

"The way I see it, I never ask God to move a mountain for me; I just ask Him for the strength to climb it. All my life, I didn't let nothin' get in my way, and I still don't," says Sylvia Woods, describing the secret of her success. "My dad died when I was only four days old. I was raised by my mother and my grandmother, and I watched them work so hard to make a life for my sister and me. I vowed to do better to make them proud of me."

Over the past 30 years, Sylvia has done more than inspire her own family. She has parlayed a small counter top luncheonette into a multi-million dollar, family-owned and -operated New York restaurant in the heart of Harlem. Her home-style barbecued ribs, stewed chicken and dumplings, and smothered pork chops and collard greens, along with her new line of nationally distributed soul food products, have attracted patrons from all over the United States and as far away as Japan to Sylvia's Restaurant on Lenox Avenue and 127th Street and earned her the sobriquet, "the Queen of Soul Food."

Woods was born in her mother's two-bedroom farmhouse in rural Hemingway, South Carolina, in 1926. She spent much of her childhood planting and weeding tobacco and beans and watching her mother and grandmother work as midwives in the small towns that dotted the fertile landscape between the Black and Lynches rivers in the eastern part of the state.

"I used to sit at home watching them prepare birthing bed-pans," Sylvia reminisces, her smooth, expressive face, quick-silver smile, and expansive gestures making her seem much younger than her 68 years. Paying no heed to the employees whisking in and out of her office, she spreads several pages of newspaper over the checkbooks and papers cluttering her desk. "They looked just like this," she adds, curling the pages of the New York *Daily News* together at the edges to form an example of the crude paper trays that her grandmother would use to catch the blood shed by mothers in childbirth. "I said to myself, 'No way I'm going to be a midwife.'"

Thus, at fifteen, armed with little more than an eighth-grade education, Sylvia moved to 131st Street in Manhattan to share an apartment with her mother, who had traveled north and found a job in a local laundry to earn enough money to try and make a better life for Sylvia and her sister. "We were poor in South Carolina and we were poor in New York, but you don't miss what you don't have. I thought I had a good life in those first years in New York," Sylvia says.

During the 1940s and '50s, she traveled back and forth between New York to South Carolina and tried her hand running a small beauty shop in her hometown. Then, in 1944, she married her husband, Herbie. "We'll be married 50 years soon," Sylvia adds. "He's the same cute guy I met picking beans for 25 cents a crate in a patch in Hemingway when I was eleven years old and he was just twelve."

She and Herbie found an apartment of their own and Sylvia took a series of odd jobs, first in a silk-screening factory, then in a hat factory, and finally doing domestic work for wealthy white families on the East Side of Manhattan. Her pleasures were simple: a dress to wear for a night out at popular Harlem nightclubs like the Cotton Club or the Savoy, an evening spent telling stories by the fire or listening to radio broadcasts of Joe Louis's boxing matches, and finally, the births of the first three of her four children.

"Taking care of others came natural to me," she recalls. "I watched my grandmother go into the smokehouse on our farm in Hemingway and wrap up a bit of meat for the new mothers she had delivered, and I remember my mama tearing up our old bed sheets to sew little white cotton clothes for the new-born babies. I grew up watching the struggle of two widowed women who still made time to help their neighbors. I wanted to do the same, but I just had to do it better.

"It was also important to me that I pleased my mama. My grandmother always praised my mama and said, 'I got the best child in the world.' I wanted to make sure that my mama was just as proud of me as her mama was of her. Maybe that's because I never knew my daddy. I never even saw a picture of him. The only thing I had from him was a little white-covered Bible he gave my mama to give to me. But over the years, I have often felt that my daddy was lookin' out for me, sending me people who would look after me."

It was 1954 when Sylvia encountered the first of what she thinks of as her "guardian angels." In fact, rarely does she take any credit for the choices she has made or the confidences she has inspired, preferring instead to thank God or her father's spirit for sending her way people who would look out for her.

She applied for a job as a waitress at Johnson's Luncheon-ette, the restaurant that would ultimately become the original location of Sylvia's Restaurant. "I lied and told Mr. Johnson I had waitressing experience from back home," Sylvia says, shaking her head in disbelief. "Of course, he knew I was lying because there were no restaurants in Hemingway, South Caro-lina. But what he said was, 'Girl, you got a lot of nerve. I like that. You just listen to what I say and I'll make you the best waitress there ever was.'" It wasn't long before Sylvia was all but running the place.

Johnson, in need of cash to buy a restaurant and resort in upstate New York, asked Sylvia if she wanted to buy him out in 1967. "I thought, 'Me? Own a restaurant?' But Johnson saw something in me that I didn't even see in myself. I think he knew that nothing would stop me once I got goin'. When I told him I had no money, he told me, 'Borrow it! No one uses their own hard-earned cash. That's what loans are for.'

He convinced me to get my mama to mortgage our farm in Hemingway and between that and some cash Mama had hidden under the mattress, we came up with the down payment."

By August of the following year, Johnson's Luncheonette had become Sylvia's Restaurant, a simple diner with a steam table displaying the day's fare. The table, a counter top piled high with chicken, ribs, yams, and other home-cooked specialties, was a leftover from the early days of Johnson's luncheonette, when many of the patrons preferred to select their own food rather than stare at a menu they did not have the skills to read. The early 1960s, Sylvia recalls, were the leanest years. Her oldest son Van went off to college, but her two younger children were still home and in need of after-school care, and Sylvia was pregnant again.

These were not the best of times for many in that neighborhood. In the 1960s Harlem was a hotbed of drug abuse. Heroin addicts had made Lenox Avenue their home, and Sylvia's corner became a convenient hang-out for strung-out locals who spent their time getting high, dealing drugs, and frightening Sylvia and many of her regular customers. "I remember thinking we would go under," says Sylvia of the long hours she worked, taking only waitress tips for salary. "Herbie was driving a taxi to help support the five of us. Every day we had another leak in our roof, and I remember thinking, 'I just can't go under. I won't.' When the knocks get harder, I just get tougher and keep movin.'"

In 1967, Sylvia decided to escape the dripping water that mysteriously collected on her ceiling every day at noon and move her restaurant a couple of doors down Lenox Avenue, away from the increasingly dangerous corner of 127th Street. "Our landlord was a very nice man. He got me a lawyer and found some friends to lend me money at only a few pennies above the bank's interest rate. We borrowed $65,000, bought two buildings, and expanded . . . Maybe some people would consider me foolish, but I simply trusted him. I looked at that landlord like I look at myself and believed he wouldn't cheat me . . . And he got me a good deal. That's been a theme in my life. There are people who have looked after me."

Sylvia's next guardian angel came in the form of a woman. In 1979, Gael Greene, the restaurant critic for *New York*, came in for a sampling of Sylvia's home-cooked chicken and ribs and wrote the review that changed Sylvia's forever. Until she met Greene, Sylvia was unaware of the power of New York's restaurant reviewers — the small, influential band of newspaper and magazine writers whose carefully chosen words can make or break a restaurant virtually overnight. The review in *New York* was particularly important since the magazine's well-heeled readers like to spend their disposable income on new and interesting night spots.

"This white woman came in askin' a lot of questions and wantin' to see my kitchen," explains Sylvia. "I remember feeling embarrassed that such a fine, well-dressed lady would want to come into my dinky little restaurant. But I showed her around. There wasn't much to see — just a linoleum floor, a Formica counter, and some red plastic bar stools. The next week, out came an article called 'Uptown Saturday Night.' Gael Greene put Sylvia's on the map with that article. Suddenly the locals that had been sitting at our counter for years were joined by white folks from all over the city."

And the rest is pretty much history. In the years that followed Greene's review, just about every major New York newspaper and magazine as well as countless international publications wrote features about Sylvia's Restaurant. "I remember one old, retired black man who came to see us," Sylvia added. "He said, 'I'm mad as hell, Sylvia. For so many years I've lived up here and I never heard of you. I had to see your write-up in *New York* while I was in my dentist's waiting room. I'm gonna make sure you get written up — not just by the white magazines, but by the black papers, too.' And he sent a bunch of the black newspaper writers to see us."

Celebrities such as film director Spike Lee, singer Janet Jackson, the Reverend Jesse Jackson, baseball player Darryl Strawberry, and boxer Mike Tyson stopped by to get a look at the restaurant Sylvia promised would "taste like home and sound like heaven," and the word kept spreading. "I wanted the restaurant to be a place where everyone would feel at home.

The food would taste like what people ate at home and the environment would be peaceful, calm and serene — just like heaven. And it worked."

Next, a number of tourist organizations approached Sylvia to design a special meal for inclusion in their tour packages. What began as the occasional visit by ten or fifteen Europeans quickly became family-style meals for groups of 200. Busses filled with travelers from as far away as Japan filled the modest space with hungry patrons, anxious for a taste of Sylvia's "world famous, talked-about barbecue ribs special," as well as her oxtail, pork chitterlings, southern fried chicken, candied yams, cow peas and rice, and other recipes originally cooked by Sylvia and now prepared under the guidance of her head chef, South Carolina-born Ruth Gulley.

"All my recipes came with me from South Carolina," insists Sylvia. "My mother taught me to cook when I was eight and I use some of those same simple recipes without too many trimmings. Ruth has been with us for 20 years and she has kept the spirit of my original recipes. The only changes we've made over the years were done to please the more health-conscious, like reducing the amount of pork fat."

As business boomed in the 1980s, Sylvia bought three more buildings on Lenox Avenue between 126th and 127th Street, adding two simply furnished dining rooms and a larger catering hall. She also established such regular events as a Sunday Gospel Brunch. Pretty soon, the Woods family owned the entire block, with the exception of the church on the corner. With the fast expansion, son Kenneth and daughters Bedelia and Trinez pitched in full-time to help Sylvia, Herbie, and Van run the business. "It was my son Van's idea to expand," says Sylvia. "And I felt, why not keep movin'?"

Indeed, it was this thinking that led, in 1992, to the creation of Sylvia's Food Products, Inc. With her new venture, Sylvia has opened a food plant in New Jersey and is distributing a variety of African-American seasonings, sauces, cereals, and food mixes to supermarkets and gourmet food shops across America. Plans are currently underway to expand distribution to Japan.

The business is still run by Sylvia and her husband, their children, and grandchildren. Although her mother died in 1987, she was able to enjoy much of her daughter's success. And the whole family still goes down to the farm in Hemingway in the summer and on holidays. "I don't think of myself as a boss," says Sylvia. "To me, the word 'boss' still reminds me of my youth. The white man was 'the boss.'

"Sylvia's is one of the few restaurants completely owned by black people. I am very concerned about the fact that black people don't own many supermarkets or restaurants or hotels. I'm not in this to be rich. If I were rich, I wouldn't be Sylvia. But I do want to get bigger and better so that I can help people. I plan to stay in Harlem too because this community has been good to me. Without them I wouldn't be where I am today. I want to be a success so people will look at me and say, 'Look what Sylvia did. If she can do it, we can.'

"I was born on Groundhog Day and I'm like the groundhog. I'm always comin' out to look for the light. I went from no light to the bright light, but I don't let the bright light blind me. I want to shine in that light so that my family and friends can see me. Then I can be an inspiration to others. When other people just starting out come to me and ask for my advice, boys or girls, I tell them all the same thing: Be willing, able, and determined. Have strength, and, most of all, put your faith in God."

Hanging on a wall of Sylvia's Restaurant, amidst framed newspaper and magazine clippings from three decades, countless community service awards, and stylized portraits of Martin Luther King, Josephine Baker, Jesse Jackson, and Muhammad Ali nestles a small brass plaque that reads:

To Our Mother:
Thank you for Creating this Dream and
Paving the Way for Your Children and
Children's Children to Continue Your Dream

If Sylvia has her way, the dream will never stop.

"In the art world, you strive for creativity.
In the political world, if you get creative, you
scare the hell out of people!"

BEN NIGHTHORSE CAMPBELL

U.S. Senator from Colorado and
fine Native American jeweler

"It is an Indian belief," explains Ben Nighthorse Campbell, "that the Creator puts a secret gift or talent in each one of us. He doesn't tell us what it is, but we are supposed to find that gift in ourselves, develop it and then share it . . . I was lucky. I received several gifts."

Ben Nighthorse Campbell was also lucky enough to develop and share those gifts quite successfully. There are, after all, very few individuals whose innovative American Indian jewelry designs have won over 200 awards and are regularly sold out in chic galleries and high-priced jewelry stores across the country. And there are even fewer who can call themselves Olympic judo contestants or champion quarter horse breeders and trainers. And there's only one — besides Charles Curtis of Kansas in the 1930s — who can lay claim to being Native American as well as a member of the United States Senate.

"Most of the things that challenge me are things I never expected to be good at," says the 62-year-old Democrat from Colorado. "I never thought of myself as a great athlete, and I never expected to be able to make a living at jewelry-making. I remember trying to join my local school board and getting rejected because I was an Indian, so I certainly never expected to be a U.S. senator. I guess I like to try to win at things I don't think I can succeed at."

"Ben," as his aides call him, is sitting in his office in the Russell Senate building in Washington, D.C., just a few days before the close of the Senate session that will allow him a month-long vacation at his 120-acre ranch in Ignacio, Colorado, on the Southern Ute Indian Reservation. His office, with its Indian blankets and relics and its rough-hewn Colorado blue spruce furnishings, handmade by Campbell's son and inlaid with Navajo sand paintings, offers a startling contrast to the marble and mahogany halls of the neoclassical government offices beyond. The man behind the desk is a similar mass of contradictions. In manner, he is every inch the senator who has shaken thousands of hands, kissed countless babies, and offered innumerable interviews on his life and his political beliefs. But Campbell looks nothing like his congressional counterparts. He wears his steel-gray hair in a six-inch ponytail, eschews a pin-striped suit and wingtips in favor of a tweed sport jacket, an ornate silver bola tie, and cowboy boots, and prefers commuting to work by Harley-Davidson to taking taxis.

"I don't like Western suits; I don't like neckties; and I never wanted to buy into the whole senatorial look. I just never believed that to be in the U.S. Senate, I had to look or act like everyone else or ride in big black limousines," says Campbell, his handsome features breaking into a wide grin. He clearly enjoys his iconoclastic style and prides himself as much, if not more, on being an artist and a biker as on being an elected representative. "If you try to be like everyone else here, then you lose your sense of who you are and the self-confidence that comes with that.

"People ask me all the time, 'If you had to quit everything except *one* thing, what would you stick with?' I always tell them, 'It would be the art world.' When the bell rings here at the Senate, I'm gone. I leave Washington politics behind and follow my own way. I'm at my studio making my jewelry; I'm working on the ranch with my wife; I'm out there riding my Harley with the bikers. I'm with what I call 'real people.'"

To this day, Senator Campbell is probably best known as the jeweler Ben Nighthorse, which is his Northern Cheyenne Indian name. His innovative "Painted Mesa" jewelry, based on a combination of Native American styles and motifs and the Japanese-influenced technique of *mokume* — the layering of gold, silver, and other metals to create a wood grain effect — can be found in stores as diverse as small Native American galleries in the tiny resort town of Scottsdale, Arizona, and Fortunoff's, New York's discount jewelry emporium. Even the Franklin Mint, a company that mass markets reproduction jewelry, issued and completely sold out of 1,800 Nighthorse pendants that sold for $1,500 each, grossing $2.7 million in sales. If Campbell has his way, Harry Winston, whose fabulous precious gems grace the neck of Elizabeth Taylor, not to mention assorted members of European royalty, may soon carry some Nighthorse designs. As things now stand, Paul Newman, Robert Redford, and even President Clinton own Nighthorse creations, which range in price from $150 for a silver ring to as much as $25,000 for gold pieces studded with diamonds and other precious stones.

"I learned the basics of jewelry-making from my father, who fooled around with copper and other inexpensive metals," says Campbell, who still spends several mornings a week drafting sketches for new designs in the condominium apartment he owns several blocks from Capitol Hill. "When I get to the bench in my studio, I let a lot of things out. It's great for relieving stress. Sometimes I have dreams and I wake up in the middle of the night just to get them down on paper. Then I wait until I go home on the weekend or I'm on vacation to actually make them . . . Unfortunately, I have more ideas than I have the time to execute them."

With energy legislation and health-care reform taking up more and more hours, the jewelry business is now mostly in the hands of Campbell's wife and children. His son, Colin, is a jeweler himself and actually executes his father's designs, and his wife, Linda, and daughter, Shanan, take orders from around the country and run the Nighthorse Studio and gallery just outside his home in Ignacio.

"I'm glad my wife is running the business," says Campbell. "I don't like to work under deadline pressure or because I've been ordered to make a piece. I'm much more interested in dreaming up new ideas and making them happen . . . Several years I ago I realized I did not want my jewelry to die when I did. I have a fantastic collection of books about jewelry, and I discovered that many of the great designers like Tiffany and my favorites — Boucheron and Fabergé — coupled craftsmanship and design with the building of name-recognition through marketing. They documented their work, and, in so doing, enabled their sons or daughters to carry on their art. Fortunately, Colin has decided to be a jewelry-maker like his father so that he, or anyone apprenticed with me, can look at my original model and craft another."

Campbell is less enthusiastic about the endurance of his political career. "In the art world, you strive for creativity. In the political world, if you get creative, you scare the hell out of people! I've learned to compartmentalize to survive in Washington. I put my best political face forward . . . But I've never felt that I would be a lifetime politician." Campbell won his seat in the Senate in 1993, after three terms as a Democratic congressman from western Colorado. "When I was a congressman, I ran for three terms and said, 'That's it!' When I ran for senator from Colorado, I said, 'Two terms and that's it! And I mean it.' Because I don't worry about a long-term future in the government, I have no trouble voting my conscience. It's the people who fall in love with Washington who are in trouble. They begin to make decisions that will help them stick around."

In fact, Campbell has received the most press as a champion for Indian rights, a reputation, he says, that "comes with the territory" of being an American Indian and being a senator. In fact, when he decided to run for the Senate, he intentionally let his hair grow, despite the warnings of campaign aides who said his long hair would alienate the public. He insisted that he would wear braids on his inauguration day, but settled for the ponytail because his hair wasn't quite long enough for braids.

"I'm the only one here of Native American ancestry, and everyone knows that," he says. "The non-Indians in my state think all I want to do is work on Indian issues. On the other hand, some Indians say I'm not doing enough for them. I want to be responsive. I want to help to the limit of my abilities. Two to three times a week we get representatives of tribes in here that aren't from my state but need help. When I was in the House of Representatives, I always used to say, 'One is the wrong number of Indians in the Congress. We need more or none.' That's still true. The Indian community supported me heavily, and I want to help them. Unfortunately, I inherited a whole constituency without enough resources to take care of them."

He also gets his share of prejudice from the non-Indian community. "I get a lot of crank phone calls. People call me up and yell, 'Go back to your own people!' or write letters telling me to cut my hair. Most of them don't even have the courage to sign their names . . . One time when I was campaigning at a barbecue in Denver, I was introduced to a man who said to me, 'What am I supposed to do? Say *How*?' I told him, 'An ordinary handshake would do just fine.'"

As a congressman, Campbell successfully sought to change the name of Custer Battlefield Monument in Montana to Little Bighorn Battlefield National Monument to honor the Indians who died in battle. The change, which became official in July of 1993, had special significance for Campbell, whose great-grandfather, Black Horse, fought with Crazy Horse against General Custer at Little Bighorn. In fact, the knife his ancestor is said to have carried into battle is encased under glass next to his desk in Washington. "I [first] thought about changing the name back in 1976, when I went up there for the 100th anniversary of the Custer battle," Campbell told a reporter. "The federal agents wouldn't let us in, wouldn't let the Indians come on the grounds unless we came under their watchful, observing eyes. Everybody else could come on — except Indians. It made me so damn' mad. I said if I ever get the chance to change the name of this outfit, I'm going to do it. Somebody asked me how long I've been working on that bill; I told them 116 years."

He also sponsored successful legislation to establish the National Museum of the American Indian, which is the last major wing of the Smithsonian Institution and is slated to open by the year 2001. As fundraising chairman, he has given a piece of his jewelry to each living American president in gratitude for their serving on the board of the museum. More recently, he has taken on the Washington Redskins football team by introducing legislation that would block congressional approval of a proposed $206 million new stadium on federal land unless the team changes its name. The term "redskins," he asserts, is offensive to most Native Americans.

He strongly supports efforts to reduce unemployment on Indian reservations, as well as reforms that address the high incidence of violent crime, teenage suicide, and alcoholism in the Indian community. For the most part, he tends to fall into what he calls "the middle of the road" politically. He is conservative on fiscal matters and liberal on social issues. He adds that he has never voted a straight party line. For example, he is ardently pro-choice, but opposed to gun control. "I don't weigh the mail or test the wind before I make a decision," he has said. "You've got to do what you believe is right. I always say that if I have the right and the left both mad at me, then I must be doing something right."

Indeed, the story of Senator Campbell's journey to Capitol Hill is a multi-cultural Horatio Alger tale if ever there was one. "I had some tough times as a kid, and I've come a long way to get to where I am now. I could be some psychologist's case study on what happens to a kid who had nothing while he was growing up."

He was born in Auburn, California, the son of Albert Campbell, a North Cheyenne Indian with Pueblo and Apache blood ties whose chronic alcoholism prevented him from holding a steady job for very long. His mother, Mary, was a Portuguese immigrant who was afflicted with tuberculosis and spent most of her adult years in and out of sanatoriums. The two met in Weimar Joint Tubercular Sanitorium in Placer County, California, where Mary was a patient and Albert was working as an orderly.

Because of Mary's failing health and Albert's unpredictable bouts of alcoholism, Ben and his sister, Alberta — who died in 1974 of an overdose of pills and liquor — shuttled in and out of foster homes and St. Patrick's Catholic orphanage in Sacramento. "We were very poor and often hungry," Campbell recalls. "I remember times when all my sister and I had to eat was a can of peas . . . My father was ashamed of his own Indian blood. We were always told, 'Don't worry about it. Just keep your mouth shut.' I just didn't get a lot of guidance, and I was always getting into trouble — stealing, drinking, fighting, and all that damn' kid stuff. Sometimes my sister and I would go into Sacramento with my mother to look for my dad. We would walk along Skid Row, turning over bodies to see if any of them were him . . . Most kids grow up with an idea of what they want to be when they grow up. I grew up knowing what I *didn't* want to be — like my father."

In 1950, Campbell dropped out of Placer High School and hit the road. He and a friend hitched rides on freight trains and found work in the forests and sawmills of the Sierra Nevada. "I don't know how the hell it happened," he recalls. "We talked about riding freights, and there was a yard at Colfax where we would go and hang around and dream in our minds. I was looking at those freight trains and the next thing I knew, we were on one . . . I could have ended up in serious trouble if it hadn't been for two things. One was sports and the other was the service."

By 1951, Campbell had joined the Air Force and was stationed in Korea. During his two years in the service, he earned his high school equivalency diploma. When the war was over, he received an honorable discharge as an airman second class. He returned to California and, in 1957, earned a degree in education at San Jose State University, which he paid for by working as a migrant fruit picker and a truck driver. In the fields, he befriended several Japanese boys, who inspired in him a passion for judo. "I liked crashing around and hitting guys," he recalls. "It kept me off the streets and out of jail."

By 1960, he had become so enamored of the sport that he moved to Tokyo to enroll in Meiji University and to study judo; in those days there were few professional judo trainers in America. "Living in Japan was a wonderful experience for me," says Campbell, who supported himself by teaching English to Japanese businessmen and by taking bit parts in Japanese films as an American gangster who was trained in judo. "I completely immersed myself in Japanese culture. I wore kimonos and spoke Japanese.

"What's more, I found a similarity between the Zen culture and the Indian way. Both peoples' values are very different than [traditional] American values. Ask a person in white society, 'What is a successful man?' and he will answer: 'A man who has power — a big car, a big house, and lots of money.' Ask an Indian and he will tell you: 'A person who gives everything he has to everyone else.' They believe that if you give everything away, it will all come back to you eventually. That is the Zen way, too. Both cultures believe that you do your best not by taking, but by giving. I felt a tremendous kinship with the Japanese culture.

"The [judo] training was absolutely brutal. My nose was broken a couple of times, I lost two teeth, and I broke or dislocated just about every finger and toe I've got and suffered any number of bruises, contusions, and swollen ears. I trained five hours a day, six days a week, and learned a tremendous dedication of purpose. When you train for judo, you must learn to strip yourself completely of your ego. All of the physical activity has a metaphysical end. You dedicate yourself completely to the training, including washing the toilets of the upperclassmen and doing everything you are told to do. You learn how to take a blow, how to win, and how to lose. You develop an internal toughness that simply won't let you give up . . . Needless to say, the training and self-discipline I learned in Japan have helped me immeasurably in my political career." And Campbell's hard work on the judo mats paid off. He won a gold medal at the 1963 Pan Am Games and captained the U.S. Olympic judo team at the 1964 Tokyo games. Carrying the American flag at the closing ceremonies, he says, was an honor he still relishes as one of the highlights of his career. "But it was never about the medals," he concedes. "The real rewards — the incredible self-discipline — are lifelong."

In fact, an Indian headdress comprising 72 eagle feathers now hangs in his senate office, a gift from his Northern Cheyenne tribe to commemorate his victories on the judo mat. The Senator wore the headdress, along with red, white, and blue war paint on his face, when he rode his horse, War Bonnet, down Washington, D.C.'s Pennsylvania Avenue during his senate inaugural parade. According to the Cheyenne tradition, explains Campbell, "the headdress is a reward not for victories over others, but for doing better each time than I had done the time before . . . This kind of explains what drives me. My goal — whether it is in sports, jewelry-making, or politics — is always to create something better or more interesting. But I never really measure whether I've actually reached my goal — just how hard I tried to get to that goal."

After four years in Tokyo, Campbell returned to California, where he began teaching judo and developed his skills as a jewelry designer. As a child, he had learned some rudimentary techniques for making American Indian jewelry from his father. Mostly, he turned silver dollars and scraps of copper into concha belts. But while he was in Japan, he learned the art of *mokume,* which involves laminating different metals together, and he felt that the style could easily be adapted to Indian design. He began showing his new designs at juried shows of Native American jewelry, but his work inspired little more than skepticism from the judges, who felt his pieces shouldn't be included in traditional shows because they did not follow the style of Indian art. Undaunted, Campbell continued to design jewelry, even teaching adult jewelry-making classes to other American Indians at a local high school.

It was in a judo class in Sacramento that he met Linda Price, whose father owned a 3,000-acre ranch in Montrose,

Colorado. Price became his third wife in 1966, (Campbell's first marriage was annulled; his second ended in divorce.) Ben and Linda spent several years living on Linda's family ranch and traveling around the Southwest in a trailer they converted into a jewelry studio. For a while, he was deputy sheriff in Sacramento County, and he taught in the Elk Grove school district. He also volunteered as a counselor for Indian inmates at Folsom Prison and opened a halfway house for them.

Son Colin was born in 1969 and daughter Shanan in 1970. And in 1972, an article in *Arizona Highways* magazine identified Campbell as one of twenty Native Americans undertaking new forms of art through his jewelery-making. Suddenly, his pieces were in demand from high-priced art galleries all over the Southwest. The jeweler Ben Nighthorse became a success.

In 1977, the Campbells made their way to the Southern Ute reservation, where Ben was offered a job training champion quarter horses. Two broken ribs, one punctured lung, and a shattered arm later, he gave up riding colts. In the meantime, however, the Campbells had purchased the Ignacio ranch they still call home. Around that time, a fellow athlete and American Indian, runner Billy Mills, a gold medal winner at the Tokyo games and a resident of Rancho Cordova, California, inspired Campbell to research his background. He began making trips to Montana to explore his Northern Cheyenne roots.

In 1980, he formally adopted the name Nighthorse, which was given to him in a traditional Cheyenne ceremony. "I come from the Black Horse family — it's different in English, but in the Indian language it comes out the same," he explains. Five years later, he was inducted into the tribe's Council of 44 Chiefs. He has taken his son and daughter to the Montana reservation he calls "home" for their own rituals. "The tribal chiefs gave them their Indian names and did the honoring ceremony for them. But they dip in and out of the culture. When they get back down to Durango, they put a lot of the ceremonial stuff behind them."

His entry into politics was accidental. "I still remember trying to get on the local school board," he recalls. "I was an

Indian, and the local white ranchers weren't going to appoint no Indian to that thing even though that's where the tribe is." Nonetheless, in 1982, he walked into a local Democratic Party meeting in Ignacio to speak on behalf of a friend who was running for sheriff and when no one else wanted to run, found himself drafted as a Democratic candidate for the state House of Representatives. "I've always had an inner need to win," he says of his sudden involvement in politics. "I guess my competitive spirit got the best of me. I wanted to see how far I could go." To everyone's surprise, Campbell defeated his opponent, a local college dean. Four years later, he won his first term in the U.S. House of Representatives against the incumbent, gentleman rancher Mike Strang — and the rest is political history.

Since his election to the Senate, Campbell says, he puts in an average 80 hours of work per week, including the time spent flying to and from Colorado just about every weekend. He prides himself on keeping his phone number listed and taking constituents' calls at all hours. He spends every spare minute he can find either at the jewelry workbench, riding one of his Harleys, or helping Linda manage their ranch's 100 head of Brangus cattle, a breed that is part Brahma, part Angus and famous for their easy deliveries. "We prefer only to breed and raise cattle, he says, conceding that "they all end up at the butcher eventually." He still has a fantasy of returning to his camper to make jewelry and travel through the West, teaching jewelry-making to other Indians.

What gives him most pleasure now, however, is the volunteer work he does with a local church group and Denver street gangs such as the Crips, the Bloods, and the Inca Boys. He and a local minister take the boys on weekend outings in the neighboring mountainous countryside. "The things that make me proudest are not necessarily the things that put me in the limelight," he says. "If I can work with one kid and feel that if I hadn't gotten my hands on him, he might have landed in jail, then I feel I have been rewarded. And who knows? If you help one kid, he may help one kid, and so on . . . This is the stuff I put store in. I don't need to be appreciated because I passed a bill or because I'm the president's friend.

"What I can share from my own life is the message: 'Never give up. Don't be confined by what other people say you can or can't do. The world is made up of winners, losers, and spectators. It's okay to be either a winner or a loser but not just to stand there watching. I started at the bottom, and look where I am today.' I want every kid in America to know that this great country will give them the opportunity to make something of themselves if they are willing to work for it."

Post Script: In March of 1995, Senator Campbell announced that he was joining the Republican party. "I can no longer represent the agenda that is put forth by the [Democratic] party although I certainly agree with many of the things that Democrats stand for," he said. Senator Campbell also said that he would continue to vote as he had in the past, which has been with the Democrats 78 percent of the time, according to tallies by Congressional Quarterly.

"Giving away a portion of our profits is nice, but it is a minor thing compared to the positive social impact we can have by making the way we run our business every day a reflection of our conscious caring for the people around us."

BEN COHEN

Co-Founder of Ben & Jerry's Ice Cream

B en Cohen owes a lot to Maurice Purpore. Way back in 1981, before Ben & Jerry's, Inc. had become the innovative $140-million-a-year ice cream business it is today, Ben had what he called "a disheartening moment." The way Ben tells it, sales of the homemade Vermont ice cream he and his partner Jerry Greenfield had been selling out of a scoop shop in Burlington, Vermont had begun to take off, and the company had started distributing their product to grocery stores. The two partners had just expanded Ben & Jerry's pint-packing operations into a larger space. "When we started we had no plans to become anything besides a single homemade ice cream parlor," he recalls. "Suddenly, I realized I was the president of a big company. Jerry and I had become business-men, and I felt that we were becoming just another cog in the economic machinery. Soon we would be exploiting people."

Their immediate reaction was to put their business on the market and sell it to the highest bidder. "Then I met Maurice Purpore," says Ben. "Maurice was this great old guy who used to be a restaurateur in Brattleboro, Vermont, and he had writ-ten us an interesting letter to tell us how much he liked our ice cream. I looked him up and told him we were selling the company, and he said, 'You can't do that. That company is your baby. You made it. If there's something you don't like about business, then why don't you change it?' That's when I said to myself, 'Maurice is right. I'm going to use business as an instrument for social change.'"

Although the process may not have been quite as immediate as the decision, it wasn't long before Ben & Jerry's Homemade, Inc. became a model for a style of enterprise called "caring capitalism." The company that had virtually revolutionized the industry by bringing the world "chunk-style" ice cream in such innovative flavors as Rainforest Crunch, Chocolate Fudge Brownie, and Cherry Garcia simultaneously became known for developing an innovative corporate management policy called "linked prosperity" and using business profits to help change the world at large.

"Once Ben & Jerry's grew, I realized that business had an incredible amount of power. When business talked, people listened. And it seemed to me that we had a responsibility to use that power for social good," affirms Ben in a telephone interview, his gruff voice, hearty laughter, and *yiddische* comic interludes the perfect match to the benign, bearded face grinning next to Jerry's on the package of every company product. "That isn't to say that we didn't want to make money. If you do something well and you are able to get your product to the consumer at a price the consumer can afford, and you control your costs, then you can turn a profit. It was just that there came a point when we decided that if our business was going to make money then we were going to be a socially responsible business . . . The more you can make, the more you can give away or at least use to build programs that will help the community."

Thanks to Maurice Purpore's simple question, Ben & Jerry's developed a mission statement that holds true to this day. Formally established in 1988, the Ben & Jerry's "Statement of Mission" affirms the production of innovative, high-quality products, the development of a sound economic policy that benefits all of the company's employees and shareholders, and the commitment "to operate the company in a way that actively recognizes the central role that business plays in the structure of society by initiating innovative ways to improve the quality of life of the local, national and international community." In short, says Ben, "Our goal became to integrate concern for the community in every business decision we made."

The social actions in which the company has involved itself over the years take many forms. Ben & Jerry's purchases ingredients from suppliers who use their resources for such issues as rain forest preservation, employing the unemployed, and supporting Native American enterprise. For example, Ben & Jerry's Rainforest Crunch ice cream uses cashews and Brazil nuts from the South American Rainforest — pushing up the demand for nuts and thereby offering an alternative to destroying the Rainforest forever by ranching and clearcutting. Their Wild Maine Blueberry ice cream is made with blueberries harvested by Maine's Passamaquoddy Indian tribe; the profits help support the economic development of the tribe and the preservation of Native American culture.

Their Fudge Brownie ice cream is made with brownies baked at the Greyston Bakery of Yonkers, New York, where previously unemployed or under-skilled people are hired to work the ovens, and Greyston Community Network reinvests the profits in housing, job training, and counseling programs for homeless people. And all of the ice cream uses local Vermont milk and cream in an effort to support traditional family farming and the rural communities being destroyed by centralized factory farming, which relies on chemicals, pesticides, and environmentally hazardous industrial farming methods.

The company also prints messages that encourage positive social action on their ice cream containers. Through on-package campaigning, the company has raised money for such organizations as the Children's Defense Fund, Farm Aid, and the First Nations. "Almost every month we hear from dozens of people across the country who tell us they buy our ice cream not only because it's the best but because they believe in what we are doing," affirms Ben.

In addition, Ben & Jerry's has begun a partnerships program with non-profit organizations that advocate a change from military to human-needs spending. In fact, seven and a half percent of the company's pre-tax profits is donated to the Ben & Jerry's Foundation, which offers grants to non-profit organizations that promote creative social problem-solving.

"In recent years the board of our foundation has been run entirely by our employees," explains Ben. "They decide which organizations will receive company profits . . . We have over 600 employees, all of whom have been hired not only for being smart, capable, educated, and motivated, but also for being socially aligned with the values of the company. We think it's only fair that they decide where the profits should go."

Most recently, the company has instigated a "partnershops" program. Partnershops are Ben & Jerry's scoop shop franchises that are donated to community-minded individuals or groups, with Ben & Jerry's waiving the standard $25,000 franchise fees. An established percentage of the business profits goes to support a specific non-profit organization or program to which the particular Partnershop has committed. The five partnershops currently in operation also offer employment and job-training opportunities. For example, the Ben & Jerry's partnershop in New York City's Harlem community directs profits to support HARK Homes, a holistic program for housing homeless men while providing work and training opportunities. The partnershop in Ithaca, New York, uses the shop to provide for hands-on job experience and a business training program for kids under 21.

"Since I believe that business is the most powerful force in the world, I believe I can address certain problems by developing a new model for how to operate a business . . . That's what makes the partnershops special," reflects Ben. "Giving away a portion of our profits is nice, but it is a minor thing compared to the positive social impact we can have by making the way we run our business every day a reflection of our conscious caring for the people around us."

There was a time when Ben was pretty much apolitical. "Before Ben & Jerry's," he says, "I felt the world was screwed up but that there wasn't much I could do about it. I think what motivated me at the beginning was to find a way to express myself and earn a living without having to work for somebody else."

By the time he and Jerry, whom he had known since junior

high school, decided to open an ice cream store in Vermont in 1978, Bennet Cohen had had a long career of seeking ways to "express himself." Born in Brooklyn, New York in 1951, Ben had grown up in Merrick, Long Island, watching his father, an accountant, come home from work and eat half-gallons of ice cream directly from the carton with a soup spoon. Ben would create his own concoctions by "mushing up" his favorite candies and cookies into his ice cream.

In his senior year in high school, Ben drove an ice cream truck, selling ice cream to kids. He enrolled in Colgate University, then dropped out after a year and a half and returned to driving an ice cream truck. "I just wasn't getting anything out of college," Ben offers in characteristically terse explanation. He tried college again — first Skidmore, then the University Without Walls, then the New School in New York — taking pottery and jewelry-making classes. In fact, he never earned his undergraduate degree, attempting instead to become a professional potter. To support himself, he held various jobs, including cashier at McDonald's, Pinkerton guard at the Saratoga Raceway, and night mopper at Jamesway and Friendly's. "I used to haul my pottery to all the crafts fairs," Ben recalls. "Nobody ever bought any of it. Ever. I figured I was probably making ugly stuff and eventually decided the best thing to do was give it up."

In the early seventies, Ben moved to New York City, supporting further pottery studies by working first as a pediatric emergency room clerk on the night shift at Bellevue Hospital and then as a taxi driver. He also enrolled in courses at the New School in experimental sound recording and at NYU in art therapy. In 1974, he moved to the town of Paradox in New York's Adirondack Mountains and became a crafts teacher at the Highland Community School, a small residential school for troubled teenagers, situated on a 600-acre working farm.

He spent three years in Paradox, building his own house and working as the school cook in addition to teaching pottery, stained glass, photography, and filmmaking. Ben made two important friends while living in Paradox — his dog, Malcolm, and Jeff Furman, the school's bus driver. Armed with law and accounting degrees, Furman later helped start Ben & Jerry's, Inc. Today he is an attorney in Ithaca, New York, and as a member of the company's board of directors was influential in starting the company's Russian operations. It was in Paradox that Ben also experimented with ice-cream making with his students.

In 1977, Ben decided it was time to start a business of his own and called his pal Jerry Greenfield to join him. "We decided that if we were going into business, it would have to be a food business because eating was our favorite activity," Ben explains in earnest. "And we decided to run our business from a rural college town because that was the kind of place in which we both wanted to live. There were two possibilities — bagels or homemade ice cream. We picked bagels and thought we'd name the company UBS (an acronym for *U*nited *B*agel *S*ervice). We planned on becoming a bagel delivery service.

"Then we talked to a bagel delivery service and discovered two things. First, no one was interested in a bagel delivery service in a rural college town, and, second, it would cost us $40,000 to buy a bagel company. Ice cream was cheaper, so we decided on ice cream.

"We were looking for warm, rural college towns and started visiting them," adds Ben. "We realized every warm-weather college town already had an ice cream shop so we landed in Vermont . . . At the time, there were more cows than people in Vermont. We had this image of Vermont as a land of rolling fields and dairy farms and very little pollution. It seemed like the right place for us."

The next thing they did was to buy all the ice cream books they could find and begin researching the subject. They signed up for a $5 Penn State correspondence course that included a text called *Ice Cream,* receiving A's in the course. Thus, in 1978, certified "experts" in ice-cream making, Ben and Jerry kicked in $4,000 apiece, borrowed $4,000 from a local bank, and opened Ben & Jerry's Homemade ice cream scoop shop in a renovated gas station in downtown Burlington, Vermont.

"Jerry had a background in biochemistry, so he made all the ice cream," says Ben, who claims his business acumen was built entirely on "trial and error" and his roving experience as a scooper, taste-tester, truck driver, marketing director, sales-person, and president. "We had no real mentors. We simply talked to anyone we thought would help us. The Small Business Administration hooked us up with some people and we talked with other local businessmen."

In time, Jerry became the company's "director of mobile operations" and took charge of sales and distribution for the company, while Ben became chairman of the board of directors and ran the marketing and international development of the company. Not long after it opened, the shop became known throughout Vermont for its rich, unusual flavors, made entirely from local dairy products — and its community-oriented approach to business. Ben & Jerry's sponsored a series of free outdoor movie festivals and celebrated their anniversaries with a Free Cone Day.

The company's size and social commitment grew astronomically in the years that followed. In 1984, Ben and Jerry took the company public in Vermont, setting a precedent by discovering an obscure regulatory clause about stocks and brokering that enabled them to establish a Vermont-only public stock offering. Allowing small investors to buy small amounts of stock brought them more closely in touch with the local Vermont community. They moved their headquarters to a large plant in Waterbury, Vermont, where they now offer public tours of the ice cream-making operations. Since 1986, annual sales have increased an average of 36 percent per year. Primary earnings per share of Ben & Jerry's stock have also grown each year, from $0.20 in 1986 to an estimated $1.01 in 1993.

There are now over 100 franchised Ben & Jerry's scoop shops in eighteen states plus Washington, D.C., Canada, and Great Britain, and plans for further international distribution are well underway. The company has a licensee in Israel that manufactures and sells Ben & Jerry's through its scoop shops, and, since 1992, has been part of a joint venture in

Petrozavodsk, Karelia, making and selling ice cream through four Russian scoop shops. Ruble profits from the Russian shops are being used to fund cross-cultural exchanges.

"When we first visited Russia, we were invited to dinner at the homes of several local people," recalls Ben. "I remember sitting next to our Russian colleagues, having a great time, and thinking, 'I was raised to believe that these people are my enemies.' Our sole motivation for [starting a venture] in Russia was to create peace through understanding . . . Right off the bat, we learned that taste buds are universal. Our Heath Bar Crunch is popular in every country."

As Ben & Jerry's social commitment grew, so did the partners' beliefs in what they call "linked prosperity." From very early on Ben actively sought ways to create a management structure that would benefit the company's employees. "In our society," explains Ben, "the people on the upper end of management tend to get overpaid, and the production workers tend to get paid too little. We said we didn't want to repeat that. We wanted all of the people in our company to prosper. So we came up with a corporate salary policy that we believe is unique. Basically, the company's highest paid employee — including top corporate officers — cannot earn more than seven times what the lowest-paid full-time regular employee earns. It hasn't been easy to maintain this. We started with a ratio of five and moved it to seven, but we are still trying to work with this policy.

"Many people argue that it will be difficult to get the best quality people to run the company because we are paying below the market rate . . . Well, so far we have managed just fine. There are a lot of different things that people get out of work besides money. At our company, people's personal values are aligned with the company's, and working here gives them a chance to actualize their personal values."

Other employee benefits include an in-house daycare center for children of employees, free career planning seminars, an employee stock purchase plan, and a profit-sharing plan that allows each full-time regular employee to share in a fund into which the company deposits five percent of the company's annual pre-tax profits, with the size of the employee's share depending upon the length of service. For some, the best benefit is one that allows all employees to take home three free "factory second" pints and novelty items such as "peace pops" and "brownie bars" each day.

Despite the company's well-recognized success, Ben admits there have been "low points." He remembers, in particular, his early proposal to sell Ben & Jerry's ice cream from outdoor kiosks, an abject failure that cost the company considerable profits. "In the early days, those kinds of disasters really took a lot out of me, but I don't feel as overwhelmed now as I used to," Ben says. "For a while, we used to feel that if we could just solve the problem in front of us, then we'd be finished. We never realized there was always another problem lurking just around the corner. Now, I think, we don't expect to solve every problem . . . I remember in the early days going to see my father when he was still alive, and telling him about all the mistakes we made. He said, 'Ben, if you don't do anything, then you don't make mistakes.'"

In 1992, Ben, took a nine-month "sabbatical" to give himself a rest from the business. "I was tired of being so scheduled up. I wanted to see what it would be like not to have so many demands on my time," he explains. "I dawdled for most of it and found that time passed very quickly and that I really liked moving at a slower pace." Nonetheless, he admits, business once again occupies three quarters of his time. Now divorced, he spends most of his leisure time hiking and bike riding around his home in Williston, Vermont, or with his young daughter Aretha, who lives with her mother.

For the rest, he considers himself one of the company's best consumers, switching favorites amongst the flavors created out of suggestions from consumers, employees, and what he calls "my collective flavor unconscious." The company continues to come up with new tastes, including a series of "smooth flavors" — ice cream without Ben & Jerry's trademark "chunks." This latest product is now being advertised in a commercial directed by Spike Lee. These days, admits Ben, butter pecan, Cherry Garcia, and Rain Forest Crunch are his preferred flavors.

Ben has his own advice to anyone starting up a business: "First, always integrate your values into your business. Second, remember that you don't have to do things the way they have always been done before. The accountants and the lawyers can only tell you what's been done in the past and not how to succeed in the future. Finally, there is a spiritual aspect to business. Business is there for making money, but if you give, then you will receive. If you support the community, then the community will support you back."

Post Script: In January of 1995, Robert Holland, Jr., a corporate turnaround consultant, was appointed Ben & Jerry's new president and chief executive officer. Ben Cohen will remain the company's chairman. The ice cream company has recently suffered significant financial losses due in part, industry analysts say, to a consumer shift away from super-premium ice cream in favor of lower-fat brands. Ben says that an important reason for the company's choosing Holland as the new CEO was that he "shares the progressive social values that are a big part of Ben & Jerry's."